snacks & beverages

table of contents

save time, cut costs, eat great

Now you can beat the kitchen clock, slash grocery bills *and* serve your family the foods they crave. With *Taste of Home Ultimate Five Ingredient Recipes*, it's a cinch to do so! Take a look inside, and you'll discover 398 foolproof dishes that come together in a pinch. That's because each recipe calls for no more than five ingredients…with the exception of water, salt and pepper.* Now you can prepare piping hot casseroles, buttery biscuits, savory side dishes and finger-licking fruit pies with only an ounce of effort. In addition, you'll enjoy no-fuss appetizers, simple snacks and bake-sale sensations sure to make your contribution a hit. In fact, with *Ultimate Five Ingredient Recipes*, cooking up a winning dish has never been easier.

Snacks & Beverages 4

Salads & Dressings 38

Soups & Sandwiches 56

Beef & Pork Entrees 80

Poultry Main Dishes 96

Seafood & Meatless Suppers 112

Side Dishes & More 126

Breads, Biscuits & Baked Goods . .152

Cookies, Bars & Candy 178

Cakes & Pies 210

Delightful Desserts 230

*Due to their commonality, water, salt and pepper are not counted as items in the ingredient lists published in this book.

Ultimate
Five
Ingredient
Recipes

©2009 Reiman Media Group, Inc.
5400 S. 60th St.,
Greendale, WI 53129

All rights reserved.
Printed in U.S.A.

Taste of Home is a registered trademark of The Reader's Digest Association, Inc.

International Standard Book Number (10):
0-89821-738-7

International Standard Book Number (13):
978-0-89821-738-4

Library of Congress Catalog Number:
200921103

Pictured on Front Cover:
Savory Chicken Dinner (p. 98), Spiced Carrot Strips (p. 145) and Fresh Strawberry Pie (p. 212).

Pictured on Title and Table of Contents Pages:
Chicken in a Haystack (p. 102) and Italian Beef Sandwiches (p. 76).

Pictured on Back Cover:
Kid's Favorite Biscuits (p. 163), Simple Salsa Chicken (p. 110), Winter Warmer (p. 21), Greek Green Beans (p. 140) and Sausage Pepper Sandwiches (p. 64).

Editor in Chief: Catherine Cassidy
Vice President & Executive Editor/Books: Heidi Reuter Lloyd
Creative Director: Ardyth Cope
Food Director: Diane Werner
Senior Editor: Mark Hagen
Editor: Krista Lanphier
Art Director: Edwin Robles, Jr.
Content Production Supervisor: Julie Wagner
Design Layout Artist: Kathy Crawford
Proofreader: Linne Bruskewitz

Recipe Asset Systems: Coleen Martin, Sue A. Jurack
Premedia Supervisor: Scott Berger
Recipe Testing & Editing: Taste of Home Test Kitchen
Food Photography: Taste of Home Photo Studio
Editorial Assistant: Barb Czysz

Cover Photograph
Photographer: Dan Roberts
Food Stylist: Jim Rude
Set Stylist: Dee Dee Jacq

Chief Marketing Officer: Lisa Karpinski
Vice President/Book Marketing: Dan Fink
Creative Director/Creative Marketing: Jim Palmen

The Reader's Digest Association, Inc.
President and Chief Executive Officer: Mary G. Berner
President, RDA Food & Entertaining: Suzanne M. Grimes
President, Consumer Marketing: Dawn Zier

"Timeless Recipes from Trusted Home Cooks" is a registered trademark of Reiman Media Group, Inc. Visit our Web site at **TasteofHome.com**. For additional books or products, visit **ShopTasteofHome.com**

taste of home
Ultimate
Five
Ingredient
Recipes

baked asparagus dip 6

apple grape drink 7

brie in puff pastry 7

butterscotch coffee 8

creamy strawberry breeze 8

smoked salmon dip 9

confetti snack mix 9

apple cartwheels 10

strawberry cooler 10

black bean quesadillas 11

parmesan popcorn 11

frappe mocha 12

taffy apple dip 13

tortilla snack strips 13

chocolate banana smoothies 14

cherry yogurt smoothies 14

turkey nachos 15

coconut fruit dip 15

cheesy zucchini bites 16

crunchy cheese nibblers 16

berry yogurt shakes 17

california fried walnuts 17

easy black bean salsa 18

smooth vanilla shakes 19

asparagus in puff pastry 19

guacamole dip 20

dreamy fruit dip 20

frosty chocolate malted shakes 21

winter warmer 21

raspberry mint cooler 22

raspberry ice tea 22

easy mint hot chocolate 23

shrimp with basil-mango sauce 23

mushroom puffs 24

colorful fruit kabobs 25

fruity red smoothies 25

like 'em hot wings 26

sweet & saucy meatballs 26

sunset cooler 27

ricotta tart 27

buffet meatballs 28

springtime lime slushy 28

raspberry lemon smoothie 29

dragon dippers 29

refreshing fruit dip 30

sunny slush 31

sausage-stuffed jalapenos 31

sparkling rhubarb spritzer 32

cappuccino chip cupcakes 32

dairy delicious dip 33

special lemonade 33

pear cooler 34

speedy pizza rings 34

crunchy trail mix 35

peanut butter berry delights 35

strawberry lemonade slush 36

italian sausage mushrooms 37

banana cocoa smoothies 37

baked asparagus dip

prep/cook: 30 minutes

Since I'm from Wisconsin, I thought it was only logical to combine a vegetable with cheese, two of the things this state produces in abundance. I come from a long line of farm families and love cooking a lot!

Sandra Baratka
Phillips, Wisconsin

1 **pound diced cooked fresh asparagus, drained**

1 **cup grated Parmesan cheese**

1 **cup mayonnaise**

Snack rye bread

In a large bowl, combine the asparagus, cheese and mayonnaise. Place in a 2-cup ovenproof bowl. Bake at 375° for 20 minutes or until heated through. Serve with bread. **Yield:** about 2 cups.

apple grape drink

prep/cook: 15 minutes

Why settle for plain juice at breakfast or brunch when you can sip this fizzy morning beverage? It comes together easily by stirring together just four ingredients, and everyone loves the taste of this refreshing punch.

Deborah Butts
Union Bridge, Maryland

6 cups apple juice, chilled

3 cups white grape juice, chilled

1 can (12 ounces) frozen lemonade concentrate, thawed

1 liter club soda, chilled

In a large container, combine the juices and lemonade concentrate. Stir in club soda. Serve immediately. **Yield:** 3-3/4 quarts.

‖Ultimate**TIP**

Brie and Camembert cheese are both soft, cow's milk cheeses that originate from France. They come in the form of a round wheel with a white, edible rind and can be a variety of sizes. Their flavor is savory, salty, buttery and sometimes with a slight bitterness. The texture is creamy. At room temperature, the interior of a ripened wheel of Brie or Camembert can become runny.

---

brie in puff pastry

prep/cook: 30 minutes

This rich and stylish appetizer adds an elegant touch to any get-together.

Marion Lowery
Medford, Oregon

1 frozen puff pastry sheet, thawed

1/4 cup apricot jam

1 round (13.2 ounces) Brie *or* Camembert cheese

1 egg

1 tablespoon water

Apple slices

Roll the puff pastry into a 14-in. square. Spread jam into a 4-1/2-in. circle in center of pastry; place cheese over jam. Fold pastry around cheese; trim excess dough. Pinch edges to seal. Place seam side down on ungreased baking sheet. Beat egg and water; brush over pastry.

Cut the trimmed pastry pieces into decorative shapes and place on the top; brush with remaining egg mixture if desired. Bake at 400° for 20-25 minutes or until puffed and golden brown. Serve warm with apple slices. **Yield:** 8-10 servings.

1 cup butterscotch chips, *divided*
8 cups hot brewed coffee
1/2 cup half-and-half cream
5 to 8 tablespoons sugar
Whipped cream in a can

In a small microwave-safe bowl, heat 1/2 cup butterscotch chips at 70% power until melted, stirring occasionally. Cut a small hole in the corner of a pastry or plastic bag; insert a #4 round tip. Fill with melted chips. Pipe eight garnishes onto a waxed paper-lined baking sheet. Refrigerate until set, about 10 minutes.

In a large pitcher, stir the coffee and remaining butterscotch chips until chips are melted. Stir in the cream and sugar.

Pour the butterscotch coffee into mugs. Top each serving with the whipped cream and a butterscotch garnish. **Yield:** 8 servings (2 quarts).

butterscotch coffee

prep/cook: 20 minutes

The rich flavor of this yummy coffee is warm and inviting on chilly winter days. Individual servings are topped with whipped cream, and fun garnishes are made from melted butterscotch chips.

Taste of Home Test Kitchen
Greendale, Wisconsin

||| Ultimate**TIP**

To preserve its flavor, store fresh ground or whole bean coffee in an airtight container in the refrigerator for up to 2 weeks. Long-term storage is best done in the freezer for up to 1 year. Unopened vacuum-packed cans or packages of beans or ground coffee can be stored in a pantry for up to 1 year. For the best-tasting coffee, always brew with fresh cold water.

creamy strawberry breeze

prep: 5 minutes

Get your Christmas Day off to a refreshing start with this frothy fruit drink. For a festive touch, garnish each serving with a strawberry and a dollop of whipped topping. The pretty pink smoothie makes an attractive addition to a Yuletide brunch.

Amy Cruson
Dodge City, Kansas

2 cups whole strawberries
2 cups apple juice
3 cups whipped topping

Place half of the strawberries and apple juice in a blender; cover and process until smooth. Add half of the whipped topping; cover and process until blended. Pour into glasses. Repeat. **Yield:** 4 servings.

smoked salmon dip

prep/cook: 30 minutes

Salmon is practically a way of life here in the Pacific Northwest. My husband can make a meal of this dip. Served with crackers, it's great for holiday parties.

Doreen McDaniels
Seattle, Washington

1 can (16 ounces) pitted ripe olives, drained

8 green onions, cut into 2-inch pieces

1 can (14-3/4 ounces) pink salmon, drained, flaked and bones removed

2/3 cup mayonnaise

8 drops Liquid Smoke, optional

Place olives and onions in a blender or food processor; cover and process for about 15 seconds. Add salmon, mayonnaise and Liquid Smoke if desired; process until the dip reaches desired consistency. Chill. **Yield:** about 3 cups.

confetti snack mix

prep/cook: 5 minutes

This colorful snack mix will satisfy a "sweet tooth" or "salty tooth!" It will conquer any hunger pains.

Billie Blanton
Kingsport, Tennessee

1 package (16 ounces) plain M&M's

1 package (16 ounces) peanut M&M's

1 package (15 ounces) golden raisins

1 can (11-1/2 ounces) mixed nuts

1 package (11 ounces) butterscotch chips

Combine all ingredients in a large bowl. Transfer to airtight containers; store in a cool, dry place. **Yield:** 11 cups.

apple cartwheels

prep: 20 minutes + chilling

When you need to feed a group of children, try these stuffed apple rings. The yummy filling is an irresistible combination of creamy peanut butter, sweet honey, miniature chocolate chips and raisins.

Miriam Miller
Thorp, Wisconsin

- 1/4 **cup peanut butter**
- 1-1/2 **teaspoons honey**
- 1/2 **cup miniature semisweet chocolate chips**
- 2 **tablespoons raisins**
- 4 **medium unpeeled Red Delicious apples, cored**

In a bowl, combine peanut butter and honey; fold in chocolate chips and raisins. Fill centers of apples with peanut butter mixture; refrigerate for at least 1 hour. Cut into 1/4-in. rings. **Yield:** about 2 dozen.

strawberry cooler

prep/cook: 10 minutes

This refreshing beverage is easy to double. Just make two batches ahead of time, and add ginger ale and ice when you're ready for more!

Judy Robertson
Southington, Connecticut

- 3 **cups water**
- 5 **cups sliced fresh strawberries**
- 3/4 **to 1 cup sugar**
- 1/4 **cup lemon juice**
- 2 **teaspoons grated lemon peel**
- 1 **cup ginger ale**

In a blender, process water, strawberries, sugar, lemon juice and peel in batches until smooth. Strain the berry seeds if desired. Pour into a pitcher; stir in the ginger ale. **Yield:** 8 servings.

black bean quesadillas

prep/cook: 30 minutes

When I get home late from work as an operating room nurse, I often rely on this handy recipe. Topped with salsa and sour cream, the crisp wedges are always a hit. when I have extra time, I add chopped onion, black olives and green chilies to the beans.

Jane Epping
Iowa City, Iowa

2 **cans (15 ounces *each*) black beans, rinsed and drained**

1-2/3 **cups salsa, *divided***

10 **flour tortillas (8 inches)**

2 **cups (8 ounces) shredded Colby-Monterey Jack cheese**

2/3 **cup sour cream**

In a bowl, mash the beans; add 1 cup salsa. Place five tortillas on ungreased baking sheets; spread with bean mixture. Sprinkle with cheese; top with the remaining tortillas.

Bake at 350° for 15-18 minutes or until crisp and heated through. Cut each quesadilla into six wedges. Serve with sour cream and remaining salsa. **Yield:** 30 wedges.

‖UltimateTIP

To make popcorn on the stove, use a large pot with a loose-fitting lid. Add 1/3 cup vegetable oil for 1 cup of kernels (1 cup kernels yields 8 cups of popped popcorn). Heat the oil to 400°-460° (if the oil smokes, it's too hot). Drop in one kernel; when it pops, add the rest—just enough to create a single layer. Cover the pan and shake. When the popping slows, remove the pan from the heat.

---

parmesan popcorn

prep/cook: 10 minutes

This tasty snack is a step up flavor-wise from plain old popcorn. The grated Parmesan cheese and melted butter make it super delicious, and the hot sauce adds just the right amount of zip.

Pat Ross
Dearborn, Michigan

4 **cups popped popcorn**

2 **tablespoons grated Parmesan cheese**

2 **tablespoons butter, melted**

1/4 **teaspoon paprika**

3 **drops hot pepper sauce**

1/4 **teaspoon salt**

Place popcorn in an 8-in. square baking dish. Bake at 350° for 5 minutes or until heated through. Combine the Parmesan cheese, butter, paprika and hot pepper sauce. Pour over popcorn; toss to coat. Sprinkle with the salt. Serve warm. **Yield:** 1-2 servings.

frappe mocha

prep: 5 minutes + freezing

Using coffee ice cubes adds body to this refreshing drink. What a treat!

Beverly Coyde
Gasport, New York

- 1 **teaspoon instant coffee granules**
- 1/4 **cup boiling water**
- 1 **cup milk**
- 4-1/2 **teaspoons chocolate syrup**
- 1/2 **cup crushed ice**

Whipped topping and additional chocolate syrup, optional

Dissolve the coffee granules in water. Pour into an ice cube tray; freeze.

In a blender, combine the milk, chocolate syrup and coffee ice cubes. Cover and process until smooth. Add crushed ice; blend. Pour into chilled glasses; serve immediately. Garnish with whipped topping and additional chocolate syrup if desired. **Yield:** 2 servings.

taffy apple dip

prep/cook: 10 minutes

My mother-in-law gave me this recipe. It's simple to make, and it tastes like the real thing!

Sue Gronholz
Columbus, Wisconsin

- 1 **package (8 ounces) cream cheese, softened**
- 3/4 **cup packed brown sugar**
- 1 **tablespoon vanilla extract**
- 1/2 **cup chopped peanuts**
- 6 **apples, cut into wedges**

Beat cream cheese, brown sugar and vanilla until smooth. Spread mixture on a small serving plate; top with nuts. Serve with apple wedges. **Yield:** 6 servings.

---

tortilla snack strips

prep/cook: 20 minutes

These crispy, zippy strips are a super homemade alternative to commercial snack chips. Add a dash of cayenne pepper for an extra kick!

Karen Riordan
Fern Creek, Kentucky

- 2 **tablespoons butter, melted**
- 6 **flour tortillas (8 inches)**
- 1/2 **teaspoon ground cumin**
- 1/2 **teaspoon garlic powder**
- 1/2 **teaspoon onion salt** *or* **onion powder**

Brush butter over one side of each tortilla. Combine the seasonings; lightly sprinkle 1/4 teaspoon over each tortilla. Make two stacks of tortillas, with three in each stack. Using a serrated knife, cut each stack into nine thin strips.

Place in an ungreased 15-in. x 10-in. x 1-in. baking pan. Bake at 400° for 8-10 minutes or until lightly browned. Serve warm. **Yield:** 1-1/2 dozen.

- 2 cups cold 2% milk
- 1 package (1.4 ounces) sugar-free instant chocolate pudding mix
- 2 tablespoons vanilla extract
- 2 large ripe frozen bananas, sliced
- 2 cups coarsely crushed ice cubes

In a blender, combine the milk, pudding mix and vanilla; cover and process until blended. Add the bananas and ice; cover and process until smooth. Pour into the chilled glasses; serve immediately. **Yield: 4 servings.**

chocolate banana smoothies

prep/cook: 5 minutes

Instant pudding makes a wonderful creamy chocolate drink when blended with some frozen banana. It's fun, tasty and easy.

Katherine Lipka
Galesburg, Michigan

||UltimateTIP

Have extra bananas with brown skin? Just freeze them and use later! Peel and mash overripe bananas with 1 teaspoon of lemon juice for each banana used. Freeze in 1- or 2-cup amounts in airtight containers for up to 6 months. To use the mashed bananas in a recipe, measure about 1-1/3 cups mashed bananas for every three medium or four small bananas.

cherry yogurt smoothies

prep/cook: 5 minutes

I add some canned pie filling to create this special smoothie. This is a favorite of mine. I think the cherries and banana are an awesome combination.

Katie Sloan
Charlotte, North Carolina

- 1 cup cranberry juice
- 1 cup (8 ounces) cherry yogurt
- 1/2 cup cherry pie filling
- 1 medium ripe banana, cut into chunks
- 1 to 1-1/2 cups ice cubes

In a blender, combine all ingredients; cover and process until blended. Pour into the chilled glasses; serve immediately. **Yield: 4 servings.**

turkey nachos

prep/cook: 10 minutes

Chunks of leftover turkey are a tasty addition to this thick, cheesy dip that starts with just three items. This recipe yields two cups, but you can easily double or triple it for an extra-large party.

Gayle Lewis
Winston, Oregon

1 can (10-3/4 ounces) condensed cheddar cheese soup, undiluted

3/4 cup salsa

1 cup cubed cooked turkey *or* chicken

Tortilla chips

   Combine the soup and salsa. Bring to a boil. Reduce heat; stir in turkey; cook until heated through. Serve warm with tortilla chips. **Yield: About 2 cups.**

coconut fruit dip

prep/cook: 10 minutes

This fruit dip has a fun pineapple and coconut flavor. I usually serve it with melon slices, strawberries and grapes, but you could use whatever fruit you have on hand. It's a big hit whenever I make it.

Nancy Tanguay
Lakeville, Massachusetts

1 can (8 ounces) crushed unsweetened pineapple, undrained

3/4 cup fat-free milk

1/2 cup (4 ounces) fat-free sour cream

3/4 teaspoon coconut extract

1 package (3.4 ounces) instant vanilla pudding mix

   In a blender, combine all five ingredients; cover and process for 1 minute or until smooth. Store in the refrigerator. **Yield: 2 cups.**

cheesy zucchini bites

prep/cook: 30 minutes

Garden-fresh zucchini and cherry tomatoes are tastefully combined in these colorful snacks. They're so yummy, folks tend to hang around the appetizer tray whenever I serve these pretty party bites.

Amy Frombach
Bradford, Pennsylvania

5 medium zucchini (about 6 inches long)
4 ounces blue cheese, crumbled
3 tablespoons grated Parmesan cheese
1 teaspoon dried basil
1/8 teaspoon pepper
1 pint cherry tomatoes, thinly sliced

Cut zucchini into 3/4-in. slices. Using a melon baller or small spoon, scoop out the insides and discard, leaving the bottom intact. Place zucchini on an ungreased baking sheet; spoon 1/2 teaspoon crumbled blue cheese into each.

Combine Parmesan cheese, basil and pepper; sprinkle half over the blue cheese. Top each with a tomato slice; sprinkle with the remaining Parmesan mixture.

Bake at 400° for 5-7 minutes or until cheese is melted. Serve warm. **Yield:** 35 appetizers.

crunchy cheese nibblers

prep/cook: 25 minutes

With only five ingredients, these savory bites are easy to make and taste scrumptious.

Janis Plourde
Smooth Rock Falls, Ontario

1 cup (4 ounces) finely shredded cheddar cheese
1 cup crushed potato chips
1/2 cup all-purpose flour
1/4 cup butter, softened
1 teaspoon ground mustard

In a bowl, combine all ingredients. Shape dough into 3/4-in. balls. Place on ungreased baking sheets and flatten slightly. Bake at 375° for 5-8 minutes or until golden brown. Remove to a wire rack. Serve warm. **Yield:** about 3 dozen.

berry yogurt shakes

prep/cook: 5 minutes

We have a few raspberry bushes in our backyard. If my grandchildren don't get the berries first, I use them in recipes like this one. Of course, the kids love the mellow flavor of these shakes. So either way, they win!

Jacquie Adams
Coquitlam, British Columbia

> 2 **cartons (8 ounces *each*) reduced-fat lemon yogurt**
>
> 1-1/2 **cups fat-free milk**
>
> 1 **cup unsweetened raspberries**
>
> **Sugar substitute equivalent to 2 tablespoons sugar**

Place all ingredients in a blender; cover and process until smooth. Pour into chilled glasses; serve immediately. **Yield:** 4 servings.

california fried walnuts

prep/cook: 25 minutes

The fried walnuts are as unique as they are delicious. They make an excellent party snack and always seem to disappear fast.

Alcy Thorne
Los Molinos, California

> 6 **cups water**
>
> 4 **cups walnut halves**
>
> 1/2 **cup sugar**
>
> **Oil for frying**
>
> 1-1/4 **teaspoons salt**

In a large saucepan, bring water to a boil. Add the walnuts; boil for 1 minute. Drain; rinse under hot water. Meanwhile, in a large bowl, toss the walnuts with sugar.

In an electric skillet, heat 1/2 in. of oil to 350°. Fry walnuts for 5 minutes or until dark brown, stirring often. Drain in a colander over paper towels. Sprinkle with salt. Store in an airtight container. **Yield:** 4 cups.

easy black bean salsa

prep/cook: 15 minutes

This salsa is a staple at my house. I can make it in about 5 minutes, so it's great for quick meals or snacks. I like to stir in some sliced olives, too!

Betty Lake
Scottsdale, Arizona

1 **can (14-1/2 ounces) Mexican stewed tomatoes**

1 **can (15 ounces) black beans, rinsed and drained**

1 **can (4 ounces) chopped green chilies, undrained**

1/2 **cup chopped onion**

1/4 **cup minced fresh cilantro**

1/2 **teaspoon salt**

Drain tomatoes, reserving juice. Cut up tomatoes; place in a bowl. Add juice and all remaining ingredients; stir until combined. Cover and store in the refrigerator. Serve with tortilla chips or as an accompaniment to Mexican food. **Yield:** about 4 cups.

smooth vanilla shakes

prep/cook: 5 minutes

Rich and creamy shakes are sure to round out any meal. They also make a great anytime snack. Pudding mix, yogurt and banana make this a deliciously different treat.

Taste of Home Test Kitchen
Greendale, Wisconsin

2 cups cold milk
1/3 cup instant vanilla pudding mix
1 carton (8 ounces) vanilla yogurt
1-1/2 cups vanilla ice cream
1 small ripe banana

Place all ingredients in a blender. Cover and process until smooth. Pour into chilled glasses. Serve immediately. **Yield:** 4 servings.

asparagus in puff pastry

prep: 30 minutes + chilling | **bake:** 10 minutes

This is one of my all-time favorite appetizers. Fast and easy, the golden bites are always a huge hit. I make and freeze batches of them during asparagus season for dinner parties throughout the year.

Dianne Werdegar
Naperville, Illinois

2 cups water
24 fresh asparagus spears (about 1 pound), trimmed
1 package (8 ounces) reduced-fat cream cheese
1/2 teaspoon salt
1 package (17-1/4 ounces) frozen puff pastry dough, thawed
1/4 cup egg substitute

In a large nonstick skillet, bring water to a boil. Add the asparagus; cover and cook for 3 minutes. Drain asparagus and immediately place in ice water; drain and pat dry. Beat the cream cheese and salt until smooth; set aside.

Unfold the dough on a lightly floured surface. Cut each sheet in half widthwise. For each rectangle, spread the cream cheese mixture lengthwise over half of the dough to within 1/2 in. of edges. Arrange two rows of three asparagus spears lengthwise in a single layer over the cream cheese.

Brush edges of dough with some of the egg substitute; fold dough over filling and press edges together to seal. Cover and refrigerate for 1 hour.

Cut widthwise into 1-1/4-in. pieces. Place 1 in. apart on a baking sheet coated with cooking spray. Brush with remaining egg substitute. Bake at 425° for 8-12 minutes or until golden. Serve warm. **Yield:** 28 servings.

guacamole dip

prep/cook: 10 minutes

This area of the country has an emphasis on Mexican food, and guacamole is a favorite snack. So I decided to create my own recipe. I serve it as a dip for chips, with baked chicken or to top off a bed of fresh lettuce.

Virginia Burwell
Dayton, Texas

- 1 **large ripe avocado, peeled**
- 1/4 **cup plain yogurt**
- 2 **tablespoons picante sauce *or* salsa**
- 1 **tablespoon finely chopped onion**
- 1/8 **teaspoon salt**
- 2 **to 3 drops hot pepper sauce, optional**

Mash the avocado until smooth. Stir in the yogurt, picante sauce, onion, salt and hot pepper sauce if desired. Cover and refrigerate until serving. **Yield:** 2 servings (3/4 cup).

dreamy fruit dip

prep/cook: 10 minutes

Everyone will love this thick, buttery sensation that is served alongside apple wedges, pineapple chunks and grapes. Chill leftover dip and use as a tasty topping for toast at breakfast the next morning.

Anna Beiler
Strasburg, Pennsylvania

- 1 **package (8 ounces) cream cheese, softened**
- 1/2 **cup butter, softened**
- 1/2 **cup marshmallow creme**
- 1 **carton (8 ounces) frozen whipped topping, thawed**

Assorted fresh fruit

Beat the cream cheese and butter together until smooth. Beat in marshmallow creme. Fold in whipped topping. Serve with fruit. Store in the refrigerator. **Yield:** about 4 cups.

frosty chocolate malted shakes

prep/cook: 10 minutes

I played around with our favorite milk shake recipe to come up with this lighter version. I serve it all the time, and no one misses the extra fat or calories.

Dora Dean
Hollywood, Florida

6 cups reduced-fat frozen vanilla yogurt

3-1/2 cups fat-free milk

1/4 cup sugar-free instant chocolate drink mix

1/4 cup malted milk powder

1-1/2 teaspoons vanilla extract

In batches, process all five ingredients in a blender until smooth. Pour shakes into tall glasses. **Yield:** 10 servings.

winter warmer

prep/cook: 10 minutes

I found this beverage recipe more than 15 years ago, when I was in high school. My husband and I also enjoy it after the children go to bed.

Sally Seidel
Banner, Wyoming

2 envelopes (1 ounce *each*) instant hot cocoa mix *or* 1/2 cup instant hot cocoa mix

3 cups hot brewed coffee

1/4 cup half-and-half cream

3/4 teaspoon rum extract

1/4 cup whipped topping

In a small saucepan, whisk together the cocoa mix, coffee, cream and rum extract until heated through and cocoa is dissolved. Pour into mugs. Garnish with whipped topping. **Yield:** 2 servings.

Editor's Note: For grown-up Winter Warmers, omit the rum extract and pour 1 to 2 oz. dark rum into each mug before adding the coffee mixture.

3 cups water
1 to 1-1/2 cups chopped fresh mint
3/4 cup sugar
3 packages (10 ounces *each*) frozen sweetened raspberries, thawed
2-1/4 cups lemonade concentrate
6 cups cold water
Crushed ice

In a large saucepan, bring the water, mint and sugar to a boil. Stir until sugar is dissolved. Remove from the heat; let stand for 5 minutes. Add the raspberries and the lemonade concentrate; gently mash raspberries.

Line a strainer with four layers of cheesecloth; place over a 1-gal. container. Slowly pour the raspberry mixture into strainer; discard the pulp and mint. Add cold water to raspberry juice; stir well. Serve in chilled glasses over ice. **Yield:** 3-1/2 quarts.

raspberry mint cooler

prep/cook: 30 minutes

This beverage is lovely in the summer when mint and rasp-berries are fresh. A garnish of mint leaves and berries on the top of each serving makes them pretty.

Patricia Kile
Greentown, Pennsylvania

raspberry ice tea

prep: 10 minutes + chilling

Frozen raspberries lend fruity flavor and lovely color to this refreshing iced tea. It calls for just a few common ingredi-ents and offers make-ahead convenience.

Lois McGrady
Hillsville, Virginia

4 quarts water
1-1/2 cups sugar
1 package (12 ounces) frozen unsweetened raspberries
10 individual tea bags
1/4 cup lemon juice

In a large kettle or Dutch oven, bring water and sugar to a boil. Remove from the heat; stir until sugar is dissolved. Add the raspberries, tea bags and lemon juice. Cover and steep for 3 minutes. Strain; discard berries and tea bags.

Transfer the tea to a large container or pitcher. Refrigerate until chilled. Serve tea over ice. **Yield:** 16 servings (4 quarts).

easy mint hot chocolate

prep/cook: 10 minutes

This quick and easy beverage is perfect to serve the family on winter mornings before they head out into the cold. They'll love the minty flavor.

Sue Fisher
Northfield Falls, Vermont

6 Andes chocolate mints
16 ounces chocolate milk
Mini marshmallows, optional

In a small saucepan, melt the mints over low heat. Slowly whisk in chocolate milk until well blended; heat but do not boil. Pour into mugs; top with the mini marshmallows if desired. **Yield: 2 servings.**

||| Ultimate**TIP**

When buying mangoes, look for ones with unblemished green to yellow skin tinged with red that feel fairly firm when gently pressed. To remove the fruit, make a lengthwise cut as close to the seed as possible; trim fruit away from the seed. Score the fruit lengthwise and widthwise, without cutting through the skin. Push the skin up, turning the fruit out. Cut fruit off at the skin.

---

1 medium ripe mango *or* 2 medium peaches, peeled and sliced

2 to 4 tablespoons minced fresh basil

1 tablespoon lemon juice

12 cooked medium shrimp, peeled and deveined

1 tablespoon butter

shrimp with basil-mango sauce

prep/cook: 15 minutes

Instead of serving cold shrimp with cocktail sauce, prepare this simple basil sauce and top it with tender cooked shrimp. It's a fun and fancy appetizer.

Ken Hulme
Prescott, Arizona

In a blender or food processor, combine the mango, minced basil and lemon juice; cover and process until blended. Pour onto two serving plates; set aside.

Skewer two shrimp each onto six 4- to 6-in. metal or soaked wooden skewers, forming a heart shape. Cook in a large skillet in butter over medium-high heat for 4-5 minutes or until shrimp turn pink, turning once. Place over mango sauce. **Yield: 2 servings.**

mushroom puffs

prep/cook: 20 minutes

You can make these attractive appetizers in a jiffy with refrigerated crescent roll dough. The tasty little spirals disappear fast at parties!

Marilin Rosborough
Altoona, Pennsylvania

- 4 **ounces cream cheese, cubed**
- 1 **can (4 ounces) mushroom stems and pieces, drained**
- 1 **tablespoon chopped onion**
- 1/8 **teaspoon hot pepper sauce**
- 1 **tube (8 ounces) crescent roll dough**

In a blender, combine the cream cheese, mushrooms, onion and hot pepper sauce; cover and process until blended. Unroll crescent dough; separate into four rectangles. Press perforations to seal. Spread mushroom mixture over dough.

Roll up jelly-roll style, starting with a long side. Cut each roll into five slices; place on an ungreased baking sheet. Bake at 425° for 8-10 minutes or until puffed and golden brown. **Yield:** 20 appetizers.

colorful fruit kabobs

prep/cook: 15 minutes

These luscious fruit kabobs are perfect as a summer appetizer, snack or side dish. The citrus glaze clings well and keeps the fruit looking fresh.

Ruth Ann Stelfox
Raymond, Alberta

Assorted fruit-strawberries, seedless red grapes, cubed cantaloupe, honeydew and pineapple, and sliced kiwifruit and star fruit

- 1/3 **cup sugar**
- 2 **tablespoons cornstarch**
- 1 **cup orange juice**
- 2 **teaspoons lemon juice**

Alternately thread fruit onto skewers; set aside. In a saucepan, combine sugar, cornstarch and juices until smooth. Bring to a boil; cook and stir for 1-2 minutes or until thickened. Brush over fruit. Refrigerate until serving. **Yield:** 1 cup glaze.

fruity red smoothies

prep/cook: 5 minutes

This thick, tangy drink combines the refreshing flavors of cranberries, raspberries and strawberries. Once you start sipping it, you can't stop!

Beverly Coyde
Gasport, New York

- 1/2 **to 3/4 cup cranberry juice**
- 1 **carton (8 ounces) strawberry yogurt**
- 1-1/2 **cups frozen unsweetened strawberries**
- 1 **cup frozen unsweetened raspberries**
- 1 **to 1-1/2 teaspoons sugar**

In a blender, combine all ingredients; cover and process until smooth. Pour into chilled glasses; serve immediately. **Yield:** 2 servings.

12 whole chicken wings (about 2-1/2 pounds)
 1 bottle (2 ounces) hot pepper sauce (about 1/4 cup)
 1 to 2 garlic cloves, minced
1-1/2 teaspoons dried rosemary, crushed
 1 teaspoon dried thyme
1/4 teaspoon salt
1/4 teaspoon pepper

Cut chicken wings into three sections; discard wing tips. In a large resealable plastic bag, combine the hot pepper sauce, garlic and all seasonings. Add wings; toss to evenly coat. Transfer to a well-greased 13-in. x 9-in. baking dish.

Bake, uncovered, at 425° for 30-40 minutes or until the chicken juices run clear, turning every 10 minutes. **Yield:** 4-6 servings.

Editor's Note: Uncooked chicken wing sections (wingettes) may be substituted for whole chicken wings.

like 'em hot wings

prep: 10 minutes | **bake:** 30 minutes

These spicy chicken wings are wonderfully seasoned. They're an easy crowd-pleasing snack, particularly when served with blue cheese dressing on the side.

Myra Innes
Auburn, Kansas

sweet & saucy meatballs

prep: 15 minutes | **bake:** 40 minutes

The little tasty meatballs are perfect for party appetizers. I often double the recipes so there's plenty to go around.

Kim Brandt
Lovell, Wyoming

 1 egg
1/2 cup quick-cooking oats
 1 pound lean ground beef
1-1/2 cups water
1-1/4 cups ketchup
 1 cup sugar

||| Ultimate**TIP**

For meatballs to cook evenly, it's important for them to be the same size. An easy way to do this is by using a 1- or 1-1/2-inch cookie scoop. Scoop the meat mixture, level off the top and gently roll into a ball. Or, you can lightly pat the meat mixture into a 1-in.-thick rectangle, and cut into equal squares as there are meatballs. Gently roll each square into a ball.

In a large bowl, combine the egg with the oats. Crumble beef over mixture and mix well. Shape into 1-1/2-in. balls.

Place in a lightly greased 11-in. x 7-in. baking dish. Combine water, ketchup and sugar; pour over meatballs. Bake, uncovered, at 350° for 40-50 minutes or until meat is no longer pink. **Yield:** 4-6 servings.

sunset cooler

prep/cook: 10 minutes

You don't have to reserve store-bought strawberry syrup just for making malts and shakes. Stirred into orange juice, it gives festive flair to this tropical-tasting beverage that's a breeze to mix with crushed ice.

Taste of Home Test Kitchen
Greendale, Wisconsin

- 6 **cups crushed ice**
- 6 **cups orange juice**
- 1/2 **to 3/4 cup strawberry syrup**

In a pitcher, combine all ingredients; mix well.
Yield: 6 servings.

ricotta tart

prep: 10 minutes | **bake:** 25 minutes

Guests will think you fussed when they bite into a wedge of this cheesy tart. It's super simple to make with store-bought pie pastry.

Teri Rasey-Bolf
Cadillac, Michigan

- 2 **eggs**
- 1 **cup ricotta cheese**
- 1 **cup (4 ounces) shredded sharp cheddar cheese**
- 2 **tablespoons salsa**
- 1/2 **teaspoon salt**
- 1/2 **teaspoon pepper**

Pastry for a single-crust pie (9 inches)

In a large bowl, beat eggs. Add the cheeses, salsa, salt and pepper; mix well. Roll out pastry into a 12-in. circle on a foil-lined baking sheet. Spread with cheese mixture to within 1 in. of edge. Fold edge of pastry over outer edge of filling.

Bake the tart at 400° for 22-26 minutes or until golden brown. Let stand for 5 minutes before cutting into wedges. Refrigerate any leftovers.
Yield: 8-12 servings.

buffet meatballs

prep: 10 minutes | **cook:** 4 hours

It takes only five ingredients to fix these easy appetizers. Grape juice and apple jelly are the secrets behind the sweet yet tangy sauce that complements convenient packaged meatballs.

Janet Anderson
Carson City, Nevada

- 1 **cup grape juice**
- 1 **cup apple jelly**
- 1 **cup ketchup**
- 1 **can (8 ounces) tomato sauce**
- 4 **pounds frozen Italian-style meatballs**

In a small saucepan, combine the juice, jelly, ketchup and tomato sauce. Cook and stir over medium heat until jelly is melted; remove from the heat. Place meatballs in a 5-qt. slow cooker. Pour sauce over the top and gently stir to coat. Cover and cook on low for 4 hours or until heated through. **Yield:** about 11 dozen.

springtime lime slushy

prep: 10 minutes + freezing

I rely on a handful of ingredients to fix this lively lime beverage. With its tart flavor and slushy consistency, it's especially cool and refreshing.

Joyce Minge-Johns
Jacksonville, Florida

- 2 **packages (3 ounces *each*) lime gelatin**
- 2 **cups boiling water**
- 2 **cups cold water**
- 2 **quarts lime sherbet**
- 3 **cups ginger ale, chilled**

In a freezer container, dissolve the gelatin in boiling water. Stir in the cold water and sherbet until combined. Freeze for 4 hours or until set.

Remove from the freezer 45 minutes before serving. For each serving, place 1 cup of slush mixture in a glass; add about 1/3 cup ginger ale. **Yield:** 8 servings.

raspberry lemon smoothie

prep: 15 minutes + chilling

With the flavors of raspberry and pineapple. this cool, thirst-quencher hits the spot on a hot day.

Patricia Quinn
Omaha, Nebraska

- 2 **cups boiling water**
- 8 **lemon herbal tea bags**
- 2 **cups pineapple juice**
- 1 **pint raspberry sherbet**

Lemon slices, optional

In a teapot, pour the boiling water over the tea bags; cover and steep for 5 minutes. Discard the bags and chill the tea.

In a blender, cover and process the tea, pineapple juice and sherbet until smooth. Pour into glasses. Garnish with lemon if desired. Serve immediately. **Yield: 4 servings.**

dragon dippers

prep/cook: 30 minutes

Once you taste these crispy chips, you may never buy tortilla chips again. The homemade snacks are a snap to prepare and are perfect served with salsa.

Taste of Home Test Kitchen
Greendale, Wisconsin

- 2 **tablespoons butter, melted**
- 10 **flour tortillas (6 inches)**
- 3/4 **teaspoon garlic salt**
- 3/4 **teaspoon ground cumin**
- 3/4 **teaspoon chili powder**

Brush butter on one side of each tortilla. Combine the seasonings; sprinkle over tortillas. Cut each into eight wedges. Place on ungreased baking sheets. Bake at 400° for 6-8 minutes or until crisp. **Yield: 6-1/2 dozen.**

refreshing fruit dip

prep/cook: 5 minutes

This brightly colored fruit dip is a breeze to blend together with peaches and strawberries from the freezer. Sometimes I don't completely thaw the fruit first because I like to eat the dip cold.

Jessica Humphrey
Fort Atkinson, Wisconsin

1 package (16 ounces) frozen unsweetened sliced peaches, thawed

1 package (10 ounces) frozen sweetened sliced strawberries, thawed

1 tablespoon lemon juice

1/4 teaspoon almond extract

Assorted fresh fruit

In a food processor, combine the first four ingredients; cover and process until smooth. Serve with fruit. **Yield:** 2-1/2 cups.

sunny slush

prep/cook: 10 minutes

What a cool and refreshing drink on a hot summer's day! It's like taking a trip to the tropics.

Carol Wakley
North East, Pennsylvania

6 cups pineapple juice
4 pints lemon sherbet
24 ice cubes
1 teaspoon rum extract

In a blender, combine pineapple juice, sherbet, ice and extract in batches; cover and process until smooth. Pour into chilled glasses. **Yield:** 3 quarts.

|||UltimateTIP

For an appetizer buffet that serves as the meal, offer five or six different appetizers (including some substantial selections) and plan on eight to nine pieces per guest. If you'll also be serving a meal, two to three pieces per person is sufficient. In order to appeal to everyone's tastes and diets, have a balance of hearty and low-calorie appetizers as well as hot and cold choices.

---

1 pound bulk pork sausage
1 package (8 ounces) cream cheese, softened
1 cup (4 ounces) shredded Parmesan cheese
22 large jalapeno peppers, halved lengthwise and seeded
Ranch salad dressing, optional

In a large skillet, cook the sausage over medium heat until no longer pink; drain. Combine the cream cheese and Parmesan cheese; fold in the cooked sausage.

Spoon about 1 tablespoonful into each jalapeno half. Place in two ungreased 13-in. x 9-in. baking dishes. Bake, uncovered, at 425° for 15-20 minutes or until filling is lightly browned and bubbly. Serve with the ranch dressing if desired. **Yield: 44 appetizers.**

Editor's Note: When cutting hot peppers, such as jalapenos, disposable gloves are recommended. Avoid touching your face.

sausage-stuffed jalapenos

prep: 20 minutes | **bake:** 15 minutes

If you like appetizers with a little kick, you'll savor these zippy cream cheese- and sausage-filled jalapenos.

Rachel Oswald
Greenville, Michigan

cappuccino chip cupcakes

prep/cook: 30 minutes

I use a muffin mix, vanilla chips and instant coffee granules to make these moist morsels. With a big chocolate flavor, they are sure to garner smiles on tired faces.

Kris Presley
Summerville, South Carolina

- 1 **package (18-1/4 ounces) double chocolate muffin mix**
- 1 **cup water**
- 1 **egg**
- 2 **tablespoons instant coffee granules**
- 1 **teaspoon ground cinnamon**
- 1/2 **cup vanilla *or* white chips**

In a large bowl, combine the muffin mix, water, egg, coffee granules and cinnamon just until moistened. Fold in chips. Fill greased muffin cups three-fourths full.

Bake at 425° for 18-21 minutes or until a toothpick comes out clean. Cool for 5 minutes before removing from the pan to a wire rack. **Yield: 1 dozen.**

sparkling rhubarb spritzer

prep: 5 minutes | **cook:** 15 minutes + chilling

Folks with a rhubarb plant or two will love this recipe. It's a nice change from the usual lemonade...we enjoy it all summer long.

Sue Rebers
Campbellsport, Wisconsin

- 12 **cups chopped fresh *or* frozen rhubarb**
- 4 **cups water**
- 2-1/2 **to 3 cups sugar**
- 1 **cup pineapple juice**
- 2 **liters lemon-lime soda, chilled**

Ice cubes

In a Dutch oven, bring rhubarb and water to a boil. Boil for 15 minutes. Cool for 10 minutes; strain and reserve juice. Discard pulp. Add sugar and pineapple juice to reserved juice; stir until sugar is dissolved. Chill thoroughly. Just before serving, add soda and ice cubes. **Yield:** 3-1/2 quarts (14 servings, 1 cup per serving).

dairy delicious dip

prep: 5 minutes + chilling

Munching on fruit becomes so much more fun when there's a sweet, creamy dip to dunk your slices in. After working up an appetite playing party games, the kids enjoy this dip. I like its ease of preparation.

Karen Kenney
Harvard, Illinois

- 1 package (8 ounces) cream cheese, softened
- 1/2 cup sour cream
- 1/4 cup sugar
- 1/4 cup packed brown sugar
- 1 to 2 tablespoons maple syrup

In a small bowl, combine the softened cream cheese, sour cream, sugars and maple syrup to taste; beat until smooth. Chill. **Yield:** 2 cups.

special lemonade

prep: 15 minutes + standing

This refreshing beverage is a little different from your run-of-the-mill lemonade. The yummy recipe comes from a charming tearoom in a historic home that my mother and I enjoy visiting regularly.

Erin Schneider
St. Peters, Missouri

- 2 medium lemons
- 1-1/2 cups sugar
- 2 cups milk
- 3 cups chilled club soda
- 2 to 3 drops yellow food coloring, optional

Remove ends from lemons and discard. Remove lemon peel with a knife; set aside. Quarter lemons; squeeze juice into a bowl. Remove and discard white membrane.

Place the peel and pulp in a blender; cover and process until coarsely chopped. Add peel mixture and sugar to lemon juice; mix well. Let stand for 30 minutes.

Stir in milk. Strain lemon mixture; add club soda and food coloring if desired. Serve immediately. **Yield:** 8 servings.

pear cooler

prep/cook: 5 minutes

My daughter and I had eaten a cold fruit soup while on vacation. When we got home, we tried to create our own version, and wound up with this yummy smoothie. Everyone enjoys it.

Jeri Clayton
Sandy, Utah

- 1 **can (15-1/4 ounces) sliced pears, undrained**
- 2 **cups ice cubes**
- 1 **envelope whipped topping mix**
- 1/4 **to 1/2 teaspoon vanilla *or* almond extract, optional**

In a blender, combine all of the ingredients. Cover and process until smooth. Pour into chilled glasses; serve immediately. **Yield:** 3 servings.

‖UltimateTIP

A blender is a great kitchen appliance to own, but cleaning one can sometimes be difficult. Here's an excellent way to easily clean your blender: Fill the jar halfway with hot water, then add a small drop of dishwashing liquid. Place the cover on the blender and blend on high for 10-15 seconds. Thoroughly rinse with hot water and air-dry overnight.

---

speedy pizza rings

prep/cook: 15 minutes

I love these little spicy appetizers because they come together in a jiffy. They also have all the flavor of pizza with the added health benefits of vegetables.

Karen Hope
Miller, Missouri

- 2 **medium zucchini (about 2 inches in diameter), cut into 1/4-inch slices**
- 1 **can (8 ounces) pizza sauce**
- 1 **package (3 ounces) sliced pepperoni**
- 1 **cup (4 ounces) shredded part-skim mozzarella cheese**

Sliced jalapeno peppers and ripe olives, optional

Arrange zucchini in a single layer on a large microwave-safe plate coated with cooking spray. Microwave, uncovered, on high for 2-1/4 minutes. Spread 1 teaspoon pizza sauce on each zucchini round; top each with a slice of pepperoni.

Heat, uncovered, for 1-1/2 minutes. Sprinkle each ring with cheese, jalapenos and olives if desired. Microwave 30-50 seconds longer or until the cheese is melted. **Yield:** 10-12 servings.

Editor's Note: When cutting hot peppers, disposable gloves are recommended. Avoid touching your face. This recipe was tested in a 1,100-watt microwave.

crunchy trail mix

prep/cook: 15 minutes

This mix was the perfect item for my daughter to take to high school track meets. This colorful crowd-pleaser is crunchy, chewy and not too sweet.

Theresa Gingery
Holmesville, Nebraska

- 1 **package (16 ounces) milk chocolate M&M's**
- 1 **package (10 ounces) peanut butter chips**
- 1 **can (3 ounces) chow mein noodles**
- 1-1/2 **cups raisins**
- 1-1/4 **cups peanuts**

In a large bowl, combine all ingredients; mix well. Store in an airtight container. **Yield:** 8 cups.

- 1/2 **cup creamy peanut butter**
- 5 **tablespoons milk chocolate chips, melted and cooled**
- 2 **tablespoons whipped topping**
- 20 **to 25 large fresh strawberries**
- 5 **squares (1 ounce *each*) semisweet chocolate, melted**

Line a baking sheet with waxed paper; set aside. Combine the peanut butter, melted milk chocolate and whipped topping.

Beginning at the top right of the stem, cut each strawberry in half diagonally. Scoop out the white portion from the larger half of each berry. Spread or pipe peanut butter mixture between the two halves; press together gently.

Place on prepared pan; refrigerate for 15 minutes or until set. Dip the bottom halves of strawberries in melted semisweet chocolate. Place on pan. Refrigerate for 15-20 minutes or until set. **Yield:** 20-25 servings.

Editor's Note: Reduced-fat or generic brands of peanut butter are not recommended for this recipe.

peanut butter berry delights

prep: 20 minutes + chilling

These cream-filled, chocolate-dipped strawberries are an excellent treat for a shower or pretty party dessert. They always receive compliments.

Rose Harman
Hays, Kansas

strawberry lemonade slush

prep: 5 minutes + freezing

This refreshing fruity slush really perks up the taste buds. I have made it for Christmas, Valentine's Day, summer potlucks and other occasions, and it's so popular there is seldom any left.

Sue Jorgensen
Rapid City, South Dakota

- 3/4 **cup water**
- 3/4 **cup pink lemonade concentrate**
- 1 **package (10 ounces) frozen sweetened sliced strawberries, thawed**
- 3/4 **cup ice cubes**
- 1 **cup club soda**

In a blender, combine the water, lemonade concentrate, sliced strawberries and ice cubes. Cover and process until blended.

Pour into a freezer container. Cover and freeze for at least 12 hours or up to 3 months.

Let stand at room temperature for 1 hour before serving. Stir in club soda. Pour into chilled glasses; serve immediately. **Yield: 4 servings.**

italian sausage mushrooms

prep/cook: 25 minutes

These savory bites can be made with only a handful of items. Whether you serve them as an elegant appetizer or as a side dish, they're sure to steal the show.

Lorie Zufall
Waynesboro, Pennsylvania

- 1 **pound bulk Italian sausage**
- 24 **medium fresh mushrooms**
- 2 **packages (3 ounces *each*) cream cheese, softened**
- 4 **tablespoons minced fresh parsley, *divided***

In a large skillet, cook sausage over medium heat until no longer pink; drain. Remove and discard mushroom stems. Place caps on a microwave-safe plate. Microwave, uncovered, on high for 2 minutes; drain.

Combine the cream cheese, 3 tablespoons parsley and sausage until well blended. Spoon into mushroom caps.

Cover and microwave at 70% power for 5-7 minutes or until heated through; drain. Let stand for 5 minutes before serving. Sprinkle with remaining parsley. **Yield:** 2 dozen.

Editor's Note: This recipe was tested in a 1,100-watt microwave.

||| Ultimate**TIP**

To prepare mushrooms for cooking, gently remove dirt by rubbing with a mushroom brush or wipe them with a damp paper towel. Or quickly rinse under cold water, drain and pat dry with paper towels. Do not peel mushrooms. Trim stems. For shiitake mushrooms, remove and discard stems. Mushrooms can be eaten raw, marinated, sauteed, stir-fried, baked, broiled or grilled.

---

banana cocoa smoothies

prep/cook: 10 minutes

With its chocolaty twist, this frothy concoction appeals to folks of all ages. It's a great way to ensure youngsters get plenty of calcium-packed yogurt and milk, too.

Anne Yaeger
Houston, Texas

- 1 **cup (8 ounces) fat-free vanilla yogurt**
- 3/4 **cup fat-free milk**
- 1 **medium ripe banana, frozen and cut into chunks**
- 3 **tablespoon sugar-free chocolate drink mix**
- 1/4 **teaspoon vanilla extract**

In a blender, combine all ingredients. Cover and process until smooth. Pour into chilled glasses; serve immediately. **Yield:** 3 servings.

salads & dressings

pg. 52

sweet potato salad 40

two-bean salad 41

blue cheese salad dressing 41

raspberry tossed salad 42

italian cucumber salad 42

cool lime salad 43

tortellini toss 43

red, white and green salad 44

sweet-sour lettuce salad 44

fruit salad dressing 45

simple cabbage slaw 45

seven-layer gelatin salad 46

milly's salad dressing 46

mandarin fluff 47

old-fashioned egg salad 47

swift strawberry salad 48

speedy spinach salad 48

fruity green salad 49

baby corn romaine salad 49

tangy cucumber gelatin 50

simple salad dressing 50

fresh fruit bowl 51

catalina tomato salad 51

sparkling melon 52

hoppin' good salad 53

italian tuna pasta salad 53

grandmother's orange salad 54

thousand island dressing 54

broccoli apple salad 55

blt pasta salad 55

pg. 44

pg. 49

sweet potato salad

prep: 25 minutes + chilling

When I took this salad to a potluck dinner, several people asked me for the recipe. The sweet potatoes make it unique, and it really is delicious. I think you'll agree it's a nice change of pace from traditional potato salads.

Lettie Baker
Pennsboro, West Virginia

3 **pounds sweet potatoes, cooked, peeled and cubed**

1 **cup chopped green pepper**

1/2 **cup finely chopped onion**

1-1/2 **teaspoons salt, optional**

1/4 **teaspoon pepper**

1-1/2 **cups light *or* regular mayonnaise**

Dash hot pepper sauce

Combine the first five ingredients in a large bowl. Add mayonnaise and pepper sauce; mix well. Cover and refrigerate for at least 1 hour before serving. **Yield:** 10 servings.

two-bean salad

prep: 5 minutes + chilling

Bottled dressing adds flavor in a flash to this salad. The recipe can be doubled or even tripled for potlucks, picnics or barbecues.

Sue Ross
Casa Grande, Arizona

1 package (9 ounces) frozen cut green beans, cooked and drained
1 cup canned garbanzo beans, rinsed and drained
1/3 cup julienned red onion
1/4 cup Italian salad dressing
1/8 teaspoon salt *or* salt-free seasoning blend

In a bowl, combine beans and onion. Add dressing and salt; toss to coat. Cover and chill until serving. **Yield:** 4 servings.

‖Ultimate**TIP**

The "shelf life" of homemade salad dressings varies somewhat. Generally, vinaigrettes can be kept refrigerated for up to 2 weeks. Dairy-based dressings that contain ingredients such as buttermilk or sour cream, and that also include fresh ingredients, like chopped onion, fresh herbs, tomato sauce and chopped hard-cooked egg, will keep for up to 1 week.

---

blue cheese salad dressing

prep/cook: 5 minutes

This classic, tangy salad dressing is ready to serve in 15 minutes or less. We like the blend of flavors with the blue cheese.

Margaret Krueger
New Berlin, Wisconsin

1/2 cup plain yogurt
1/2 cup sour cream
1 tablespoon lemon juice
1 garlic clove, minced
1/8 teaspoon pepper
1/2 cup (2 ounces) crumbled blue cheese

Combine the yogurt, sour cream, lemon juice, garlic and pepper; whisk until smooth. Stir in the blue cheese. Serve over salad greens. Store in the refrigerator. **Yield:** 1-1/3 cups.

9 cups torn mixed salad greens

3 cups fresh *or* frozen unsweetened raspberries

2 tablespoons olive oil

2 tablespoons cider vinegar

4 teaspoons sugar

1/8 teaspoon salt

Dash pepper

In a large salad bowl, gently combine the salad greens and 2-3/4 cups fresh or frozen raspberries. Mash the remaining berries; strain, reserving the juice and discarding seeds. Whisk the raspberry juice, oil, vinegar, sugar, salt and pepper. Drizzle over salad; gently toss to coat. **Yield:** 12 servings.

raspberry tossed salad

prep/cook: 15 minutes

Fresh raspberries brighten this tossed green salad, making it the perfect side dish to round out a festive Yuletide menu. Raspberry juice brings a special, fruity touch to the light oil-and-vinegar dressing.

Kerry Sullivan
Longwood, Florida

italian cucumber salad

prep/cook: 10 minutes

This salad makes a perfect accompaniment to almost any soup, stew or main dish. I like to take it to potlucks, where it always goes over well.

Jane Nichols
Houston, Texas

2 medium cucumbers, peeled and sliced

1 cup halved cherry tomatoes

1 cup sliced red onion

1/2 cup chopped green pepper

1/2 cup Italian salad dressing

In a large bowl, combine all of the ingredients; cover and refrigerate until serving. Serve with a slotted spoon. **Yield:** 8 servings.

cool lime salad

prep: 20 minutes + chilling

I've made this recipe for many years. Since my husband is diabetic, one-portion recipes work out well for us.

Elnora Johnson
Union City, Tennessee

- 1/2 cup undrained canned crushed pineapple
- 2 tablespoons lime gelatin
- 1/4 cup 4% cottage cheese
- 1/4 cup whipped topping

In a small saucepan, bring pineapple to a boil. Remove from the heat and stir in gelatin until dissolved. Cool to room temperature. Stir in the cottage cheese and whipped topping; transfer to a small bowl. Chill until set. **Yield:** 1 serving.

tortellini toss

prep/cook: 30 minutes

This hearty salad can serve as a main course or side dish. The creamy Italian dressing and marinated artichoke hearts create a tangy coating for the tortellini.

Mary Ellen Pillatzhi
Buffalo, Minnesota

- 1-1/4 cups frozen cheese tortellini
- 6 cherry tomatoes, halved
- 1/4 cup sliced green onions
- 1 jar (6-1/2 ounces) marinated artichoke hearts, drained and coarsely chopped
- 1/4 cup creamy Italian salad dressing

Cook tortellini according to package directions; drain and rinse with cold water. Place in a bowl. Add the tomatoes, onions, artichokes and salad dressing; toss to coat. Refrigerate until serving. **Yield:** 2-3 servings.

1 pound small red potatoes, cooked and cubed

2 large tomatoes, diced

1 pound green beans, cut into 2-inch pieces and cooked

7 tablespoons olive oil

5 tablespoons white wine vinegar

3/4 teaspoon salt

1/2 teaspoon pepper

In a large bowl, combine potatoes, tomatoes and beans. In another bowl, combine the oil, vinegar, salt and pepper. Pour dressing over vegetables; toss to coat. Refrigerate for several hours before serving. **Yield:** 8-10 servings.

red, white and green salad

prep: 15 minutes + chilling

This crisp and cool salad is great for summertime...and it's easy to prepare! Try it at your next get-together, such as a family picnic.

Jodie McCoy
Tulsa, Oklahoma

sweet-sour lettuce salad

prep/cook: 10 minutes

This super-quick salad dressing is a breeze to shake up when you're in a hurry. Its refreshing, slightly sweet flavor compliments fresh salad greens and crispy bits of bacon quite nicely.

Lois Fetting
Nelson, Wisconsin

1/2 cup sugar

1/4 cup vinegar

2 tablespoons water

3/4 cup half-and-half cream

8 cups torn salad greens

6 bacon strips, cooked and crumbled

||| UltimateTIP

Recipes often call for a specific type of vinegar. White vinegar has a sharp flavor and is used for pickling and in recipes where a strong taste is desired. Cider vinegar is made from apples, has a fruity flavor and is used in recipes where a milder flavor is preferred. In general, if more sharpness is desired, use white vinegar. For a milder flavor, use cider vinegar.

In a jar with a tight-fitting lid, combine the sugar, vinegar and water; shake until sugar is dissolved. Add cream; shake well. Just before serving, toss greens, bacon and dressing in a large bowl. **Yield:** 8 servings.

fruit salad dressing

prep/cook: 15 minutes

Served with seasonal fruit, this citrusy dressing makes a revitalizing side dish or dessert for your next ladies' luncheon or breakfast buffet. It's a snap to make, too!

Shirley Haase
Madison, Wisconsin

2/3 **cup orange juice**
3 **tablespoons lemon juice**
1 **cup sugar**
1 **egg, lightly beaten**
Assorted fresh fruit

In a small saucepan, combine juices, sugar and egg. Bring to a boil; cook and stir for 1 minute or until thickened. Strain. Cover and refrigerate until serving. Serve with fresh fruit. **Yield:** about 1 cup.

simple cabbage slaw

prep: 5 minutes + chilling

When I was growing up, my father would make this salad as part of our Sunday dinner. Now I carry on the tradition with my own family.

Sandra Lampe
Muscatine, Iowa

4 **cups coleslaw mix**
1 **medium sweet red *or* green pepper, finely chopped**
5 **tablespoons sugar**
5 **tablespoons cider vinegar**
1/4 **cup water**
1/4 **teaspoon salt**
1/8 **teaspoon pepper**

In a large bowl, combine all ingredients and toss to coat. Cover and refrigerate for at least 4 hours or overnight. **Yield:** 6 servings.

seven-layer gelatin salad

prep: 30 minutes + chilling

Here's an eye-catching salad that my mother makes for Christmas dinner each year. You can choose different flavors to make other color combinations for specific holidays or other gatherings.

Jan Hemness
Stockton, Missouri

7 packages (3 ounces *each*) assorted flavored gelatin
4-1/2 cups boiling water, *divided*
4-1/2 cups cold water, *divided*
1 can (12 ounces) evaporated milk, *divided*
1 carton (8 ounces) frozen whipped topping, thawed
Fresh mint, sliced strawberries and kiwifruit, optional

In a small bowl, dissolve one package of gelatin in 3/4 cup boiling water. Add 3/4 cup cold water; stir. Spoon into a 13-in. x 9-in. dish coated with cooking spray. Chill until set but not firm, about 40 minutes.

In another bowl, dissolve another package of gelatin in 1/2 cup boiling water. Add 1/2 cup cold water and 1/2 cup milk; stir. Spoon over the first layer. Chill until set but not firm, about 40 minutes.

Repeat five times, alternating plain gelatin layers with creamy gelatin layers. Chill each layer until set but not firm before spooning next layer on top. Refrigerate the entire salad overnight. Just before serving, spread the top of gelatin layers with whipped topping. Cut into squares to serve. Garnish with mint and fruit if desired.
Yield: 15-20 servings.

Editor's Note: This salad takes time to prepare since each layer must be set before the next layer is added.

milly's salad dressing

prep/cook: 10 minutes

This flavorful dressing is so versatile, it can be used for fresh salad greens as well as potato salad, coleslaw and fruit salad. You'll also like the fact that it's quick and easy to prepare.

Milly Heaton
Richmond, Indiana

1 bottle (8 ounces) sweet-sour celery seed salad dressing
1 cup mayonnaise
2 tablespoons sweet pickle relish
2 tablespoons water
4 teaspoons Dijon-mayonnaise blend
3/4 teaspoon prepared horseradish

Combine all ingredients; stir until well blended. Store dressing in the refrigerator.
Yield: 2 cups.

mandarin fluff

prep/cook: 5 minutes

As easy as it is delicious, people of all ages love to bite into this creamy and refreshing fruit salad. The pecans add a crunchy touch.

Elizabeth Freise
Bryn Mawr, Pennsylvania

- 2 **cans (15 ounces *each*) mandarin oranges, well drained**
- 1 **carton (8 ounces) frozen whipped topping, thawed**
- 1/2 **cup chopped pecans**

Place the oranges in a bowl. Fold in the whipped topping. Just before serving, fold in the pecans. **Yield:** 5-6 servings.

old-fashioned egg salad

prep: 15 minutes + chilling

Here's a pared-down version of a long-time staple. You can also add a little cream cheese to the recipe for an extra-rich sandwich if you'd like.

Linda Braun, American Egg Board
Park Ridge, Illinois

- 1/4 **cup mayonnaise**
- 2 **teaspoons lemon juice**
- 1 **teaspoon dried minced onion**
- 1/4 **teaspoon salt**
- 1/4 **teaspoon pepper**
- 6 **hard-cooked eggs, chopped**
- 1/2 **cup finely chopped celery**

In a large bowl, combine the mayonnaise, lemon juice, onion, salt and pepper. Stir in eggs and celery. Cover and refrigerate. **Yield:** 3 servings.

swift strawberry salad

prep/cook: 10 minutes

A simple blend of syrup, orange juice and caramel topping forms the light dressing for the fresh berries and the crunchy cashews found in this sensational salad.

Taste of Home Test Kitchen
Greendale, Wisconsin

- **4 cups sliced fresh strawberries**
- **2 tablespoons caramel ice cream topping**
- **2 tablespoons maple syrup**
- **1 tablespoon orange juice**
- **1/3 cup cashew halves**

Place strawberries in a serving bowl. Combine caramel topping, syrup and orange juice; mix well. Drizzle over strawberries. Sprinkle with cashews. **Yield:** 4-6 servings.

speedy spinach salad

prep/cook: 10 minutes

After tasting this delicious spinach salad, no one will guess how easy it was to prepare. It's a great way to add leafy greens to your diet.

Tina Lust
Nevada, Ohio

- **4 cups torn fresh spinach**
- **1/2 cup shredded Monterey Jack cheese**
- **1/2 cup coarsely crushed butter-flavored crackers (about 8)**
- **Ranch salad dressing *or* dressing of your choice**

Place spinach in a salad bowl; top with cheese and crackers. Serve with dressing. **Yield:** 4 servings.

fruity green salad

prep/cook: 10 minutes

I'm a beekeeper and always looking for new ways to use honey. I've found that when I put honey in dressing, I don't need to add oil, which cuts down on the fat. This salad goes well with any entree.

Hope Ralph
Woburn, Massachusetts

  6 cups torn mixed salad greens *or*
    1 package (10 ounces) fresh
    spinach, torn

  2 medium ripe pears, thinly sliced

1/3 cup dried cherries *or* cranberries

1/4 cup balsamic vinegar

  2 tablespoons honey, warmed

1/4 teaspoon salt

1/8 teaspoon pepper

In a salad bowl, toss the greens, pears and cherries. Combine the vinegar, honey, salt and pepper. Drizzle over salad and toss to coat. Serve immediately. **Yield:** 4 servings.

baby corn romaine salad

prep/cook: 10 minutes

My kids really enjoy this fresh, green salad that is made with romaine lettuce, broccoli, baby corn and crumbled bacon. The bottled dressing makes it a convenient and quick-to-fix dish.

Kathryn Maxson
Mountlake Terrace, Washington

  6 cups torn romaine

  2 cups fresh broccoli florets

  1 can (15 ounces) whole baby corn, rinsed,
    drained and cut into 1/2-inch pieces

  3 tablespoons crumbled cooked bacon

1/2 cup fat-free Caesar *or* Italian salad
    dressing

In a large salad bowl, combine the romaine, broccoli, corn and bacon. Drizzle with the dressing; toss to coat. **Yield:** 6 servings.

1 **package (3 ounces) lemon gelatin**
1/2 **cup boiling water**
1 **medium cucumber, peeled and diced**
4 **green onions, chopped**
1 **cup (8 ounces) 4% cottage cheese**
1/2 **cup mayonnaise**

In a bowl, dissolve the gelatin in boiling water. Add the cucumber and onions. Stir in cottage cheese and mayonnaise until blended. Pour into two 1-1/2-cup molds coated with cooking spray. Refrigerate overnight or until set. Unmold just before serving. **Yield:** 2 servings.

tangy cucumber gelatin

prep: 10 minutes + chilling

A friend shared this recipe with me years ago. She had a vegetable garden and always had a good yield of cucumbers. This pleasant, comforting salad is the right amount for one or two. The cucumber and green onions give a nice, refreshing crunch in contrast to the gelatin.

Bernadeane McWilliams
Decature, Illinois

|||Ultimate**TIP**

To loosen gelatin from a mold, first gently pull the gelatin away from the top edge with a moistened finger. Then dip the outside of the mold up to its rim in a sink or large pan of warm water for a few seconds or until the edges begin to release from the side of the mold. Place a plate over the mold and invert. Carefully lift the mold from the salad.

simple salad dressing

prep/cook: 5 minutes

A friend created this mild and light dressing that's a snap to whip up with on-hand ingredients. Whenever I serve it, someone asks for the recipe.

Joan Rose
Langley, British Columbia

1/2 **cup olive oil**
1/4 **cup sugar**
3 **tablespoons cider vinegar**
1 **tablespoon minced fresh parsley**
1/2 **teaspoon salt**
1/4 **teaspoon pepper**
Salad greens and vegetables of your choice

Combine the first six ingredients in a jar with a tight-fitting lid; shake until blended. Store in the refrigerator. Shake well before serving; drizzle over salad of your choice. **Yield:** about 1 cup.

fresh fruit bowl

prep: 15 minutes + chilling

The glorious colors of summer fruit make this a great salad. Slightly sweet and chilled, it makes a nice accompaniment to a grilled entree.

Marion Kirst
Troy, Michigan

- **8 to 10 cups fresh melon cubes**
- **1 to 2 tablespoons white corn syrup**
- **1 pint fresh strawberries**
- **2 cups fresh pineapple chunks**
- **2 oranges, sectioned**

In a large bowl, combine the melon cubes and corn syrup. Cover and refrigerate overnight. Just before serving, stir in the remaining fruit. **Yield: 3-4 quarts.**

catalina tomato salad

prep: 10 minutes + chilling

I'm a tomato lover, and this is my favorite summertime salad. With its sweet dressing and tangy olives, the unique blend disappears almost immediately at picnics and barbecues.

Lora Billmire
Spokane, Washington

- **6 cups chopped plum tomatoes**
- **1 jar (5-1/4 ounces) pimiento-stuffed olives, drained and halved**
- **3/4 cup Catalina salad dressing**
- **1 small onion, chopped**
- **1/4 to 1/2 teaspoon pepper**

In a bowl, combine all ingredients. Cover and refrigerate for at least 2 hours. **Yield: 8 servings.**

sparkling melon

prep/cook: 10 minutes

Cold and citrusy lemon-lime soda adds a refreshing twist to a summer melon medley. Topped with vanilla yogurt and a sprig of mint, the quick fruit salad makes an elegant side dish or dessert.

Janet Twigg
Campbellford, Ontario

1/2 medium honeydew, cut into cubes

1/2 medium cantaloupe, cut into cubes

1 can (12 ounces) lemon-lime soda, chilled

1 cup vanilla yogurt

Fresh mint, optional

Place the melon cubes in dessert dishes. Pour lemon-lime soda over the melon. Top with yogurt. Garnish with mint if desired. **Yield:** 8 servings.

hoppin' good salad

prep: 10 minutes + chilling

Anything containing cream cheese is always a winner with me. And this recipe is no exception. With that yummy ingredient plus tangy oranges, gelatin and fluffy marshmallows, this salad is always a hit with those who try it.

Gail Kuntz
Dillon, Montana

- 1 package (8 ounces) cream cheese, softened
- 1 package (3 ounces) orange gelatin
- 1-1/2 cups boiling water
- 2 cans (15 ounces *each*) mandarin oranges, drained
- 1 cup heavy whipping cream, whipped
- 1-1/2 cups miniature pastel marshmallows, *divided*

In a large bowl, combine the cream cheese and gelatin powder. Stir in water until the gelatin is dissolved. Refrigerate for 1 hour or until thickened, stirring frequently. Set aside 10-12 mandarin oranges for garnish.

Fold whipped cream, 3/4 cup marshmallows and remaining oranges into gelatin mixture. Transfer to a 2-1/2-qt. serving bowl. Sprinkle with the remaining marshmallows.

Chill the salad until firm. Garnish with the reserved oranges. **Yield:** 8-10 servings.

italian tuna pasta salad

prep: 10 minutes + chilling

My husband is fond of fish, so I'm always looking for new recipes. When we had this dish at an Italian friend's home, I was able to write down the recipe. It is a good choice for potluck suppers or picnics.

Mary Dennis
Bryan, Ohio

- 1-1/2 cups cooked small shell pasta
- 1 cup shredded carrots
- 1 cup shredded zucchini
- 1 can (6 ounces) light water-packed tuna, drained
- 6 tablespoons creamy Italian salad dressing

In a large bowl, combine the cooked pasta, carrots, zucchini, drained tuna and salad dressing. Cover and refrigerate for 2 hours or overnight. **Yield:** 2 servings.

1 can (11 ounces) mandarin oranges
1 can (8 ounces) crushed pineapple
Water
1 package (6 ounces) orange gelatin
1 pint orange sherbet, softened
2 bananas, sliced

Drain oranges and pineapple, reserving juices. Set oranges and pineapple aside. Add water to juices to measure 2 cups. Place in a saucepan and bring to a boil; pour over gelatin in a large bowl. Stir until gelatin is dissolved. Stir in sherbet until smooth.

Chill the salad until partially set (watch carefully). Fold in the oranges, pineapple and bananas. Pour into an oiled 6-cup mold. Chill until firm. **Yield:** 8-10 servings.

grandmother's orange salad

prep: 20 minutes + chilling

When the weather starts turning warm, this cool, fruity salad is just right. It adds beautiful color to any meal and appeals to appetites of all ages!

Ann Eastman
Santa Monica, California

||| UltimateTIP

When making gelatin salad, always use canned or cooked pineapple. Fresh pineapple and kiwifruit will prevent the salad from setting. If your gelatin mixture sets too fast and you've passed the partially set step, place the bowl of gelatin in a pan of warm water and stir until softened. Chill again until the consistency of unbeaten, uncooked egg whites.

thousand island dressing

prep/cook: 10 minutes

This creamy dressing has a fresh taste that complements any tossed salad.

Elizabeth Hunter
Prosperity, South Carolina

3/4 cup fat-free plain yogurt
3 tablespoons chili sauce
1 tablespoon sweet pickle relish
Sugar substitute equivalent to 3/4 teaspoon sugar

In a small bowl, whisk together all ingredients. Refrigerate until serving. **Yield:** 1 cup.

broccoli apple salad

prep/cook: 10 minutes

I don't remember where I discovered this recipe, but my husband and I agree that it's one of our favorite salads. It's nutritious, tasty and adds flair to any meal. The yogurt gives it a unique flavor. For extra crunch, I often add chopped walnuts.

Vera Schmidt
Celina, Ohio

- 2 **cups broccoli florets**
- 1 **large red apple, chopped**
- 1/2 **cup vanilla yogurt**
- 1/4 **cup raisins**
- 1 **tablespoon chopped onion**

In a medium serving bowl, combine all ingredients. Cover and refrigerate until serving. **Yield:** 2 servings.

blt pasta salad

prep/cook: 25 minutes

Crisp bacon, chopped tomato and fresh greens give a packaged pasta salad mix terrific flavor. I make this easy salad for lots of potlucks and always come home with an empty dish.

Ellie Marsh
Lewistown, Pennsylvania

- 1 **package (6.2 ounces) pasta salad mix**
- 1 **medium tomato, seeded and chopped**
- 6 **bacon strips, cooked and crumbled**
- 5 **cups torn lettuce**

Prepare the pasta salad mix according to package directions. Stir in the tomato and bacon. Serve over lettuce. **Yield:** 6 servings.

country cabbage soup 58
curried zucchini soup 59
ham 'n' cheddar corn bread 59
chicken rice soup 60
pigs in a blanket .60
italian grilled cheese 61
abc vegetable soup 61
green chili grilled cheese 62
spicy potato soup 62
avocado bacon sandwiches 63
grilled pbj sandwiches 63
sausage pepper sandwiches 64
egg drop soup 65
reuben burgers .65
chilled blueberry soup 66
meat loaf sandwiches 66
italian pork hoagies 67
tomato hamburger soup 67
beef onion soup 68
jalapeno swiss burgers 68
new england clam chowder 69
stuffed spinach loaf 69
spinach sausage soup 70
mushroom meatball soup 71
beef 'n' cheese tortillas 71
creamy tomato soup 72
prosciutto provolone panini 72
spicy fish soup .73
salsa chicken soup 73
tomato soup with a twist 74
salsa sloppy joes 74
seasoned turkey burgers 75
cream of spinach soup 75
italian beef sandwiches 76
thanksgiving turkey sandwich 77
quick pizza soup 77
lemon chicken soup 78
taco turkey wraps 78
barbecued beef sandwiches 79
stuffed bacon burgers 79

country cabbage soup

prep: 5 minutes | **cook:** 45 minutes

Here's an old-fashioned favorite that my mother-in-law shared with me. Try stirring in some shredded carrots or frozen mixed vegetables if you like. And if you want to stretch the number of servings a bit, add 2 cups of cooked rice or pasta.

Vicky Catullo
Youngstown, Ohio

- 2 **pounds ground beef**
- 2 **cans (28 ounces *each*) stewed tomatoes**
- 1 **medium head cabbage, shredded**
- 2 **large onions, chopped**
- 6 **celery ribs, chopped**

Salt and pepper to taste

In a large saucepan, cook beef over medium heat until no longer pink; drain. Add the tomatoes, cabbage, onions and celery; bring to a boil. Reduce heat; simmer, uncovered, for 25 minutes or until vegetables are tender. Stir in the salt and pepper. **Yield:** 12-14 servings (3-1/4 quarts).

curried zucchini soup

prep/cook: 30 minutes + cooling

This soup, a recipe given to me by one of my daughters-in-law, is a special treat when used from the freezer on a cold winter's day. It calls to mind memories of the "zucchini summer" that was, and gives hope of the "zucchini summer" yet to be!

Ruth McCombie
Etobicoke, Ontario

2 pounds zucchini, sliced (about 4 medium)
5 green onions, chopped
4 cups chicken broth
1 to 2 tablespoons butter, optional
1-1/2 teaspoons curry powder
1 teaspoon salt
1/8 teaspoon cayenne pepper

In a large saucepan or Dutch oven, combine all ingredients. Cover and simmer until zucchini is soft, about 15 minutes. Puree in batches in a blender on low speed; return to pan and heat through. **Yield:** 6-8 servings (2 quarts).

|||UltimateTIP

Adding a garnish to soup before serving it to your family or guests adds a splash of color, as well as flavor and texture. Easy ideas include: finely chopped green onions or chives, minced fresh parsley, shredded cheddar cheese, grated or shredded Parmesan cheese, a dollop of sour cream or yogurt, and plain or seasoned croutons.

---

2 packages (8-1/2 ounces *each*) corn bread/muffin mix
2/3 cup milk
2 eggs
1/4 pound thinly sliced deli ham
6 slices cheddar cheese

In a bowl, combine the corn bread mixes, milk and eggs. Pour half of the batter into an 11-in. x 7-in. baking dish coated with cooking spray. Layer with ham and cheese; carefully spread remaining batter over the top.

Bake at 400° for 20-25 minutes or until a toothpick inserted near the center comes out clean. Serve warm. **Yield:** 10 servings.

ham 'n' cheddar corn bread

prep/cook: 25 minutes

Not your ordinary corn bread, this hearty recipe is filling enough to be eaten as if it were a sandwich. It goes great with a soup or salad.

Christa Habegger
Greenville, South Carolina

pigs in a blanket

prep/cook: 25 minutes

These baked hot dog sandwiches appeal to kids of all ages. Even my husband, Allan, admits to enjoying every bite! We like to dip them in ketchup and mustard.

Linda Young
Longmont, Colorado

- 1 **tube (8 ounces) refrigerated crescent rolls**
- 8 **hot dogs**
- 1 **egg, beaten**
- 1 **tablespoon water**

Caraway seeds

Carrots and celery sticks, optional

Separate crescent dough into triangles. Place hot dogs at wide end of triangles and roll up. Place on an ungreased baking sheet. Combine egg and water; brush over rolls. Sprinkle with caraway and press lightly into rolls. Bake at 375° for 12-15 minutes or until golden. Serve with carrots and celery if desired. **Yield:** 4 servings.

chicken rice soup

prep: 15 minutes | **cook:** 30 minutes

There's nothing more comforting on a cold day than a nice hot bowl of chicken soup. As hearty as it is easy, this soup will chase the winter chills away.

Tracy Fischler
Tallahassee, Florida

- 8 **cups chicken broth**
- 3 **celery ribs, sliced**
- 1 **small onion, chopped**

Salt and pepper to taste

- 2 **cups cubed cooked chicken**
- 1 **cup uncooked long grain rice**

In a large saucepan, combine broth, celery, onion, salt and pepper; bring to a boil. Reduce heat; cover and simmer for 10 minutes. Add chicken and rice; bring to a boil. Reduce heat; cover and simmer for 20-25 minutes or until the rice is tender. **Yield:** 8-10 servings (2-1/2 quarts).

italian grilled cheese

prep/cook: 15 minutes

Provolone cheese, tomato slices and basil leaves make up the satisfying filling for these flame-broiled sandwiches. Lightly brushed with Italian salad dressing, they're sure to become family favorites.

Melody Biddinger
Costa Mesa, California

- 8 **fresh basil leaves**
- 8 **thin tomato slices**
- 4 **slices provolone cheese**
- 4 **slices Italian bread (1/4 inch thick)**
- 2 **tablespoons prepared Italian salad dressing**

Layer the basil, tomato and cheese on two slices of bread. Top with remaining bread. Brush outsides of sandwiches with salad dressing. Grill, uncovered, over medium heat for 3-4 minutes on each side. **Yield:** 2 servings.

abc vegetable soup

prep/cook: 30 minutes

All you need for this down-home soup is a handful of ingredients, including fun alphabet pasta and convenient frozen veggies. It's ideal for cold nights.

Taste of Home Test Kitchen
Greendale, Wisconsin

- 1/2 **cup uncooked alphabet pasta**
- 3 **cans (14-1/2 ounces each) beef broth**
- 1 **package (16 ounces) frozen mixed vegetables**
- 1/2 **teaspoon dried thyme**
- 1/2 **teaspoon dried basil**
- 1/4 **teaspoon pepper**

Cook the pasta according to package directions. In a large saucepan, combine the remaining ingredients. Bring to a boil. Reduce heat; cover and simmer for 5 minutes or until vegetables are tender. Drain pasta; stir into soup. **Yield:** 6-8 servings.

spicy potato soup

prep: 5 minutes | **cook:** 1 hour 5 minutes

This recipe originally came courtesy of m
sister-in-law, who is from Mexico. Bu
since she prefers her foods much spicie
than we do, I've cut back on the heat b
reducing the amount of hot pepper sauce

Audrey Wa
Industry, Pennsylvani

- 1 **pound ground beef**
- 4 **cups cubed peeled potatoes**
  (1/2-in. cubes)
- 1 **small onion, chopped**
- 3 **cans (8 ounces** *each***) tomato**
  sauce
- 4 **cups water**
- 2 **teaspoons salt**
- 1-1/2 **teaspoons pepper**
- 1/2 **to 1 teaspoon hot pepper**
  sauce

In a Dutch oven or large kettle
cook the ground beef over medium
heat until no longer pink; drain. Add
the potatoes, onion and tomato sauce
Stir in the water, salt, pepper and hot
pepper sauce; bring to a boil. Reduce
heat and simmer for 1 hour or unti
the potatoes are tender and the soup
has thickened. **Yield:** 6-8 servings
(2 quarts).

green chili grilled cheese

prep/cook: 10 minutes

An old favorite gets a Southwestern twist in these savory
sandwiches. I enjoy making grilled cheese often during the
summer months when it's too hot to use the oven. It makes
a nice light lunch or dinner.

Emily Hockett
Federal Way, Washington

- 4 **slices bread**
- 4 **slices cheddar cheese**
- 1 **can (4 ounces) chopped**
  green chilies, drained
- 2 **tablespoons butter, softened**

Top two slices of bread with two
slices of cheese; sprinkle with chilies.
Top with the remaining bread. Butter
the outsides of sandwiches.

In a large skillet or griddle, toast
sandwiches until bread is lightly
browned on both sides or until lightly
browned. **Yield:** 2 servings.

avocado bacon sandwiches

prep/cook: 20 minutes

If you like BLTs, then you'll love this easy-to-make recipe. When I'm craving a good sandwich without a lot of fuss, it always hits the spot.

Alva Snider
Fallbrook, California

1 pound sliced bacon, halved

2 medium ripe avocados, sliced

Salt and pepper to taste

1/3 cup mayonnaise

1 tablespoon lemon juice

8 slices whole wheat bread, toasted

Cook bacon until crisp; drain on paper towels; set aside. Gently toss avocados with salt and pepper. Combine mayonnaise and lemon juice; spread over toast. Top with avocado and bacon. **Yield:** 8 sandwiches.

|||Ultimate**TIP**

Avocados are easiest to peel and slice when they are ripe yet firm. Cut the avocado in half lengthwise. Twist the halves in opposite directions to separate. Tap the seed with the blade of a sharp knife and rotate to loosen the seed and lift it out. Scoop out the flesh from each half with a large spoon, staying close to the peel. Slice and dip in lemon juice to prevent from turning brown.

grilled pbj sandwiches

prep/cook: 10 minutes

I was going to make grilled cheese sandwiches one day and had already buttered several slices of bread when I found I was out of cheese. So I pulled out some peanut butter and jelly, and the result was this tasty version of a popular classic.

Barb Trautmann
Ham Lake, Minnesota

4 tablespoons peanut butter

2 tablespoons strawberry jam

4 slices English muffin *or* white toasting bread

2 tablespoons butter, softened

Confectioners' sugar, optional

Spread peanut butter and jam on two slices of bread; top with the remaining bread. Butter the outsides of sandwiches; cook in a large skillet over medium heat until golden brown on each side. Dust with confectioners' sugar if desired. **Yield: 2 servings.**

sausage pepper sandwiches

prep: 5 minutes | **cook:** 7 hours

Green bell peppers and onions add a fresh taste to this zippy sausage filling for sandwiches. My mother gave me this recipe. It's simple to assemble, and it's gobbled up quickly.

Suzette Gessel
Albuquerque, New Mexico

5 **Italian sausage links (4 ounces *each*)**
1 **medium green pepper, cut into 1-inch pieces**
1 **large onion, cut into 1-inch pieces**
1 **can (8 ounces) tomato sauce**
1/8 **teaspoon pepper**
6 **hoagie *or* submarine sandwich buns, split**

In a large skillet, brown sausage links over medium heat. Cut into 1/2-in. slices; place in a 3-qt. slow cooker. Stir in the green pepper, onion, tomato sauce and pepper.

Cover and cook on low for 7-8 hours or until sausage is no longer pink and vegetables are tender. Use a slotted spoon to serve on buns. **Yield:** 6 servings.

egg drop soup

prep/cook: 15 minutes

We start many stir-fry meals with this easy soup, which cooks in just minutes flat. There are many recipe variations, but we like the addition of cornstarch to thicken the soup and give it a rich, golden color.

Amy Corlew-Sherlock
Lapeer, Michigan

- **3 cups chicken broth**
- **1 tablespoon cornstarch**
- **2 tablespoons cold water**
- **1 egg, lightly beaten**
- **1 green onion, sliced**

In a large saucepan, bring broth to a boil over medium heat. Combine cornstarch and water until smooth; gradually stir into broth. Bring to a boil; cook and stir for 2 minutes or until thickened.

Reduce heat. Drizzle beaten egg into hot broth, stirring constantly. Remove from the heat; stir in onion. **Yield:** 4 servings.

reuben burgers

prep/cook: 20 minutes

A Rueben sandwich was always my first choice when eating out, until I found this recipe in a local newspaper. Our daughters used to make these when they were in charge of preparing a meal. I usually had all the ingredients on hand, so it didn't take long to get everything on the table.

Betty Ruenholl
Syracuse, Nebraska

- **1/4 cup sauerkraut**
- **1/4 teaspoon caraway seeds**
- **1/2 pound ground pork**
- **2 slices Swiss cheese (3/4 ounce *each*)**
- **2 hamburger buns, split and toasted**

In a small saucepan, heat sauerkraut and caraway seeds; keep warm. Shape pork into two patties. Grill, uncovered, over medium heat or broil 4-6 in. from heat for 6-8 minutes on each side or until meat juices run clear.

Top each patty with cheese; continue cooking until cheese is melted. Drain sauerkraut. Place patties on buns; top with sauerkraut. Replace bun tops. **Yield:** 2 servings.

1/2 **cup sugar**

2 **tablespoons cornstarch**

2-3/4 **cups water**

2 **cups fresh** *or* **frozen blueberries**

1 **cinnamon stick (3 inches)**

1 **can (6 ounces) frozen orange juice concentrate**

In a large saucepan, combine sugar and cornstarch. Gradually stir in water until smooth. Bring to a boil over medium heat; cook and stir for 2 minutes or until thickened.

Add blueberries and cinnamon stick; return to a boil. Remove from the heat. Stir in orange juice concentrate until thawed. Cover and refrigerate for at least 1 hour. Discard cinnamon stick. **Yield: 4 servings.**

chilled blueberry soup

prep: 5 minutes | **cook:** 10 minutes + chilling

With 100 blueberry bushes in my garden, I'm always looking for recipes calling for this sweet-tart fruit. So I was delighted when my granddaughter shared this one with me. I like to garnish servings with a little sour cream.

Edith Richardson
Jasper, Alabama

meat loaf sandwiches

prep/cook: 10 minutes

Dijon mustard provides the lively flavor in these hot and hearty sandwiches. Because they are so easy to prepare, you can have a hot meal ready in minutes. I've made them for lunch and dinner.

Wendy Moylan
Chicago, Illinois

1 **jar (12 ounces) beef gravy**

4 **slices bread**

2 **teaspoons butter**

2 **teaspoons Dijon mustard**

4 **slices cooked meat loaf, warmed**

|||Ultimate**TIP**

Leftover meat loaf tastes great, if not better than the first time around. And it can be used in a variety of ways. Cut leftover meat loaf into thick slices and store each slice in its own freezer bag. The next time you make a soup or even pizza, simply thaw the number of slices you need, cut into pieces and add to the recipe. The slices are also great for sandwiches.

In a small saucepan, heat the gravy. Toast bread if desired; spread with butter and mustard. Top with meat loaf slices. Serve with gravy. **Yield: 4 sandwiches.**

italian pork hoagies

prep/cook: 20 minutes

I like to prepare these quick toasted sandwiches whenever I have extra pork. I spread pizza sauce over hoagie buns before adding sliced pork, Italian salad dressing and mozzarella cheese.

Jackie Hannahs
Fountain, Michigan

- 6 hoagie buns, split
- 1/2 cup pizza sauce
- 12 slices cooked pork (1/4 inch thick and 2 ounces *each*)
- 1/2 cup Italian salad dressing
- 1/2 cup shredded part-skim mozzarella cheese

Place bottom and top halves of buns, cut side up, on an ungreased baking sheet. Spread pizza sauce on the bottom half of each bun. Top with pork; drizzle with salad dressing. Sprinkle with cheese.

Bake at 350° for 5-10 minutes or until cheese is melted and tops of buns are lightly toasted. Replace bun tops. **Yield:** 6 servings.

tomato hamburger soup

prep: 5 minutes | **cook:** 4 hours

As a full-time teacher, I only have time to cook from scratch a few nights each week. This recipe makes a big enough batch to feed my family for two nights.

Julie Kruger
St. Cloud, Minnesota

- 1 can (46 ounces) V8 juice
- 2 packages (16 ounces *each*) frozen mixed vegetables
- 1 pound ground beef, cooked and drained
- 1 can (10-3/4 ounces) condensed cream of mushroom soup, undiluted
- 2 teaspoons dried minced onion

Salt and pepper to taste

In a 5-qt. slow cooker, combine the first five ingredients; mix well. Cover and cook on high for 4 hours or until heated through. Season with salt and pepper. **Yield:** 12 servings (3 quarts).

jalapeno swiss burgers

prep/cook: 30 minutes

Mexican culture greatly influences our cuisine, and we eat a lot of spicy foods. In this recipe, the mellow flavor of Swiss cheese cuts the heat of the jalapenos.

Jeanine Richardson
Floresville, Texas

- **2 pounds ground beef**
- **4 slices Swiss cheese**
- **1 small onion, thinly sliced**
- **2 to 3 pickled jalapeno peppers, seeded and julienned**
- **4 hamburger buns, split**

Shape beef into eight thin patties. Top four patties with cheese, onion and jalapenos. Top with remaining patties; press edges firmly to seal. Grill, covered, over medium-hot heat for 8-9 minutes on each side or until no longer pink. Serve on buns. **Yield:** 4 servings.

Editor's Note: When cutting hot peppers, disposable gloves are recommended. Avoid touching your face.

beef onion soup

prep/cook: 10 minutes

I live alone, so I'm always looking for ways to use up leftovers like beef. This soup makes a quick lunch or dinner along with fresh veggies or a crisp green salad.

Barbara Zowada
Sheridan, Wyoming

- **1 can (10-1/2 ounces) French onion soup**
- **1 cup cubed cooked beef**
- **2 slices French bread (3/4 inch thick), toasted**
- **1/3 cup shredded Monterey Jack cheese**
- **2 teaspoons shredded Parmesan cheese, optional**

Prepare soup according to package directions; add beef. Ladle into two 2-cup ovenproof bowls. Top each with a French bread slice. Sprinkle with Monterey Jack cheese and Parmesan cheese if desired. Broil 4-6 in. from the heat until cheese is melted. **Yield:** 2 servings.

new england clam chowder

prep/cook: 15 minutes

While vacationing in the New England states, we enjoyed a delicious clam chowder. When we arrived home, I wanted to savor the same flavor with the least amount of effort and time. That's how this shortcut was born. Top bowls with some shredded cheddar if you like.

Rosann Mcwherter
Dublin, California

 1 can (10-3/4 ounces) condensed
   New England clam chowder, undiluted

1-1/3 cups milk

 1 can (6-1/2 ounces) chopped clams,
   drained

 2 tablespoons sherry *or* chicken broth

 1 tablespoon butter

In a large saucepan, combine the first five ingredients. Bring to a boil. Reduce heat; cover and simmer for 5 minutes. **Yield:** 3 servings.

 1 pound bulk Italian sausage

1/2 teaspoon salt

1/2 teaspoon dried basil

 1 loaf (1 pound) frozen bread dough, thawed

 1 package (10 ounces) frozen spinach,
   thawed and well-drained

 2 cups (8 ounces) shredded mozzarella
   cheese

In a large skillet, cook sausage over medium heat until no longer pink; drain. Sprinkle with salt and basil. Roll out bread dough to a 13-in. x 10-in. rectangle. Sprinkle with meat mixture. Top with spinach; sprinkle with cheese. Roll up jelly-roll style, starting with a long side; pinch seams to seal and tuck ends under.

Place seam side down on a greased baking sheet. Bake at 350° for 25-30 minutes or until crust is golden brown. Serve warm. Refrigerate leftovers. **Yield:** 10 servings.

stuffed spinach loaf

prep: 15 minutes | **bake:** 25 minutes

My mom made this recipe once years ago and I always remembered how good it tasted! So I made it myself from memory, and it was a big hit! Folks who think they don't like spinach are in for a surprise when they try it.

Anita Harmala
Howell, Michigan

spinach sausage soup

prep/cook: 30 minutes

Chock-full of potatoes, Italian sausage and spinach, this hearty soup is sure to disappear fast. Not only is it delicious and quick, but it freezes well. It's easy to adjust the amount of broth to suit your family's preference.

Bonita Krugler
Anderson, Indiana

1 **pound bulk Italian sausage**

4 **cans (14-1/2 ounces *each*) chicken broth**

8 **small red potatoes, quartered and thinly sliced**

1 **envelope Italian salad dressing mix**

2 **cups fresh spinach *or* frozen chopped spinach**

In a large skillet, brown the Italian sausage over medium heat. Meanwhile, in a Dutch oven or large pot, combine the broth, potatoes and salad dressing mix. Bring to a boil; cover and simmer for 10 minutes or until the potatoes are tender.

Drain sausage. Add the sausage and spinach to broth mixture; heat through. **Yield:** 10 servings (2-1/2 quarts).

mushroom meatball soup

prep/cook: 10 minutes

After a busy day of running errands and cleaning, I wanted something fast but hearty for dinner. I combined prepared meatballs with canned soup, mushrooms and seasonings. My husband loved my creation and thought I spent hours preparing it.

Sue Fuller
Quincy, Michigan

2 cans (10-3/4 ounces *each*) condensed cream of mushroom soup, undiluted

2-2/3 cups milk

1/2 teaspoon dried oregano

1/8 to 1/4 teaspoon pepper

24 frozen cooked Italian meatballs (1/2 ounce *each*), thawed

1 jar (4-1/2 ounces) sliced mushrooms, drained

In a large saucepan, whisk the soup, milk, oregano and pepper until blended. Add the meatballs and mushrooms. Cover and cook until heated through. **Yield:** 6 servings.

|||Ultimate**TIP**

Have an opened package of tortillas in the refrigerator? Here is one sweet and one savory way to use them up in a jiffy. Brush the tortillas with butter, sprinkle with herbs or cinnamon-sugar and bake on a cookie sheet until crisp. Or just let the tortillas dry on racks until brittle, then crumble into small pieces to use on soups or salads in place of croutons.

beef 'n' cheese tortillas

prep: 10 minutes + chilling

I like to take these sandwiches along on our many outings. They can be made in advance and don't get soggy. You'll appreciate the convenience...your family and friends will love the great taste!

Myra Innes
Auburn, Kansas

1/2 cup garlic-herb cheese spread

4 flour tortillas (10 inches)

3/4 pound thinly sliced cooked roast beef

20 to 25 whole spinach leaves

11 to 12 sweet banana peppers

Spread about 2 tablespoons cheese spread over each tortilla. Layer with roast beef and spinach. Remove seeds from peppers and slice into thin strips; arrange over spinach. Roll up each tortilla tightly; wrap in plastic wrap. Refrigerate until ready to serve. **Yield:** 4 servings.

prosciutto provolone panini

prep/cook: 25 minutes

For a quick lunch or supper, try this fancy, "up-town" take on traditional grilled cheese sandwiches. They're fast and easy but sophisticated enough for entertaining. I sometimes replace the fresh sage with 1 tablespoon of Italian seasoning for a tasty variation. Enjoy!

Candy Summerhill
Alexander, Arkansas

- **8 slices white bread**
- **8 slices provolone cheese**
- **4 thin slices prosciutto**
- **3 tablespoons olive oil**
- **3 tablespoons minced fresh sage**

On four slices of bread, layer a slice of cheese, a slice of prosciutto and a second slice of cheese. Top with remaining bread. Brush both sides of sandwiches with oil; sprinkle with sage. Cook in a panini maker or indoor grill until bread is toasted and cheese is melted. **Yield: 4 servings.**

creamy tomato soup

prep/cook: 10 minutes

A few handy pantry items inspired me to create this fresh-tasting tomato soup. It's super easy, requires just a few ingredients...and tastes oh-so-good!

Gail Westing
Landfill, Minnesota

- **1 can (8 ounces) tomato sauce**
- **1 tablespoon butter**
- **1/8 to 1/4 teaspoon onion powder**
- **Dash pepper**
- **2 cups milk**

In a saucepan, combine the first four ingredients. Bring to a simmer over medium heat. Gradually stir in milk; cook and stir until heated through (do not boil). **Yield: 2 servings.**

spicy fish soup

prep/cook: 25 minutes

Salsa packs a punch in this soup recipe, which we like to serve with warm homemade bread slices.

Linda Murry
Allenstown, New Hampshire

- 2 cans (14-1/2 ounces *each*) chicken broth
- 2-1/2 cups water
- 2/3 cup uncooked instant rice
- 1-1/2 cups salsa
- 1 package (10 ounces) frozen corn
- 1 pound frozen cod, thawed and cut into 2-inch pieces

In a large saucepan, bring the broth, water and rice to a boil. Reduce heat; cover and simmer for 5 minutes. Add the salsa and corn; return to a boil. Add fish. Reduce heat; cover and simmer for 5 minutes or until fish flakes easily with a fork. **Yield:** 8 servings (about 2-1/4 quarts).

salsa chicken soup

prep/cook: 30 minutes

You wouldn't guess that this quick-and-easy soup is low in fat. Since my husband loves spicy foods, I sometimes use medium or hot salsa in this recipe for extra zip.

Becky Christman
Bridgeton, Missouri

- 1/2 pound boneless skinless chicken breasts, cubed
- 1 can (14-1/2 ounces) chicken broth
- 1-3/4 cups water
- 1 to 2 teaspoons chili powder
- 1 cup frozen corn
- 1 cup salsa

In a large saucepan, combine chicken, broth, water and chili powder. Bring to a boil. Reduce heat; cover and simmer for 5 minutes. Add corn; return to a boil. Reduce heat; simmer, uncovered, for 5 minutes or until chicken is no longer pink and corn is tender. Add salsa and heat through. **Yield:** 6 servings.

1 can (10-3/4 ounces) condensed tomato soup, undiluted
1 tablespoon creamy peanut butter
1-1/3 cups milk
2 tablespoons shredded cheddar cheese
Additional cheddar cheese

In a saucepan, combine the soup and peanut butter. Gradually stir in milk. Add cheese; cook and stir until peanut butter and cheese are melted and soup is heated through. Garnish with the additional cheese. **Yield: 2 servings.**

tomato soup with a twist

prep/cook: 15 minutes

In 1932, our junior high school cooking class teacher taught us a simple recipe starting with a can of tomato soup. As I was preparing tomato soup for lunch recently, I remembered those two additional ingredients. I had forgotten what a tasty difference the peanut butter and cheese make.

Eleanor Stamen
Whitehall, Pennsylvania

|||UltimateTIP

Ground beef is labeled using the cut of meat that it is ground from, such as ground chuck or ground round. It can also be labeled according to the fat content of the ground meat or the percentage of lean meat to fat, such as 85% or 90% lean. The higher the percentage, the leaner the meat. Select ground beef that is bright red in color and is in a tightly sealed package.

salsa sloppy joes

prep/cook: 30 minutes

When I was looking for a quick-and-easy way to spice up my sloppy joe recipe, I decided to add a little salsa. Everyone who's tried these sandwiches really likes them.

Mary Banninga
Austin, Minnesota

3 pounds ground beef
1 cup chopped onion
1 jar (16 ounces) salsa
1 can (15 ounces) sloppy joe sauce
16 to 20 hamburger buns, split

In a large skillet, cook beef and onion over medium heat until meat is no longer pink; drain. Stir in salsa and sloppy joe sauce; bring to a boil. Reduce heat; cover and simmer for 20 minutes. Spoon about 1/2 cup onto each bun. **Yield: 16-20 servings.**

seasoned turkey burgers

prep: 20 minutes | **broil:** 10 minutes

This fun mixture of turkey and dressing tastes almost like Thanksgiving on a bun. These moist burgers are great alone, but my family likes them best with lettuce, onion, tomato and a dab of mayonnaise on a whole wheat bun.

Vicki Engeldardt
Grand Rapids, Michigan

1/2 **cup herb-seasoned stuffing croutons**

1 **pound ground turkey breast**

1 **small onion, finely chopped**

5 **hamburger buns, split**

Lettuce leaves, onion, tomato slices and fat-free mayonnaise, optional

Crush or process stuffing croutons into fine crumbs. Combine the crumbs, turkey and onion. Shape into five patties.

Broil or grill over medium-hot heat for 8-10 minutes, turning once. Serve on buns with lettuce, onion, tomato and mayonnaise if desired. **Yield: 5 servings.**

cream of spinach soup

prep/cook: 15 minutes

This rich, creamy soup tastes as if a professional chef made it. I often use drained canned spinach in the recipe; frozen spinach works well, too.

Patricia Bradley
Rohnert Park, California

1 **package (1.8 ounces) leek soup and dip mix**

1 **package (10 ounces) frozen leaf spinach, thawed, drained and chopped**

1 **cup (8 ounces) sour cream**

1/4 **teaspoon ground nutmeg**

Lemon slices

Prepare the soup mix according to package directions. Stir in the spinach. Cover and simmer for 2 minutes. Remove from the heat; stir in the sour cream and nutmeg. Garnish with lemon slices. **Yield: 4 servings.**

italian beef sandwiches

prep: 15 minutes | **cook:** 7 hours

Before leaving for work, I often put these ingredients in the slow cooker. Supper is ready when I get home. This hearty recipe is also good to take to a get-together.

Carol Allen
McLeansboro, Illinois

1 **boneless beef chuck roast (3 to 4 pounds), cut in half**

3 **tablespoons dried basil**

3 **tablespoons dried oregano**

1 **cup water**

1 **envelope onion soup mix**

10 **to 12 Italian rolls *or* sandwich buns**

Place roast in a 5-qt. slow cooker. Combine basil, oregano and water; pour over roast. Sprinkle with soup mix.

Cover and cook on low for 7-8 hours or until meat is tender. Remove meat; shred with a fork and keep warm. Strain broth and skim fat. Serve meat on rolls; use broth for dipping if desired. **Yield:** 10-12 servings.

thanksgiving turkey sandwich

prep/cook: 10 minutes

I created this recipe after sampling a similar sandwich at a nearby restaurant. At first, my husband turned up his nose. But after one bite, he was converted!

Jeanne Imbrigiotta
Pennington, New Jersey

2 tablespoons cream cheese, softened
2 slices multigrain bread
1 tablespoon hot pepper jelly
3 slices thinly sliced deli *or* cooked turkey

Spread cream cheese on both slices of bread; spread jelly over cream cheese. Place turkey on one slice; cover with the remaining slice. **Yield:** 1 sandwich.

---

1 pound ground beef
2 cans (26 ounces *each*) condensed tomato soup, undiluted
6-1/2 cups water
1 jar (28 ounces) spaghetti sauce
1 tablespoon Italian seasoning
2 cups (8 ounces) shredded cheddar cheese
Additional shredded cheddar cheese, optional

In a soup kettle or Dutch oven, cook beef over medium heat until no longer pink; drain. Add soup, water, spaghetti sauce and Italian seasoning; bring to a boil. Reduce heat; simmer, uncovered, for 15 minutes. Add cheese; cook and stir until melted. Garnish with additional cheese if desired. **Yield:** 16 servings (4 quarts).

Editor's Note: Make Quick Pizza Soup a complete, satisfying meal by serving it with grilled cheese or sub sandwiches.

quick pizza soup

prep: 5 minutes | **cook:** 35 minutes

My kids first sampled this soup in the school cafeteria. It was so good they couldn't stop talking about it, so I knew I had to get the recipe. This quick and easy soup warms us up on cold winter evenings.

Penny Lanxon
Newell, Iowa

lemon chicken soup

prep/cook: 10 minutes

For years, I made Greek chicken soup from scratch. My daughter devised this super simple version that she and her family can enjoy when time's short. Lemon juice makes the delicious difference.

Joan Fotopoulo
Turah, Montana

- 1 can (11-1/2 ounces) condensed chicken with rice soup, undiluted
- 1 can (10-3/4 ounces) condensed cream of chicken soup, undiluted

2-1/4 cups water

- 1 cup diced cooked chicken, optional
- 1 to 2 tablespoons lemon juice

Pepper to taste

Minced fresh parsley, optional

In a large saucepan, combine soups and water; cook until heated through. Add the chicken if desired. Stir in lemon juice and pepper. Garnish with parsley if desired. **Yield:** 4-5 servings.

taco turkey wraps

prep/cook: 10 minutes

I get lots of compliments whenever I bring these roll-ups to potluck lunches. Sour cream, taco seasoning and shredded Mexican cheese bring south-of-the-border flair to ordinary deli turkey.

Kathy Neidermann
Holland, Michigan

- 2/3 to 3/4 cup sour cream
- 2 tablespoons taco seasoning

- 6 flour tortillas (8 inches), warmed
- 1 cup (4 ounces) shredded Mexican cheese blend
- 1/2 pound thinly sliced deli turkey breast

Combine sour cream and taco seasoning. Spread over tortillas. Sprinkle with cheese. Top with turkey; roll up. **Yield:** 6 servings.

barbecued beef sandwiches

prep/cook: 15 minutes

With only three ingredients, our food staff confirms that you can assemble these sandwiches in short order. Use store-bought barbecue sauce to flavor your leftover beef if you like. (This recipe works fine with deli roast beef, too.)

Taste of Home Test Kitchen
Greendale, Wisconsin

- 2 **cups shredded cooked roast beef**
- 1 **bottle (18 ounces) barbecue sauce**
- 5 **kaiser rolls, split**

In a large saucepan, combine the beef and barbecue sauce; heat through. Serve on rolls. **Yield:** 5 servings.

- 1-1/2 **pounds ground beef**
- 1 **envelope onion soup mix**
- 1/4 **cup water**
- 6 **slices (1 ounce *each*) process American cheese**
- 6 **bacon strips**
- 6 **hamburger buns, toasted**

In a bowl, combine ground beef, soup mix and water. Shape into 12 thin patties. Place a cheese slice on six patties. Cover each with another patty. Pinch edges to seal. Wrap a strip of bacon around each; fasten with a wooden toothpick.

Grill, uncovered, for 8-10 minutes, turning once, or until burgers reach desired doneness. Discard toothpicks. Serve on buns. **Yield:** 6 servings.

stuffed bacon burgers

prep/cook: 25 minutes

Everyone comes running when they hear the sizzle, and smell the wonderful aroma, of these burgers on the grill. Nothing else captures the taste of summer.

Johnnie McLeod
Bastrop, Louisiana

beef & pork entrees

Save a Penny Casserole 82

Hamburger Skillet Supper 83

Vegetable Beef Pie 83

Tortellini Carbonara 84

Enchilada Casserole 84

Pepperoni Rigatoni 85

Roast Beef and Gravy 85

Mozzarella Ham Stromboli 86

Zippy Pork Chops 87

Hamburger Casserole 87

Chili Barbecue Chops 88

Maple Ham Steak 88

Sausage Hash 89

Beef & Rice Enchiladas 89

Berry Barbecue Pork Roast 90

Spinach Rice Ham Bake 90

Sugar-Glazed Ham 91

Beef Veggie Casserole 91

Fiesta Rib Eye Steaks 92

Sweet and Savory Ribs 92

Barbecued Baby Back Ribs 93

Tailgate Sausages 93

Flavorful Beef Brisket 94

Slow-Cooked Swiss Steak 94

Marmalade Baked Ham 95

Spinach Ravioli Bake 95

pg. 95

save a penny casserole

prep: 10 minutes | **bake:** 30 minutes

At the office where I worked years ago, the women often shared our favorite recipes during the lunch hour. This casserole came from a co-worker, and my family has enjoyed it for some 30 years ever since. Besides being easy and quick to prepare, it's very economical. It's a perfect contribution to church suppers and potlucks, and it's a real time-saver on busy days.

Janice Miller
Worthington, Kentucky

- **1 pound ground beef**
- **1 can (10-3/4 ounces) condensed cream of mushroom soup, undiluted**
- **1 can (14-3/4 ounces) spaghetti in tomato sauce with cheese**
- **1 can (15 ounces) mixed vegetables, drained**
- **1 cup (4 ounces) shredded cheddar cheese, optional**

In a large skillet, cook beef until no longer pink; drain. Stir in the soup, spaghetti and vegetables. Transfer to an ungreased 11-in. x 7-in. baking dish.

Bake, uncovered, at 350° for 30 minutes or until heated through. Sprinkle with cheese if desired; bake 5 minutes longer or until cheese is melted. **Yield:** 4-6 servings.

hamburger skillet supper

prep/cook: 15 minutes

When time is tight, this one-dish wonder is a surefire way to beat the clock. I created it while looking for a new stovetop meal. You can easily double the ingredients for a larger group.

Donna Gardner
Ottumwa, Iowa

1 pound ground beef

1 package (3 ounces) ramen noodles

2 cups water

2 cups frozen mixed vegetables, thawed

In a skillet, cook beef until no longer pink; drain. Add noodles with contents of seasoning packet and water. Bring to a boil; cook for 3 minutes or until noodles are tender. Add the vegetables and cook until tender, about 3 minutes. **Yield:** 4 servings.

||| Ultimate**TIP**

To make a fluted edge on a double-crust pie, trim the pastry to 1 inch. Turn the overhang under to form the built-up edge. Position your index finger on the edge of the crust, pointing out. Place your thumb and index finger of your other hand on the outside edge and pinch dough around the index finger to form a V-shape. Continue around the edge.

Pastry for double-crust pie
   (9 inches)

1 pound ground beef, cooked
   and drained

1 can (16 ounces) mixed
   vegetables, drained *or* 1-1/2
   cups frozen mixed vegetables

1 can (10-3/4 ounces)
   condensed cream of onion
   soup, undiluted

1/2 teaspoon pepper

Line a 9-in. pie plate with bottom pastry; trim pastry even with edge. In a large bowl, combine the beef, vegetables, soup and pepper. Spoon into crust. Roll out the remaining pastry to fit top of pie. Place over filling; trim, seal and flute edges. Cut slits in top. Bake at 400° for 30-35 minutes or until crust is golden brown. **Yield:** 4-6 servings.

vegetable beef pie

prep: 15 minutes | **bake:** 30 minutes

Like most country folks, I have plenty of busy days, so I depend on easy recipes that also taste great. This simple meat pie originally called for a homemade crust, but I use store-bought pastry to beat the clock.

Valorie Hall Walker
Bradley, South Carolina

1 package (9 ounces) refrigerated cheese tortellini

8 bacon strips, cooked and crumbled

1 cup heavy whipping cream

1/2 cup minced fresh parsley

1/2 cup grated Parmesan cheese

Cook the tortellini according to package directions. Meanwhile, in another saucepan, combine the bacon, cream, parsley and cheese; cook over medium heat until heated through.

Drain the tortellini; toss with the cream sauce. Serve immediately. **Yield:** 4 servings.

tortellini carbonara

prep: 10 minutes | **cook:** 30 minutes

My creamy carbonara calls for only a handful of ingredients and comes together in mere moments. For fast preparation, just simmer the rich bacon and Parmesan cheese sauce in one pan while boiling the packaged tortellini to perfection in another. Add more cheese or additional parsley to the sauce to fit your family's taste.

Cathy Croyle
Davidsville, Pennsylvania

|||Ultimate**TIP**

Always check the date on packages of vacuum-sealed bacon to make sure it's fresh. The date reflects the last date the bacon can be sold. Once opened, a package of bacon should be used within a week. For long-term storage, freeze up to 1 month. An easy way to cook bacon is to bake it. Line a baking sheet with foil, top it with bacon and bake at 400° until crisp.

enchilada casserole

prep: 20 minutes | **cook:** 6 hours

Tortilla chips and a side salad turn this casserole into a mouth-watering meal.

Denise Waller
Omaha, Nebraska

1 pound ground beef

2 cans (10 ounces *each*) enchilada sauce

1 can (10-3/4 ounces) condensed cream of onion soup, undiluted

1/4 teaspoon salt

1 package (8-1/2 ounces) flour tortillas, torn

3 cups (12 ounces) shredded cheddar cheese

In a skillet, cook beef over medium heat until no longer pink; drain. Stir in enchilada sauce, soup and salt.

In a 3-qt. slow cooker, layer a third of the beef mixture, tortillas and cheddar cheese. Repeat the layers twice. Cover and cook on low for 6-8 hours or until heated through. **Yield:** 4 servings.

pepperoni rigatoni

prep/cook: 30 minutes

My friend and I created this flavorful recipe as a main dish for the cafeteria at work. It has also become a favorite among teenagers at our church, who make a beeline for it at potlucks.

Becky Fisk
Ashland City, Tennessee

1 package (16 ounces) rigatoni *or* large tube pasta

1 jar (28 ounces) spaghetti sauce

1 package (3-1/2 ounces) sliced pepperoni, halved

2 cups (8 ounces) shredded Monterey Jack cheese

Cook pasta according to package directions; drain. Add spaghetti sauce and toss to coat. Place half in a greased shallow 3-qt. microwave-safe dish. Top with half of the pepperoni and cheese. Repeat layers.

Cover the casserole and microwave on high for 5-7 minutes or until heated through and the cheese is melted. Let stand for 5 minutes before serving. **Yield:** 6-8 servings.

Editor's Note: This recipe was tested in a 1,100-watt microwave.

roast beef and gravy

prep: 15 minutes | **cook:** 8 hours

This is by far the simplest way to make roast beef and gravy. On busy days, I can put this main dish in the slow cooker and forget about it. My family likes it with mashed potatoes and fruit salad.

Abby Metzger
Larchwood, Iowa

1 boneless beef chuck roast (3 pounds)

2 cans (10-3/4 ounces *each*) condensed cream of mushroom soup, undiluted

1/3 cup sherry *or* beef broth

1 envelope onion soup mix

Cut roast in half; place in a 3-qt. slow cooker. In a large bowl, combine the remaining ingredients; pour over roast. Cover and cook on low for 8-9 hours or until meat is tender. **Yield:** 8-10 servings.

mozzarella ham stromboli

prep: 20 minutes | **bake:** 20 minutes

The original recipe for this savory bread called for salami, but I use ham instead. People are always amazed that it only takes about 15 minutes to assemble. I usually serve it with tomato soup on the side for a filling meal.

Janice Brightwell
Jeffersonville, Indiana

- **1 tube (11 ounces) refrigerated crusty French loaf**
- **2 cups (8 ounces) shredded part-skim mozzarella cheese**
- **1/4 pound thinly sliced deli ham**
- **1 tablespoon butter, melted**
- **1 tablespoon grated Parmesan cheese**

On a lightly floured surface, unroll dough at seam. Pat dough into a 14-in. x 12-in. rectangle. Sprinkle mozzarella cheese over dough to within 1/2 in. of edges. Top with a single layer of ham. Roll up tightly from a short side; pinch seam to seal. Place seam side down on an ungreased baking sheet. Brush top of loaf with butter; sprinkle with Parmesan cheese.

Bake at 375° for 20-25 minutes or until golden brown. Cool on a wire rack for 5 minutes. Cut stromboli with a serrated knife. **Yield:** 6 servings.

zippy pork chops

prep: 10 minutes + chilling | **grill:** 10 minutes

Try this simple grilled recipe the next time you need to feed your family in a hurry. The full-flavored herb rub sparks the taste of these tender boneless chops that cook in no time. You can even try it on chicken as well.

Donna Glascoe
Dayton, Ohio

4 teaspoons chili powder
1-1/2 teaspoons dried oregano
2 garlic cloves, minced
3/4 teaspoon ground cumin
6 boneless pork loin chops (3/4 inch thick)

Combine the chili powder, oregano, garlic and cumin; gently rub over both sides of pork chops. Cover and refrigerate for at least 2 hours.

Grill, covered, over medium-hot heat for 5-7 minutes on each side or until a meat thermometer reads 160°. **Yield:** 6 servings.

hamburger casserole

prep: 10 minutes | **cook:** 50 minutes

This recipe is such a hit that it's traveled all over the country! My mother originated the recipe in Pennsylvania, I brought it to Texas when I married, I'm still making it in California and my daughter treats her friends to this "oldie" in Colorado. It's hearty, yet simple to prepare.

Helen Carmichall
Santee, California

2 pounds lean ground beef
4 pounds potatoes, peeled and sliced 1/4 inch thick
1 large onion, sliced
1 teaspoon salt, optional
1/2 teaspoon pepper
1 teaspoon beef bouillon granules
1 cup boiling water
1 can (28 ounces) diced tomatoes, undrained

In a Dutch oven, layer half of the meat, potatoes and onion. Sprinkle with half of the salt if desired and pepper. Repeat layers. Dissolve bouillon in water; pour over all. Top with tomatoes. Cover and cook over medium heat for 45-50 minutes or until potatoes are tender. **Yield:** 10 servings.

1/2 cup Italian salad dressing
1/2 cup barbecue sauce
  2 teaspoons chili powder
  4 bone-in pork chops (3/4 inch thick and 7 ounces *each*)

In a small bowl, combine the salad dressing, barbecue sauce and chili powder. Pour 1/2 cup marinade into a large resealable plastic bag; add the pork chops. Seal bag and turn to coat; refrigerate for at least 1 hour. Cover and refrigerate remaining marinade.

Drain and discard marinade. In a large skillet coated with cooking spray, brown chops on both sides over medium heat; drain. Add reserved marinade. Bring to a boil. Reduce heat; cover and simmer for 5-7 minutes or until a meat thermometer reaches 160°. **Yield:** 4 servings.

chili barbecue chops

prep: 5 minutes + marinating | **cook:** 20 minutes

It's a snap to jazz up store-bought Italian salad dressing with barbecue sauce and chili powder to make the easy marinade for pork chops. They're simmered on the stovetop for just a few minutes, so I can get them on the table in no time.

Tonya Fitzgerald
West Monroe, Louisiana

|||UltimateTIP

There are four grades of maple syrup that are available to consumers. Grade A Light Amber is light and mild; Grade A Light Medium is a bit darker with more maple flavor; Grade A Dark Amber is even darker and more flavorful; and Grade B is very dark with a strong maple flavor. Deciding which one to use is simply a matter of personal preference.

maple ham steak

prep/cook: 15 minutes

Three ingredients and 15 minutes are all you need for this hearty meal that serves six people. Add some corn bread and a salad and dinner is ready. Save the leftover ham for sandwiches the next day, or serve it with eggs for breakfast.

Jean Tayntor
Eaton, New York

  1 bone-in fully cooked ham steak (about 2 pounds and 3/4 inch thick)
1/2 cup maple syrup, *divided*

Grill ham steak, uncovered, over medium-hot heat for 5-7 minutes on each side, basting frequently with 1/4 cup syrup. Warm remaining syrup to serve with ham. **Yield:** 6 servings.

sausage hash

prep: 10 minutes | **cook:** 30 minutes

I always keep plenty of bulk pork sausage on hand so when I need a quick supper, I can grab this handy recipe. The colorful vegetables give this dish a perky look to match its flavor.

Virginia Krites
Cridersville, Ohio

- 1 pound bulk pork sausage
- 1 medium onion, chopped
- 2 medium carrots, grated
- 1 medium green pepper, chopped
- 3 cups diced cooked potatoes
- 1/2 teaspoon salt
- 1/4 teaspoon pepper

In a large skillet, cook the sausage over medium heat until no longer pink; drain. Add the onion, carrots and green pepper; cook until tender. Stir in the potatoes, salt and pepper. Reduce heat; cook and stir for 20 minutes or until lightly browned and heated through. **Yield:** 6 servings.

beef & rice enchiladas

prep: 30 minutes | **bake:** 10 minutes

With a toddler in the house, I look for foods that are a snap to make. Loaded with beef, cheese and a flavorful rice mix, these enchiladas come together without any fuss. But they're so good that guests think I spent hours in the kitchen.

Jennifer Smith
Colona, Illinois

- 1 package (6.8 ounces) Spanish rice and vermicelli mix
- 1 pound ground beef
- 2 cans (10 ounces *each*) enchilada sauce, *divided*
- 10 flour tortillas (8 inches), warmed
- 4 cups (16 ounces) shredded cheddar cheese, *divided*

Prepare the rice mix according to package directions. Meanwhile, in a large skillet cook beef over medium heat until no longer pink; drain. Stir in Spanish rice and 1-1/4 cups enchilada sauce.

Spoon about 2/3 cup beef mixture down the center of each tortilla. Top each with 1/3 cup cheddar cheese; roll up.

Place in an ungreased 13-in. x 9-in. baking dish. Top with the remaining enchilada sauce and cheddar cheese. Bake, uncovered, at 350° for 8-10 minutes or until the cheese is melted. **Yield:** 10 enchiladas.

1 boneless rolled pork loin roast (3 pounds)
1/4 teaspoon salt
1/4 teaspoon pepper
4 cups fresh *or* frozen cranberries
1 cup sugar
1/2 cup orange juice
1/2 cup barbecue sauce

berry barbecued pork roast

prep: 15 minutes | **bake:** 1 hour + standing

Moist and tender, this elegant pork roast topped with a thick, ruby-red cranberry barbecue sauce is sure to please dinner guests! Leftovers make great sandwiches.

Doris Heath
Franklin, North Carolina

Sprinkle roast with salt and pepper. Place with fat side up on a rack in a shallow roasting pan. Bake, uncovered, at 350° for 45 minutes.

In a medium saucepan, combine the cranberries, sugar, orange juice and barbecue sauce. Bring to a boil. Reduce heat to medium-low; cook and stir for 10-12 minutes or until the cranberries pop and the sauce is thickened.

Brush some of the sauce over the roast. Bake 15-20 minutes longer or until a meat thermometer reads 160°, brushing often with sauce. Let stand for 10 minutes before slicing. Serve with the remaining sauce. **Yield: 12 servings.**

spinach rice ham bake

prep: 10 minutes | **bake:** 25 minutes

When I was in college, my best friend gave me this casserole recipe. It became a staple in my house when my children were toddlers because it was an easy way for them to eat rice. We still enjoy it today.

Ramona Parris
Marietta, Georgia

8 ounces process cheese (Velveeta), cubed
1/2 cup milk
3 cups cooked rice
2 cups cubed fully cooked ham

1 package (10 ounces) frozen chopped spinach, thawed and squeezed dry

In a microwave-safe bowl, combine the cheese and milk. Microwave, uncovered, on high for 1-1/2 minutes or until cheese is melted; stir until smooth. Stir in the rice, ham and spinach. Transfer to a greased 1-1/2-qt. baking dish. Cover and bake at 350° for 25-30 minutes or until heated through. **Yield:** 3 servings.

Editor's Note: This recipe was tested in a 1,100-watt microwave.

sugar-glazed ham

prep: 5 minutes | **bake:** 2 hours

My old-fashioned sugar glaze gives ham a pretty, golden-brown coating just like Grandma used to make. The mustard and vinegar complement the brown sugar and add tangy flavor.

Carol Battle
Heathsville, Virginia

- 1 fully cooked bone-in ham (5 to 7 pounds)
- 1 cup packed brown sugar
- 2 teaspoons prepared mustard
- 1 to 2 tablespoons cider vinegar

Score ham about 1/2-in. deep with a sharp knife. Place ham on a rack in a shallow baking pan. Bake at 325° for 2 to 2-1/2 hours (20 minutes per pound). Combine brown sugar, mustard and enough vinegar to make a thick paste. During the last hour of baking, brush glaze on ham every 15 minutes. **Yield:** 10-14 servings.

beef veggie casserole

prep/cook: 25 minutes

This satisfying stew is a breeze to fix because it uses left-over roast beef and refrigerated biscuits.

Patti Keith
Ebensburg, Pennsylvania

- 1 envelope mushroom gravy mix
- 3/4 cup water
- 2 cups cubed cooked beef
- 2 cups frozen mixed vegetables
- 2 medium potatoes, peeled, cubed and cooked
- 1 tube (12 ounces) refrigerated buttermilk biscuits, separated into 10 biscuits

In a large saucepan, combine gravy mix and water until smooth. Bring to a boil; cook and stir for 1 minute or until thickened. Stir in the beef, vegetables and potatoes; heat through.

Transfer to a greased 8-in. square baking dish. Top with the biscuits. Bake, uncovered, at 400° for 12-16 minutes or until bubbly and biscuits are golden brown. **Yield:** 5 servings.

8 flour tortillas (6 inches)
8 boneless beef rib eye steaks
   (3/4 inch thick)
1/4 cup lime juice
1 cup (4 ounces) shredded
   Colby-Monterey Jack cheese
2 cups salsa

Place tortillas on a sheet of heavy duty foil (about 18 in. x 12 in.). Fold foil around tortillas and seal tightly; set aside.

Drizzle both sides of steaks with lime juice. Grill, covered, over medium-hot heat for 7-9 minutes on each side or until meat reaches desired doneness (for medium-rare, a meat thermometer should read 145°; medium, 160°; well-done, 170°).

Place tortillas on outer edge of grill; heat for 5-6 minutes, turning once. Sprinkle cheese over steaks; serve with salsa and warmed tortillas. **Yield:** 8 servings.

fiesta rib eye steaks

prep/cook: 30 minutes

Here's a great recipe for grilling out or to prepare on camping trips. Adapt it for the indoors by cooking the steaks in a skillet and heating the tortillas in a warm oven.

Jodee Harding
Granville, Ohio

sweet and savory ribs

prep: 5 minutes | **cook:** 8 hours

My husband and I love barbecue ribs, but with our conflicting schedules, we rarely have time to fire up the grill. Instead, we let the slow cooker do the work for us. By the time we get home from work, the ribs are tender, juicy and ready to devour.

Kandy Bingham
Green River, Wyoming

||| UltimateTIP

Pork ribs come in a variety of styles. Country-style ribs are meaty and come from the rib end of the pork loin. Baby back ribs come from the blade and center section of the pork loin and are smaller than spareribs, which are curved ribs from the belly and are the least meaty of the ribs. St. Louis-style ribs are spareribs with the breastbone removed.

1 large onion, chopped
2-1/2 to 3 pounds boneless country-style
   pork ribs
1 bottle (18 ounces) honey barbecue
   sauce
1/3 cup maple syrup
1/4 cup spicy brown mustard
1/2 teaspoon salt
1/4 teaspoon pepper

Place onion in a 5-qt. slow cooker. Top with the ribs. Combine the barbecue sauce, syrup, mustard, salt and pepper; pour over ribs. Cover and cook on low for 8-9 hours or until the meat is tender. **Yield:** 6-8 servings.

barbecued baby back ribs

prep: 10 minutes | **cook:** 1 hour 35 minutes

This recipe came about by accident when I was making ribs for company and discovered I didn't have enough sauce. I combined the ingredients on hand and came up with this special version.

Jamie Barnett
Syracuse, Missouri

- 4 **pounds pork baby back ribs**
- 1/2 **teaspoon salt**
- 1/4 **teaspoon pepper**
- 3/4 **cup barbecue sauce**
- 1/3 **cup honey-Dijon barbecue sauce**
- 1/3 **cup ketchup**
- 1/4 **cup honey**

Cut the ribs into serving size pieces; place in a Dutch oven and cover with water. Add salt and pepper; bring to a boil. Reduce heat; cover and simmer for 1-1/4 hours or until ribs are just tender. Do not overcook.

Meanwhile, combine barbecue sauces, ketchup and honey. Drain ribs and transfer to grill. Grill, uncovered, over medium heat, basting both sides several times with sauce, for 8-10 minutes or until ribs are tender and well-glazed. **Yield:** 6 servings.

tailgate sausages

prep/cook: 20 minutes

You'll need just a handful of items to fix these tasty sandwiches. Fully cooked sausages are stuffed with cheese and a homemade relish, then wrapped in foil.

Taste of Home Test Kitchen
Greendale, Wisconsin

- 1/2 **cup giardiniera**
- 1/2 **teaspoon sugar**
- 4 **cooked Italian sausage links**
- 4 **slices provolone cheese, cut into strips**
- 4 **brat buns *or* hot dog buns, split**

In a small food processor, combine giardiniera and sugar; cover and process until blended. Make a lengthwise slit three-fourths of the way through each sausage to within 1/2 in. of each end. Fill with giardiniera mixture and cheese.

Place sausages in buns; wrap individually in a double thickness of heavy-duty foil (about 12 in. x 10 in.). Grill, uncovered, over medium-hot heat for 8-10 minutes or until heated through and cheese is melted. **Yield:** 4 servings.

flavorful beef brisket

prep: 20 minutes | **bake:** 3 hours + chilling

A memorable part of my wedding day was the supper my mom prepared. This moist, fork-tender brisket is a popular entree hearty appetites appreciate.

Jamie Gurney
Odessa, Missouri

1 beef brisket (about 5 pounds
2 tablespoons canola oil
1 medium onion, sliced
Salt and pepper to taste
1 cup water
1 bottle (18 ounces) barbecue sauce

In a Dutch oven, brown beef in o on both sides over medium-hig heat; drain. Top with onion, salt an pepper. Add water; cover and bake a 325° for 2-1/2 hours or until tender.

Remove beef. Cool for 5 minutes cover and refrigerate overnight.

Discard the onion and cookin liquid. Slice the meat 1/4 in. thic across the grain; place in a roastin pan. Drizzle with the barbecue sauce Cover and bake at 325° for 30-4 minutes or until heated through **Yield:** 16-18 servings.

Editor's Note: This is a fresh bee brisket, not corned beef. Refrigeratin the beef overnight makes it possibl to slice it very thinly.

slow-cooked swiss steak

prep: 10 minutes | **cook:** 6 hours

This is a favorite of mine because I flour and season the steaks and refrigerate them overnight. The next morning, I just put the ingredients in the slow cooker, and I have a delicious dinner waiting for us when I arrive home from work.

Sarah Burks
Wathena, Kansas

2 tablespoons all-purpose flour
1/2 teaspoon salt
1/4 teaspoon pepper
1-1/2 pounds boneless beef round steak, cut into six pieces
1 medium onion, cut into 1/4-inch slices
1 celery rib, cut into 1/2-inch slices
2 cans (8 ounces *each*) tomato sauce

In a large resealable plastic bag, combin the flour, salt and pepper. Add the steak; sea bag and toss to coat.

Place the onion in a greased 3-qt. slow cooker. Top with the steak, celery and tomat sauce. Cover and cook on low for 6-8 hours o until meat is tender. **Yield:** 6 servings.

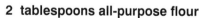

marmalade baked ham

prep: 15 minutes | **bake:** 1-1/2 hours

My family loves the flavor that orange marmalade, beer and brown sugar give this ham. Scoring the ham and inserting whole cloves gives it an appealing look with little effort.

Clo Runco
Punxsutawney, Pennsylvania

- 1 **boneless fully cooked ham (3 to 4 pounds)**
- 12 **to 15 whole cloves**
- 1 **can (12 ounces) beer *or* beef broth**
- 1/4 **cup packed brown sugar**
- 1/2 **cup orange marmalade**

Place ham on a rack in a shallow roasting pan. Score the surface of the ham, making diamond shapes 1/2 in. deep; insert a clove in each diamond.

Pour the beer or broth over ham. Rub brown sugar over surface of ham. Cover and bake at 325° for 1-1/4 hours.

Spread with marmalade. Bake, uncovered, for 15-25 minutes longer or until a meat thermometer reads 140°. **Yield:** 12-14 servings.

spinach ravioli bake

prep: 5 minutes | **bake:** 40 minutes

This entree is unbelievably simple to prepare yet tastes delicious. The fact that it calls for frozen ravioli—straight from the bag without boiling or thawing—saves so much time.

Susan Kehl
Pembroke Pines, Florida

- 2 **cups spaghetti sauce**
- 1 **package (25 ounces) frozen Italian sausage ravioli *or* ravioli of your choice**
- 2 **cups (8 ounces) shredded part-skim mozzarella cheese**
- 1 **package (10 ounces) frozen chopped spinach, thawed and squeezed dry**
- 1/4 **cup grated Parmesan cheese**

Place 1 cup spaghetti sauce in a greased shallow 2-qt. baking dish. Top with half of the frozen ravioli, mozzarella cheese, spinach and Parmesan cheese. Repeat layers.

Bake, uncovered, at 350° for 40-45 minutes or until heated through and cheese is melted. **Yield:** 4-6 servings.

savory chicken dinner 98
wild rice mushroom chicken 99
honey baked chicken 99
baked lemon chicken 100
dilled turkey breast 100
chicken salsa pizza 101
barbecue jack chicken 101
chicken in a haystack 102
party chicken 102
garlic chicken penne 103
grilled chicken with peach sauce 103
spaghetti with homemade turkey sausage 104
easy chicken and noodles 104
apricot-glaze chicken 105
honey mustard chicken 105
chicken in baskets 106
breaded turkey slices 107
baked swiss chicken 107
stuffing-coated chicken 108
ranch turkey pasta dinner 108
pesto chicken pasta 109
southern fried chicken 109
grilled chicken cordon bleu 110
simple salsa chicken 110
cranberry chicken 111
pecan-crusted chicken 111

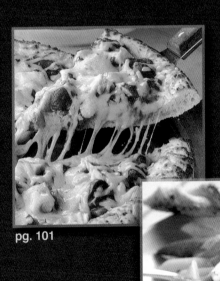

pg. 101

pg. 103

savory chicken dinner

prep: 10 minutes | **bake:** 45 minutes

No one would guess that these moist chicken breasts and tender potatoes are seasoned with herb- and garlic-flavored soup mix. The meal-in-one is simple to assemble, and it all bakes in one dish so there's little cleanup.

Leslie Adams
Springfield, Missouri

- 2 **envelopes savory herb with garlic soup mix**
- 6 **tablespoons water**
- 4 **boneless skinless chicken breast halves (6 to 8 ounces *each*)**
- 2 **large red potatoes, cubed**
- 1 **large onion, halved and cut into small wedges**

In a small bowl, combine soup mix and water; pour half into a large resealable plastic bag. Add chicken. Seal bag and toss to coat. Pour the remaining soup mix in another large resealable plastic bag. Add potatoes and onion. Seal bag and toss to coat.

Drain and discard marinade from the chicken. Transfer to a greased 13-in. x 9-in. baking dish. Pour the potato mixture with marinade over chicken.

Bake, uncovered, at 350° for 40-45 minutes or until vegetables are tender and a meat thermometer reads 170°, stirring vegetables occasionally. **Yield:** 4 servings.

wild rice mushroom chicken

prep: 15 minutes | **cook:** 30 minutes + freezing

I use a wild rice mix to put a tasty spin on a traditional chicken and rice bake. On busy nights, it's a snap to toss together with leftover chicken or turkey.

Jacqueline Graves
Lawrenceville, Georgia

- 2 **packages (6 ounces *each*) long grain and wild rice mix**
- 8 **boneless skinless chicken breast halves**
- 5 **tablespoons butter, *divided***
- 1 **large sweet red pepper, chopped**
- 2 **jars (4-1/2 ounces *each*) sliced mushrooms, drained**

Prepare rice according to package directions. Meanwhile, in a large skillet, cook chicken in 3 tablespoons butter for 10 minutes on each side or until browned and juices run clear. Remove chicken and keep warm.

Add remaining butter to pan drippings; saute red pepper until tender. Stir in mushrooms; heat through. Add to rice. Serve four chicken breasts with half of the rice mixture.

Place remaining chicken in a greased 11-in. x 7-in. baking dish; top with remaining rice mixture. Cool. Cover and freeze for up to 3 months.

To use the frozen casserole: Thaw in the refrigerator. Cover and bake at 350° for 35-40 minutes or until heated through. **Yield:** 2 casseroles (4 servings each).

- 2 **bone-in chicken breast halves (8 ounces *each*)**
- 2 **tablespoons butter**
- 1/2 **cup honey**
- 1/2 **teaspoon salt**
- 1 **tablespoon prepared mustard**

Place the chicken halves in a greased or foil-lined 9-in. square baking pan. Bake, uncovered, at 325° for 30 minutes.

Meanwhile, in a small saucepan, combine remaining ingredients; cook and stir over low heat until well blended and heated through. Pour over chicken.

Bake, uncovered, 30-35 minutes longer or until a meat thermometer reaches 170°. Baste before serving. **Yield:** 2 servings.

honey baked chicken

prep: 5 minutes | **bake:** 1 hour

After our children left home, I had to learn to cook all over again. I began to economize on food purchases by buying meat in quantity and freezing extras for future menus. My husband especially loves this chicken recipe, which I pared down to fit our current lifestyle.

Helen Whelan
Jarrettsville, Maryland

3 tablespoons butter, melted
2 tablespoons lemon juice
1 garlic clove, minced
1/2 teaspoon salt
1/4 teaspoon pepper
1/2 cup seasoned bread crumbs
4 boneless skinless chicken
   breast halves (4 ounces *each*)

In a shallow dish, combine the butter, lemon juice, garlic, salt and pepper. Place bread crumbs in another dish. Dip chicken in butter mixture, then coat with crumbs.

Place in a greased 13-in. x 9-in. baking dish. Drizzle with remaining butter mixture. Bake, uncovered, at 350° for 25-30 minutes or until juices run clear. **Yield:** 4 servings.

baked lemon chicken

prep: 10 minutes | **bake:** 25 minutes

This lovely chicken is as good the next day as it is right out of the oven. It's moist, tender and lemony with a nice crunch. It makes a wonderful meal with scalloped or baked potatoes and a fresh green salad on the side. It's a delicious picnic entree as well.

Marion Lowery
Medford, Oregon

||| UltimateTIP

Buying skinned and boned chicken breasts can cut up to 15 minutes off your cooking time. Save money by buying larger packages, wrapping individually or in family-sized portions and freezing. Allow 1/4 to 1/3 pound of boneless chicken per serving. When checking chicken breasts for doneness, use an instant-read thermometer. Breasts should register 170°.

dilled turkey breast

prep/cook: 15 minutes

Sliced turkey is delightful when served in a creamy sauce such as this. Try it with mashed potatoes or a tasty side dish of steamed vegetables.

Nancy Bohlen
Brookings, South Dakota

1 can (10-3/4 ounces) condensed
   cream of mushroom soup, undiluted
3/4 cup chicken broth
3/4 cup sour cream
1 tablespoon dill weed
Sliced cooked turkey, warmed

In a saucepan, combine soup, broth, sour cream and dill. Cook until heated through but do not boil. Arrange turkey slices on a platter; pour sauce over slices and serve immediately. **Yield:** 6-8 servings.

chicken salsa pizza

prep/cook: 20 minutes

This zippy pizza is sure to become the most-requested version in the house. The cooked chicken and a prebaked crust make it quick, easy and oh-so-good.

Mrs. Guy Turnbull
Arlington, Massachusetts

1 prebaked Italian bread shell crust
(14 ounces)

2 cups (8 ounces) shredded cheddar
cheese, *divided*

1 jar (11 ounces) salsa

1 cup cubed cooked chicken

Place bread shell on an ungreased 12-in. pizza pan. Sprinkle with 3/4 cup of cheese. Top with salsa, chicken and remaining cheese. Bake at 450° for 8-10 minutes or until cheese is bubbly. **Yield: 4 servings.**

barbecue jack chicken

prep/cook: 25 minutes

Zesty pepper Jack cheese from the deli and convenient bottled barbecue sauce are all you need to dress up the simple grilled chicken breasts.

Taste of Home Test Kitchen
Greendale, Wisconsin

4 boneless skinless chicken breast halves
(6 ounces *each*)

4 slices pepper Jack cheese

1 cup barbecue sauce

Carefully cut a pocket in each chicken breast half. Fill with cheese; secure with metal or soaked wooden skewers.

Grill chicken, covered, over medium heat or broil 4 in. from the heat for 6-8 minutes on each side or until juices run clear, basting frequently with barbecue sauce. **Yield: 4 servings.**

1 can (10-3/4 ounces) condensed cream of chicken soup, undiluted

2 cups cubed cooked chicken

1/2 cup water

Hot cooked rice

TOPPINGS:

Cooked peas, raisins, pineapple tidbits, shredded cheddar cheese, sliced ripe olives, chow mein noodles *and/or* mandarin oranges

In a microwave-safe bowl, combine the soup, chicken and water. Cover and microwave on high for 2-3 minutes or until heated through. Serve over rice. Top with toppings of your choice. **Yield:** 4 servings.

Editor's Note: This recipe was tested in a 1,100-watt microwave.

chicken in a haystack

prep/cook: 15 minutes

This is probably one of the quickest meals in my recipe file and a wonderful way to please picky eaters. Youngsters will love "stacking" their favorite toppings over this rich chicken and rice combo.

Helle Watson
Thornton, Colorado

party chicken

prep: 10 minutes | **bake:** 35 minutes

After trying this at a church dinner, I knew it would be well liked by family and friends. The dish combines tender chicken with dried beef in a creamy sauce.

Eva Snyder Widmyer
Lahmansville, West Virginia

1 package (2-1/2 ounces) thinly sliced dried beef

8 boneless skinless chicken breast halves

1 can (10-3/4 ounces) condensed cream of celery soup, undiluted

1 cup (8 ounces) sour cream

Hot cooked rice, optional

|||Ultimate**TIP**

When preparing rice, make extra. Packaged in freezer containers or heavy-duty resealable plastic bags, cooked rice will keep in the freezer for up to 6 months. To reheat, add 2 tablespoons of liquid for each cup of rice; microwave or cook in a saucepan until heated through. Leftover rice also makes a great dessert. Just add yogurt and your favorite fruit.

In a greased 13-in. x 9-in. baking dish, arrange beef slices to evenly cover bottom of dish. Top with chicken breasts. Combine the soup and sour cream; pour over chicken.

Bake, uncovered, at 350° for 35 minutes or until the chicken juices run clear. Serve over rice if desired. **Yield:** 8 servings.

garlic chicken penne

prep/cook: 20 minutes

All it takes is four ingredients and 20 minutes to have this hearty dish ready to eat. I think the garlicky sauce ties the chicken, snap peas and pasta together nicely.

Anne Nock
Avon Lake, Ohio

- **8 ounces uncooked penne pasta**
- **1-1/2 cups frozen sugar snap peas**
- **1 package (1.6 ounces) garlic-herb pasta sauce mix**
- **1 package (6 ounces) sliced cooked chicken**

In a large saucepan, cook pasta in boiling water for 6 minutes. Add peas; return to a boil. Cook for 4-5 minutes or until pasta is tender. Meanwhile, prepare sauce mix according to package directions.

Drain pasta mixture; add chicken. Drizzle with sauce and toss to coat. **Yield:** 4 servings.

- **1 cup sugar**
- **2 tablespoons cornstarch**
- **1 cup water**
- **2 tablespoons peach *or* orange gelatin**
- **1 medium peach, peeled and finely chopped**
- **4 boneless skinless chicken breast halves (4 ounces *each*)**

In a small saucepan, combine the sugar, cornstarch and water until smooth. Bring to a boil over medium heat; cook and stir for 2 minutes. Remove from heat. Stir in gelatin powder and chopped peach; mix well until gelatin powder is dissolved. Set aside 1 cup for serving.

Grill chicken, uncovered, over medium heat for 3 minutes on each side. Baste with some of the remaining peach sauce. Continue grilling for 6-8 minutes or until meat juices run clear, basting and turning several times. Serve with the reserved peach sauce. **Yield:** 4 servings.

grilled chicken with peach sauce

prep/cook: 30 minutes

This recipe was adapted from a pie filling I often use. I've served the juicy chicken and fruity sauce many times to family and friends, and folks always seem to like it.

Beverly Minton
Milan, Michigan

1 pound ground turkey

1 teaspoon fennel seed, crushed

1 teaspoon water

1/2 teaspoon salt

1/2 teaspoon pepper

1 jar (27 ounces) spaghetti sauce

12 ounces spaghetti, cooked and drained

In a large bowl, combine the ground turkey, fennel seed, water, salt and pepper. Cover and refrigerate overnight. Crumble into bite-size pieces into a large skillet. Cook over medium heat until no longer pink. Stir in spaghetti sauce and heat through. Serve with hot spaghetti. **Yield:** 6 servings.

spaghetti with homemade turkey sausage

prep: 10 minutes + chilling | **cook:** 10 minutes

This speedy, hearty dish is quite tasty. You get the rich flavor by allowing the turkey and spices to blend overnight, so whatever you do, don't skip that step!

Shirley Goodson
West Allis, Wisconsin

easy chicken and noodles

prep/cook: 15 minutes

Here's a stovetop supper you can have on the table in mere minutes. Canned soup makes the sauce a snap to throw together while the noodles boil. It's comforting and inexpensive, too.

Shirley Heston
Lancaster, Ohio

||| UltimateTIP

To cook pasta and noodles evenly and avoid boil-overs, always cook in a large kettle or Dutch oven. It's best not to cook more than 2 pounds of pasta at a time. For 8 ounces, bring 3 quarts water to a full rolling boil. To flavor, add 1 tablespoon salt if desired. Cook pasta noodles until "al dente," or firm yet tender. Avoid overcooking, which can result in a mushy texture.

1 can (10-3/4 ounces) condensed cream of chicken soup, undiluted

3/4 cup milk

1/3 cup grated Parmesan cheese

1/8 teaspoon pepper

3 cups cooked wide egg noodles

2 cups cubed cooked chicken

In a large saucepan, combine the soup, milk, Parmesan cheese and pepper. Stir in the noodles and chicken; heat through. **Yield:** 4 servings.

apricot-glaze chicken

prep/cook: 30 minutes

My husband knows what's on the supper menu when our boys drive home from college. This entree has become our homecoming tradition. Best of all, it can be adjusted to serve any number of people.

Retha Kaye Naylor
Frankton, Indiana

- **2 boneless skinless chicken breast halves**
- **1/4 cup mayonnaise**
- **1/4 cup apricot preserves**
- **2 tablespoons dried minced onion**

Place chicken in a greased 9-in. square baking dish. Combine the mayonnaise, preserves and onion; spoon over chicken. Bake, uncovered, at 350° for 25-minutes or until chicken juices run clear. **Yield:** 2 servings.

honey mustard chicken

prep/cook: 30 minutes

The whole family enjoys my saucy chicken that I serve over rice, so I make it often. It cooks up so tender and juicy that I sometimes serve the chicken on sandwich rolls with lettuce and tomato.

Heather Wray
Portville, New York

- **4 boneless skinless chicken breast halves (4 ounces *each*)**
- **1 jar (12 ounces) chicken gravy**
- **4 teaspoons Dijon mustard**
- **2 to 3 teaspoons honey**

Hot cooked rice, optional

In a large skillet coated with cooking spray, cook chicken over medium-high heat for 5 minutes on each side. Combine the gravy, mustard and honey; pour over chicken. Bring to a boil. Reduce heat; cover and simmer for 8-12 minutes or until the chicken juices run clear. Serve with rice if desired. **Yield:** 4 servings.

chicken in baskets

prep/cook: 25 minutes

My family loves this delicious meal, and I enjoy the fact that it all starts with packaged pastry shells, canned soup and frozen chicken and vegetables.

Cheryl Miller
Robesonia, Pennsylvania

1 **package (10 ounces) frozen puff pastry shells**

1 **can (10-3/4 ounces) condensed cream of chicken soup, undiluted**

1 **package (9 ounces) frozen diced cooked chicken, thawed**

1 **cup frozen mixed vegetables, thawed**

3/4 **cup milk**

Bake pastry shells according to package directions. Meanwhile, in a microwave-safe bowl, combine the soup, chicken, vegetables and milk. Cover and microwave on high for 4-5 minutes or until bubbly. Cut the top off each pastry shell; fill with chicken mixture. Replace tops. **Yield:** 3 servings.

breaded turkey slices

prep/cook: 20 minutes

Stovetop dinners are a snap to fix on busy nights, and this turkey supper is wonderful. Serve the succulent cutlets with a side of buttered noodles or a green salad.

Julie Jahnke
Green Lake, Wisconsin

2 eggs

3 tablespoons milk

2 cups seasoned bread crumbs

1/2 teaspoon salt

1-1/2 pounds turkey breast cutlets

1/2 cup butter, cubed

In a shallow bowl, beat the eggs and milk. In another shallow bowl, combine bread crumbs and salt. Dip turkey slices in egg mixture, then coat with crumb mixture.

In a large skillet, melt butter; brown turkey for about 2 minutes on each side or until juices run clear. **Yield:** 6 servings.

‖ UltimateTIP

When cooking with wine, a general rule of thumb is to use a wine that you feel comfortable drinking. It's best to stay away from bottles of "cooking wine," because they have added salt and preservatives that don't add a pleasant flavor to dishes. Excellent white wines for cooking are Sauvignon Blanc and Chardonnay. Good red wines to cook with are Merlot and Cabernet.

---

6 boneless skinless chicken breast halves (1-1/2 pounds)

1 can (10-3/4 ounces) condensed cream of chicken soup, undiluted

1/2 cup white wine *or* chicken broth

6 slices Swiss cheese

1 cup crushed seasoned croutons

Place the chicken in a greased 13-in. x 9-in. baking dish. In a small bowl, combine the soup and wine or broth; pour over chicken. Top with cheese and sprinkle with croutons.

Bake, uncovered, at 350° for 35-40 minutes or until chicken juices run clear. **Yield:** 6 servings.

baked swiss chicken

prep: 5 minutes | **bake:** 35 minutes

I use canned soup, white wine, Swiss cheese and crushed croutons to dress up chicken breasts at my home. The creamy sauce is excellent with garlic mashed potatoes or rice. This easy entree is always a winner.

Beverly Roberge
Bristol, Connecticut

1-1/2 **cups stuffing mix, finely crushed**

2 **tablespoons grated Parmesan cheese**

1/4 **cup butter, melted**

1 **garlic clove, minced**

5 **boneless skinless chicken breast halves (6 to 8 ounces each)**

In a shallow dish, combine the stuffing crumbs and the Parmesan cheese. In another shallow dish, combine butter and garlic. Dip chicken in butter mixture, then coat with stuffing mixture. Place in a greased 13-in. x 9-in. baking dish.

Sprinkle with remaining stuffing mixture and drizzle with remaining butter mixture. Bake, uncovered, at 350° for 40-45 minutes or until chicken juices run clear. **Yield:** 5 servings.

stuffing-coated chicken

prep: 15 minutes | **bake:** 45 minutes

I found this recipe in an old church cookbook, and it quickly became one of my favorites. While at work, I use the microwave to reheat leftovers for lunch. When the aroma of garlic and Parmesan cheese grabs the attention of co-workers, they ask for the recipe.

Patricia Inman
Litchfield, Minnesota

||Ultimate**TIP**

You can use either shredded or grated Parmesan in equal proportions in your favorite recipes. If you decide to buy a chunk of Parmesan cheese and grate your own, be sure to use the finest section on your grating tool. Or, you can use a food processor. Simply cut the Parmesan cheese into 1-inch cubes and process 1 cup of cubes at a time on high until finely grated.

---

ranch turkey pasta dinner

prep/cook: 20 minutes

This entree is a great way to showcase leftover turkey. If I have chicken on hand, I use it instead. Try sprinkling grated cheese over the top of each helping for extra flavor.

Peggy Key
Grant, Alabama

2-1/2 **cups uncooked penne pasta**

6 **to 8 tablespoons butter, cubed**

1 **envelope ranch salad dressing mix**

1 **cup frozen peas and carrots, thawed**

3 **cups cubed cooked turkey**

Cook penne pasta according to package directions. Meanwhile, in a large skillet, melt butter. Stir in salad dressing mix until smooth. Add peas and carrots; cook and stir for 2-3 minutes. Drain pasta and add to skillet. Stir in turkey; cook for 3-4 minutes or until heated through. **Yield:** 4 servings.

pesto chicken pasta

prep/cook: 20 minutes

It's never been easier to bring a bit of Italy to the table than it is with this change-of-pace recipe. Mix up your dinner routine a bit and serve this specialty tonight.

Taste of Home Test Kitchen
Greendale, Wisconsin

- 1 package (16 ounces) cellentani *or* spiral pasta
- 2 cups cubed cooked rotisserie chicken
- 1 cup chopped fresh tomatoes
- 1 container (7 ounces) prepared pesto
- 1/4 cup pine nuts, toasted

Cook pasta according to package directions. Meanwhile, in a nonstick skillet, saute chicken and tomatoes for 2 minutes. Stir in pesto; heat through. Drain pasta; toss with chicken mixture. Sprinkle with pine nuts. **Yield:** 6 servings.

southern fried chicken

prep: 10 minutes | **cook:** 35 minutes

This dish was a happy accident. I discovered at the last minute that I didn't have enough all-purpose flour for coating the chicken, so I used pancake mix instead. Everyone adored the twist of flavor.

Patricia Gowen
Amherst, Virginia

- 1 cup pancake mix
- 2 to 3 teaspoons salt
- 1/4 teaspoon pepper
- 1/4 teaspoon paprika
- 1 broiler/fryer chicken (3 to 4 pounds), cut up

Oil for deep-fat frying

In a large resealable plastic bag, combine the pancake mix, salt, pepper and paprika. Add chicken, a few pieces at a time; shake to coat.

Heat 2 in. of oil in an electric skillet or deep-fat fryer to 375°. Fry chicken, a few pieces at a time for 6 minutes on each side or until golden brown and juices run clear. **Yield:** 4-6 servings.

- **6 boneless skinless chicken breast halves (4 ounces *each*)**
- **6 slices Swiss cheese**
- **6 thin slices deli ham**
- **3 tablespoons olive oil**
- **3/4 cup seasoned bread crumbs**

Flatten the chicken to 1/4-in thickness. Place a slice of cheese an ham on each to within 1/4 in. edges. Fold in half; secure wit toothpicks. Brush with oil and roll i bread crumbs.

Grill, covered, over medium-ho heat for 7-9 minutes on each side o until chicken is no longer pink Remove toothpicks. **Yield: 6 servings**

grilled chicken cordon bleu

prep: 20 minutes | **grill:** 15 minutes

These special chicken bundles are absolutely delicious. You can assemble them up to 8 hours in advance and keep them in the refrigerator until you're ready to cook them. Then just place them on the grill shortly before dinner.

Shawna McCutcheon
Homer City, Pennsylvania

|||Ultimate**TIP**

Before you head to your backyard for some fun outdoor cooking, refresh your grilling skills with these tips. Bring foods to a cool room temperature before grilling—cold foods may burn on the outside before the interior is cooked. Before grilling meats, trim excess fat to avoid flare-ups. And use tongs to turn meat instead of a fork to avoid piercing and losing juices.

simple salsa chicken

prep: 10 minutes | **bake:** 25 minutes

My husband and I prefer our food a little spicier than our children do, so one evening I baked plain chicken for the kids and created this dish for us. My husband liked it so well that it is now a regular menu item at our house. It doubles easily for larger families, too.

Jan Cooper
Troy, Alabama

- **2 boneless skinless chicken breast halves (5 ounces *each*)**
- **1/8 teaspoon salt**
- **1/3 cup salsa**
- **2 tablespoons taco sauce**
- **1/3 cup shredded Mexican cheese blend**

Place chicken in a shallow 2-qt. baking dish coated with cooking spray. Sprinkle with salt. Combine salsa and taco sauce; drizzle over chicken. Sprinkle with cheese.

Cover and bake at 350° for 25-30 minutes or until the chicken juices run clear. **Yield: 2 servings.**

cranberry chicken

prep: 5 minutes + marinating | **cook:** 1 hour

It's easy to cook chicken to serve any number of people, and now that we're a two-person household, we have chicken often. I made up this recipe because I love cranberries. The dish is tangy and tart...an interesting combination of flavors. We like it with hot rice on the side.

Angelina Lenhart
Concord, California

1/2 cup cranberry juice
2 tablespoons soy sauce
2 tablespoons Worcestershire sauce
2 garlic cloves, minced
2 bone-in chicken breast halves

In a resealable plastic bag, combine the first four ingredients. Add chicken and turn to coat. Seal bag and refrigerate 8 hours or overnight. Place chicken and marinade in a small ungreased baking pan. Bake, uncovered, at 350° for 1 hour or until meat juices run clear. **Yield:** 2 servings.

---

3 egg whites
1 package (4.2 ounces) seasoned coating mix
1/2 cup chopped pecans
1/8 teaspoon Chinese five-spice powder
6 boneless skinless chicken breast halves (4 ounces *each*)

In a shallow bowl, lightly beat the egg whites. In another shallow bowl, combine the coating mix, pecans and five-spice powder. Dip chicken into egg whites, then roll into coating mixture.

Place in a greased 15-in. x 10-in. baking pan. Bake, uncovered, at 400° for 25 minutes or until chicken juices run clear and a meat thermometer reaches 170°. **Yield:** 6 servings.

pecan-crusted chicken

prep: 10 minutes | **bake:** 25 minutes

After tasting a similar dish at a restaurant, I created these impressive baked chicken breasts with a pecan coating. For a special night, I recommend them with mashed sweet potatoes and a side of cooked canned cherries. No one will be disappointed.

Ramona Parris
Marietta, Georgia

seafood & meatless suppers

pg. 114

crumb-topped haddock 114
firecracker shrimp 115
italian bow tie bake 115
italian orange roughy 116
greek grilled catfish 116
tarragon flounder 117
pesto halibut 117
lazy lasagna 118
caribbean rice 'n' shrimp 119
minty peach halibut 119
trout baked in cream 120
vegetarian pasta 120
tomato salmon bake 121
tomato spinach spirals 121
blackened fish salad 122
tomato macaroni casserole 123
honey grilled shrimp 123
bbq chip-crusted orange roughy 124
honey walleye .124
baked cod 125
budget macaroni and cheese 125

pg. 123

pg. 115

crumb-topped haddock

prep: 5 minutes | **bake:** 35 minutes

With only five ingredients, this creamy fish entree with a crispy topping is a breeze to make.

Debbie Solt
Lewistown, Pennsylvania

2 **pounds haddock *or* cod fillets**

1 **can (10-3/4 ounces) condensed cream of shrimp soup, undiluted**

1 **teaspoon grated onion**

1 **teaspoon Worcestershire sauce**

1 **cup crushed butter-flavored crackers (about 25 crackers)**

Arrange fillets in a greased 13-in. x 9-in. baking dish. Combine the soup, onion and Worcestershire sauce; pour over fish.

Bake, uncovered, at 375° for 20 minutes. Sprinkle with the cracker crumbs. Bake 15 minutes longer or until fish flakes easily with a fork. **Yield:** 6-8 servings.

firecracker shrimp

prep/cook: 20 minutes

The marinade, which comes together in minutes, turns into a sweet and spicy glaze as these delightful shrimp sizzle on the grill.

Mary Tallman
Arbor Vitae, Wisconsin

1/2 cup apricot preserves
1 teaspoon canola oil
1 teaspoon soy sauce
1/2 teaspoon crushed red pepper flakes
1 pound uncooked large shrimp, peeled and deveined

Combine the apricot preserves, oil, soy sauce and pepper flakes. Thread shrimp onto metal or soaked wooden skewers.

Grill, uncovered, over medium heat or broil 4 in. from the heat for 2-3 minutes on each side or until shrimp turn pink, basting frequently with apricot mixture. **Yield:** 10-12 servings.

|||UltimateTIP

Opened cheese, such as part-skim mozzarella, should be wrapped with waxed paper, then wrapped again with a tight seal of plastic wrap or foil. Mozzarella cheese stored this way in the refrigerator at a temperature of 34° to 38° will keep for several weeks. If mold develops, trim off the mold plus 1/2 inch extra of cheese and discard it. The rest of the cheese can be eaten.

---

8 ounces uncooked bow tie pasta
1 jar (16 ounces) garlic and onion spaghetti sauce
1 envelope Italian salad dressing mix
2 cups (8 ounces) shredded part-skim mozzarella cheese

Cook the pasta according to the package directions; drain. In a large bowl, combine the spaghetti sauce and salad dressing mix. Add the pasta; toss to coat.

Transfer to a greased shallow 2-qt. baking dish. Sprinkle with cheese. Bake, uncovered, at 400° for 15-20 minutes or until heated through. **Yield:** 4 servings.

italian bow tie bake

prep: 20 minutes | **bake:** 15 minutes

Served with a green salad and garlic bread, this is one of the easiest dinners I prepare for my family. They love the four-ingredient main dish because it tastes as if I worked on it for hours. They don't even miss the meat!

Lisa Blackwell
Henderson, North Carolina

4 orange roughy fillets (6 ounces *each*)

1/4 teaspoon lemon-pepper seasoning

1/4 teaspoon salt

1/4 cup finely chopped onion

1/4 cup finely chopped celery

1 can (14-1/2 ounces) Italian diced tomatoes, undrained

Arrange fish fillets in an ungreased 13-in. x 9-in. baking dish. Sprinkle with lemon-pepper and salt. Cover with onion and celery. Top with the tomatoes. Bake at 350° for 30-40 minutes or until fish flakes easily with a fork. **Yield:** 4 servings.

italian orange roughy

prep: 5 minutes | **bake:** 30 minutes

This dish is delicious, foolproof and very low in fat. I prepare it on weeknights when I need a quick supper, but I've also used it for company meals. The Italian tomatoes and lemon-pepper seasoning give the mild fillets a little zest.

Michelle Haerr
Eureka, Illinois

greek grilled catfish

prep/cook: 30 minutes

Temperatures here on the Gulf Coast are moderate year-round, so we grill out a lot. My husband, Larry, came up with this recipe by experimenting. Our whole family likes the unique taste of this dish.

Rita Futral
Starkville, Mississippi

|||UltimateTIP

Feta is a white, salty, semi-firm cheese. Traditionally it was made from sheep or goat's milk but is now also made with cow's milk. After feta is formed in a special mold, it's sliced into large pieces, salted and soaked in brine. Although feta cheese is mostly associated with Greek cooking, "feta" comes from the Italian word "fette," meaning slice of food.

---

6 catfish fillets (8 ounces *each*)

Greek seasoning to taste

4 ounces feta cheese, crumbled

1 tablespoon dried mint

2 tablespoons olive oil

Sprinkle both sides of fillets with Greek seasoning. Sprinkle each fillet with 1 rounded tablespoon feta cheese and 1/2 teaspoon mint. Drizzle 1 teaspoon oil over each. Roll up fillets and secure with toothpicks.

Grill over medium heat for 20-25 minutes or until fish flakes easily with a fork. Or, place fillets in a greased baking dish and bake at 350° for 30-35 minutes or until fish flakes easily with fork. **Yield:** 6 servings.

tarragon flounder

prep/cook: 30 minutes

Tarragon is one of my favorite herbs. It, along with butter and other ingredients, turns regular fish fillets into an elegant and delicious main dish.

Donna Smith
Fairport, New York

1/4 **pound flounder fillet**

1/4 **cup chicken broth**

1 **tablespoon butter, melted**

1-1/2 **teaspoons minced fresh tarragon**
or **1/2 teaspoon dried tarragon**

1/2 **teaspoon ground mustard**

Place fillets in a greased 11-in. x 7-in. baking dish. Combine the remaining ingredients; pour over the fish. Bake, uncovered, at 350° for 20-25 minutes or until fish flakes easily with a fork. Remove to a serving plate with a slotted spatula. Serve immediately. **Yield:** 1 serving.

pesto halibut

prep/cook: 20 minutes

The mild flavor of the fish pairs well with the pesto. It takes only 5 minutes to get the fish fillets ready for the oven, so you can start on your choice of side dishes. Nearly anything goes well with this fish.

April Showalter
Milwaukee, Wisconsin

2 **tablespoons olive oil**

1 **envelope pesto sauce mix**

1 **tablespoon lemon juice**

6 **halibut fillets (4 ounces *each*)**

Combine the oil, sauce mix and lemon juice; brush over both sides of fillets. Place in a greased 13-in. x 9-in. baking dish.

Bake, uncovered, at 450° for 12-15 minutes or until fish flakes easily with a fork. **Yield:** 6 servings.

lazy lasagna

prep/cook: 30 minutes

When my family is craving the hearty flavor of lasagna but I don't have time to make it, this quick-to-fix meatless version does the trick.

Carol Mead
Los Alamos, New Mexico

1 cup spaghetti sauce

3/4 cup shredded part-skim mozzarella cheese

1/2 cup 4% cottage cheese

1-1/2 cups cooked wide noodles

2 tablespoons grated Parmesan cheese

Warm the spaghetti sauce; stir in the mozzarella and cottage cheeses. Fold in the noodles. Pour into two 2-cup baking dishes coated with cooking spray. Sprinkle with Parmesan cheese.

Bake, uncovered, at 375° for 20 minutes or until bubbly. **Yield:** 2 servings.

caribbean rice 'n' shrimp

prep/cook: 25 minutes

A convenient packaged rice mix plus vegetables and shrimp create a tasty and quick meal for busy cooks.

Taste of Home Test Kitchen
Greendale, Wisconsin

- 1 package (8 ounces) Caribbean rice mix
- 6 cups water
- 1/2 pound fresh asparagus, trimmed and cut into 1-inch pieces
- 1 pound uncooked medium shrimp, peeled and deveined
- 1 medium tomato, chopped

Prepare rice mix according to the package directions, omitting the chicken. Meanwhile, in a large saucepan, bring the water to a boil. Add asparagus; cover and cook for 2 minutes. Stir in shrimp; cook for 2-3 minutes or until shrimp turn pink. Drain. Add asparagus, shrimp and tomato to rice; toss gently. **Yield:** 4 servings.

minty peach halibut

prep/cook: 20 minutes

I knew this golden entree was a winner when my mother-in-law, who owns every cookbook imaginable, asked for the recipe. I flavor thick halibut steaks with a deliciously different sauce that is made with an easy combination of fresh mint and peach preserves.

Dawn Mayford
Granite City, Illinois

- 1 jar (10 ounces) peach preserves
- 2 teaspoons minced fresh mint
- 4 halibut steaks (6 ounces *each*)
- 1/2 teaspoon salt
- 1/4 teaspoon pepper

In a small saucepan, combine preserves and mint. Bring to a boil; cook and stir for 2 minutes. Remove from the heat; set aside. Sprinkle fish with salt and pepper.

Broil 4 in. from the heat for 5 minutes. Spoon half of peach mixture over fish. Broil 1 minute longer; turn, Broil 3-4 minutes more or until fish flakes easily with a fork, basting once with remaining peach mixture. **Yield:** 4 servings.

6 **trout fillets (about 3-1/2 ounces** *each***)**
2 **tablespoons lemon juice**
1 **teaspoon dill weed**
1/2 **teaspoon salt**
1/8 **teaspoon pepper**
1 **cup heavy whipping cream**
2 **tablespoons seasoned bread crumbs**

Place the trout in a greased 13-in. x 9-in. baking dish. Sprinkle with lemon juice, dill, salt and pepper. Pour the heavy cream over all. Sprinkle with bread crumbs. Bake, uncovered, at 350° for 11-15 minutes or until fish flakes easily with a fork. **Yield:** 4-6 servings.

trout baked in cream

prep/cook: 20 minutes

Here's a quick and delicious way to serve trout. It's definitely one of our family's favorites.

Ann Nace
Perkasie, Pennsylvania

vegetarian pasta

prep/cook: 25 minutes

I add a can of beans to noodles to create this fast, flavorful lunch fare. You can use any type of pasta you have on hand to make this filling dish.

Mary Feichtel
Binghamton, New York

2 **cups uncooked angel hair pasta**
1 **can (15-1/2 ounces) great northern beans, rinsed and drained**
3 **tablespoons butter**
1/4 **teaspoon garlic salt, optional**
1/4 **cup shredded Parmesan** *or* **Romano cheese**

UltimateTIP

There's no question about it, heavy cream lends an undeniably rich flavor to many foods. However, at 100 calories and 11 grams of fat per 2 tablespoons, it can be a calorie and fat buster! Substituting an equal amount of half-and-half for the heavy cream generally works quite well. That's a savings of 60 calories and 8 grams of fat per 2 tablespoons.

Cook the pasta according to package directions. Meanwhile, place the beans in a microwave-safe dish; cover and microwave on high for 1-1/4 minutes or until heated through.

Drain pasta; transfer to a large serving bowl. Add butter and garlic salt if desired; toss until butter is melted. Add beans and cheese; toss to coat. Serve immediately. **Yield:** 4 servings.

Editor's Note: This recipe was tested in a 1,100-watt microwave.

tomato salmon bake

prep/cook: 30 minutes

I was looking for a healthy alternative to beef and chicken when I found this recipe and decided to personalize it. My husband doesn't usually like fish unless it's fried, but he loves the Italian flavor in this dish. Serve it with a green salad for a great meal any time of year.

Lacey Parker
Gainesville, Virginia

4 **salmon fillets (6 ounces *each*)**

1 **can (14-1/2 ounces) diced tomatoes, drained**

1/2 **cup sun-dried tomato salad dressing**

2 **tablespoons shredded Parmesan cheese**

Hot cooked rice

Place salmon in a greased 13-in. x 9-in. baking dish. Combine tomatoes and salad dressing; pour over salmon. Sprinkle with Parmesan cheese.

Bake, uncovered, at 375° for 20-25 minutes or until fish flakes easily with a fork. Serve with rice. **Yield:** 4 servings.

tomato spinach spirals

prep/cook: 25 minutes

A great side dish or meatless main course, this pasta pleaser comes together in a snap. And at less than a dollar per serving, it's affordable as well. I make extra so I can have it for lunch the next day.

Janet Montano
Temecula, California

1 **package (8 ounces) spiral pasta**

1 **package (10 ounces) frozen creamed spinach**

1 **can (14-1/2 ounces) diced tomatoes, undrained**

3 **tablespoons grated Romano cheese, *divided***

3 **tablespoons grated Parmesan cheese, *divided***

1/2 **teaspoon salt**

Cook pasta according to package directions. Meanwhile, prepare spinach according to package directions. Drain pasta; place in a large bowl. Add the spinach, tomatoes, 2 tablespoons of Romano cheese, 2 tablespoons of Parmesan cheese and salt; toss to coat. Sprinkle with the remaining cheeses. **Yield:** 6 servings.

blackened fish salad

prep/cook: 25 minutes

A handful of convenience items, including pasta salad from the deli and Cajun-style fish fillets from the freezer section, make it a snap to put together this easy and delicious main dish.

Taste of Home Test Kitchen
Greendale, Wisconsin

2 **packages (7.6 ounces *each*) frozen Cajun blackened grilled fish fillets**

1 **pound deli pasta salad**

1 **cup fresh baby spinach**

2 **tablespoons grated Parmesan cheese**

Bake fish fillets according to package directions. Meanwhile, in a large bowl, toss the pasta salad and spinach. Divide among four salad plates. Cut fish into slices; arrange over salad. Sprinkle with Parmesan cheese. **Yield:** 4 servings.

||| Ultimate**TIP**

When buying prepackaged fish, be sure it is tightly wrapped with no air space or liquid between the fish and wrapping. Frozen fish should be frozen solid. The package should not contain ice crystals or water stains. The fish should not have any discoloration due to freezer burn. Frozen fish should be thawed in its original package in the refrigerator. Do not refreeze.

tomato macaroni casserole

prep/cook: 15 minutes

I dress up cooked macaroni with four flavorful ingredients. This dish is one of my husband's favorites.

Karen Smith
Thornton, Colorado

- **4 cups cooked elbow macaroni**
- **1 can (14-1/2 ounces) diced tomatoes, drained**
- **1 can (10 ounces) diced tomatoes and green chilies, undrained**
- **1 cup (4 ounces) shredded Colby-Monterey Jack cheese, *divided***
- **6 bacon strips, cooked and crumbled**

In a greased 11-in. x 7-in. microwave-safe dish, combine the macaroni, tomatoes and 3/4 cup cheese; mix well. Cover and microwave on high for 2 to 2-1/2 minutes; stir. Cover and heat 45 seconds longer. Sprinkle with bacon and remaining cheese. Microwave, uncovered, for 20-40 seconds longer or until cheese is melted. Let stand for 5 minutes before serving. **Yield: 4 servings.**

Editor's Note: This recipe was tested in a 1,100-watt microwave.

honey grilled shrimp

prep: 10 minutes + marinating | **grill:** 10 minutes

My husband received this super-simple recipe from a man who sold shrimp at the fish market. It's now our family's favorite shrimp recipe. We even serve it to company...with great success. Enjoy!

Lisa Blackwell
Henderson, North Carolina

- **1 bottle (8 ounces) Italian salad dressing**
- **1 cup honey**
- **1/2 teaspoon minced garlic**
- **2 pounds uncooked medium shrimp, peeled and deveined**

Combine the salad dressing, honey and minced garlic; set aside 1/2 cup. Pour the remaining marinade into a large resealable plastic bag; add the shrimp. Seal the bag and turn to coat; refrigerate for 30 minutes. Cover and refrigerate the reserved marinade for basting later on.

Coat grill rack with cooking spray before starting the grill. Drain and discard the marinade. Thread shrimp onto eight metal or soaked wooden skewers. Grill, uncovered, over medium heat for 1 to 1-1/2 minutes on each side. Baste with reserved marinade. Grill 3-4 minutes longer or until shrimp turn pink, turning and basting frequently. **Yield: 8 servings.**

4 orange roughy fillets
(6 ounces *each*)

3 tablespoons lemon juice

1 tablespoon butter, melted

1/2 cup crushed barbecue potato
chips

Tartar sauce, optional

Place fish fillets in a greased 13-in. x 9-in. baking dish. Combine the lemon juice and butter; pour over fillets. Top with crushed potato chips.

Bake, uncovered, at 400° for 20-25 minutes or until fish flakes easily with a fork. Serve with tartar sauce if desired. **Yield:** 4 servings.

bbq chip-crusted orange roughy

prep/cook: 25 minutes

This easy and delectable recipe actually converted me into a fish lover. It was given to me by a fishmonger decades ago and is frequently requested by family and friends. Even those who generally do not like fish like this recipe! Tilapia or other white fish are easy and excellent substitutions for the orange roughy fillets.

Geraldine Buba
Palos Hills, Illinois

||| UltimateTIP

If your family's not wild about fish, start with some of the milder flavored types. Cod, haddock, flounder, sole and walleye are all pleasantly mild and have a delicate texture. Fish with more distinctive flavors and firmer textures include halibut, red snapper, orange roughy, catfish, sea bass, trout and salmon. To avoid bones, purchase fillets, the boneless sides of the fish.

honey walleye

prep/cook: 20 minutes

Our state is known as the "Land of 10,000 Lakes," so fishing is a favorite recreation here. This recipe has been a quick way to prepare all the fresh walleye that's been hooked by the anglers in our family.

Kitty McCue
St. Louis Park, Minnesota

1 egg

2 teaspoons honey

2 cups crushed butter-flavored crackers
(about 45 to 50)

1/2 teaspoon salt

4 to 6 walleye fillets (1-1/2
to 2 pounds)

1/3 to 1/2 cup canola oil

In a shallow bowl, beat the egg; add honey. In a plastic bag, combine the crackers and salt. Dip fish in egg mixture, then place in bag and shake until coated.

In a skillet, cook fillets in oil for 3-5 minutes per side or until golden and fish flakes easily with a fork. **Yield:** 4-6 servings.

baked cod

prep/cook: 20 minutes

These fish fillets bake in no time! Brushed with ranch salad dressing and coated with seasoned stuffing crumbs and parsley, the cod fillets are moist and flavorful.

Taste of Home Test Kitchen
Greendale, Wisconsin

- 1 **cup seasoned stuffing croutons, crushed**
- 1 **tablespoon minced fresh parsley**
- 2 **cod fillets (6 ounces *each*)**
- 1 **tablespoon reduced-fat ranch salad dressing**

Refrigerated butter-flavored spray

In a shallow bowl, combine the crushed croutons and parsley. Brush the cod with salad dressing, then coat with crumb mixture. Spritz with butter-flavored spray.

Place in an 11-in. x 7-in. baking dish coated with cooking spray. Bake, uncovered, at 400° for 10-15 minutes or until fish flakes easily with a fork. **Yield:** 2 servings.

budget macaroni and cheese

prep/cook: 20 minutes

You can't beat this comforting casserole for pleasing the family and going easy on the budget. It's a classic and satisfying meatless entree.

Debbie Carlson
San Diego, California

- 1 **package (7 ounces) elbow macaroni**
- 3 **tablespoons butter**
- 3 **tablespoons all-purpose flour**
- 1/4 **teaspoon salt**

Dash pepper
- 1 **cup milk**
- 1 **cup (4 ounces) shredded cheddar cheese**

Cook the macaroni according to package directions. Meanwhile, in a large saucepan, melt the butter over medium-low heat. Add the flour, salt and pepper; stir until smooth. Gradually add the milk. Bring to a boil; cook and stir for 2 minutes or until thickened. Remove from the heat; stir in cheese until melted.

Drain pasta. Add to the cheese mixture; toss to coat. **Yield:** 4 servings.

side dishes & more

pg. 138

creamy mushroom bow ties 128
garlic lemon butter 129
hollandaise sauce 129
double cheddar hash browns 130
cheddar cheese sauce 130
baked carrots 131
broccoli casserole 131
herbed potato wedges 132
kettle gravy 132
italian mixed vegetables 133
cheese potato puff 133
asparagus with blue cheese sauce 134
perfect scalloped oysters 135
beans with celery bacon sauce 135
pear cranberry sauce 136
creamy parmesan sauce 136
ballpark baked beans 137
garlic brussels sprouts 137
potatoes supreme 138
baked cranberry relish 138
cheesy hash brown bake 139
skillet ranch vegetables 139
greek green beans 140
dill mustard 140
herbed corn on the cob 141
savory soup spuds 141
sunday dinner mashed potatoes 142
broccoli with mock hollandaise 143
zucchini corn medley 143
homemade noodles 144
spiced honey butter 144
spiced carrot strips 145
italian vegetable saute 145
vegetable rice medley 146
cran-apple sauce 146
spiced pineapple 147
basil cherry tomatoes 147
broccoli with orange sauce 148
seasoned fries 149
snappy peas 'n' mushrooms 149
sweet-and-sour mustard 150
brussels sprouts with pecans 150
buttery peas and carrots 151
parmesan noodles 151

creamy mushroom bow ties

prep/cook: 20 minutes

This pasta dish has become one of our favorites. It's so easy! But it tastes like it took much longer in the kitchen than it does. Some of our friends don't eat red meat, so I sometimes serve this as a meatless main dish. It's wonderful with a salad and a loaf of French bread.

Dodi Mahan Walker
Peachtree City, Georgia

- 6 **cups uncooked bow tie pasta**
- 1 **pound sliced fresh mushrooms**
- 1/2 **teaspoon salt**
- 1/4 **teaspoon pepper**
- 2 **tablespoons butter**
- 1 **package (4.4 ounces) garlic-herb cheese spread**
- 1/4 **cup chicken broth**

Cook the pasta according to package directions. Meanwhile, in a large skillet, saute the mushrooms, salt and pepper in butter until tender. Add cheese spread and broth; cook and stir until blended. Drain pasta; add to skillet and toss to coat. **Yield:** 9 servings.

garlic lemon butter

prep/cook: 10 minutes

This tangy flavored butter offers a nice change from plain butter and gives a refreshing new taste to an ear of corn. When I serve this on the side during fresh corn season, the same question always gets asked: "What's in the butter that makes it so delicious?"

Margie Wampler
Butler, Pennsylvania

- 1/2 cup butter, softened
- 1 garlic clove, minced
- 1 teaspoon minced fresh parsley
- 2 to 3 teaspoons grated lemon peel
- 1/4 teaspoon salt, optional
- **Pepper to taste**

Mix all ingredients until smooth. Spread on hot corn on the cob or dab on any cooked vegetables. **Yield:** 1/2 cup.

||| Ultimate**TIP**

To keep fresh parsley in the refrigerator for several weeks, wash the entire bunch in warm water, shake off all excess moisture, wrap in a paper towel and seal in a plastic bag. If you need a longer storage time, remove the paper towel and place the sealed bag in the freezer. Then simply break off and crumble the amount of parsley you need for soups, stews and other cooked dishes.

---

hollandaise sauce

prep/cook: 30 minutes

This rich, lemony sauce is typically served with Eggs Benedict. But it's also delicious served over green vegetables. In this case, the classic sauce adds an elegant touch to fresh steamed asparagus.

Taste of Home Test Kitchen
Greendale, Wisconsin

- 3 egg yolks
- 1/4 cup water
- 2 tablespoons lemon juice
- 1/2 cup cold butter, cut into 8 pieces
- 1/8 teaspoon salt
- 1/8 teaspoon paprika
- **Dash white pepper**

In a small heavy saucepan or double boiler, whisk together the egg yolks, water and lemon juice. Cook and stir over low heat until the mixture begins to thicken, bubbles around edges and reaches 160°, about 20 minutes. Add butter to yolk mixture, one piece at a time, whisking after each addition until butter is melted. Remove from the heat; stir in the salt, paprika and pepper. Serve immediately. **Yield:** 1 cup.

1 can (10-3/4 ounces) condensed cream of onion soup, undiluted

1 can (10-3/4 ounces) condensed cheddar cheese soup, undiluted

1 package (30 ounces) frozen shredded hash brown potatoes

2 cups (8 ounces) shredded cheddar cheese

1 cup crushed cornflakes

double cheddar hash browns

prep: 10 minutes | **bake:** 1 hour

This comforting side dish starts with convenient frozen hash browns and two kinds of canned soup. Shredded cheddar cheese and crunchy cornflake crumbs are the fast finishing touches to this easy potato bake.

Renee Hatfield
Marshallville, Ohio

In a large bowl, combine the soups. Stir in the hash browns. Pour into a greased 2-1/2-qt. baking dish. Sprinkle with cheddar cheese and cornflake crumbs. Cover and bake at 350° for 50 minutes. Uncover; bake 10 minutes longer or until golden. **Yield:** 8 servings.

---

cheddar cheese sauce

prep/cook: 15 minutes

This speedy sauce is perfect over vegetables, omelets or any items made tastier with melted cheddar. Surprise your family tonight by drizzling some on baked potatoes.

Taste of Home Test Kitchen
Greendale, Wisconsin

||| Ultimate**TIP**

When buying potatoes, look for those that are firm, well-shaped and free of blemishes. Avoid potatoes that are wrinkled, cracked or sprouting. If kept in a cool, dark, well-ventilated place, most potatoes will keep for up to 2 weeks. However, new potatoes should be used within 4 days of purchase. Generally, three medium russet potatoes equal one pound.

1/2 cup butter

1/2 cup all-purpose flour

1 teaspoon salt

1/2 teaspoon pepper

4 cups milk

2 cups (8 ounces) shredded cheddar cheese

6 hot baked potatoes

In a saucepan over medium heat, melt butter. Stir in flour, salt and pepper until smooth. Gradually add milk. Bring to a boil; cook and stir for 2 minutes or until thickened. Reduce heat; add the cheese. Cook and stir until cheese is melted.

Serve 1-1/2 cups of cheese sauce with the baked potatoes. Refrigerate remaining sauce. **Yield:** 5-1/2 cups.

baked carrots

prep: 10 minutes | **bake:** 1 hour

These carrots are compatible with most any meal. The chicken broth gives them great flavor. Whenever I serve this simple dish, there are never any leftovers. For a unique variation of mashed potatoes, mash the vegetable combination with the potatoes—it's delicious!

Eleanore Hill
Fresno, California

- 1 **pound carrots, cut into sticks**
- 1 **bunch green onions with tops, chopped**
- 1 **cup chicken broth**

Place the carrots and onions in an ungreased 1-qt. casserole; pour chicken broth over all. Cover and bake at 325° for 1 hour. **Yield:** 6 servings.

broccoli casserole

prep: 20 minutes | **bake:** 35 minutes

Everybody who has tried this side dish absolutely raves about it. My friends and family who don't even like the taste of broccoli beg me to make it.

Elaine Hubbard
Pocono Lake, Pennsylvania

- 2 **packages (16 ounces *each*) frozen broccoli florets**
- 1 **can (10-3/4 ounces) condensed cream of mushroom soup, undiluted**
- 1 **cup (8 ounces) sour cream**
- 1-1/2 **cups (6 ounces) shredded sharp cheddar cheese, *divided***
- 1 **can (6 ounces) french-fried onions, *divided***

Cook broccoli according to package directions; drain well. In a large saucepan, combine the soup, sour cream, 1 cup cheese and 1-1/4 cups onions. Cook over medium heat for 4-5 minutes or until heated through. Stir in the broccoli.

Pour into a greased 2-qt. baking dish. Bake, uncovered, at 325° for 25-30 minutes or until bubbly. Sprinkle with the remaining cheese and onions. Bake 10-15 minutes longer or until cheese is melted. **Yield:** 6-8 servings.

3 tablespoons grated Parmesan cheese

1 tablespoon dried basil

1/4 teaspoon salt, optional

1/4 teaspoon pepper

1 large unpeeled baking potato, cut into wedges

2 teaspoons canola oil

In a shallow bowl, combine the Parmesan cheese, basil, salt if desired and pepper. Brush the cut sides of the potato wedges with oil; dip into the cheese mixture.

Place in a greased 8-in. square pan. Bake, uncovered, at 400° for 20-25 minutes or until tender. **Yield: 2 servings.**

herbed potato wedges

prep/cook: 30 minutes

I'm a widower and cook mainly for myself. This recipe is simple and I've used it many times. Since it makes enough for two, I'll wrap half of the baked potato wedges in foil and freeze them for another time. Then I simply warm them in the toaster oven or microwave.

R.V. Taibbi
Honolulu, Hawaii

kettle gravy

prep/cook: 10 minutes

This recipe can be used to thicken pan juices that form when meats, such as a whole chicken or pot roast, are cooked in a roasting pan with water or broth.

Taste of Home Test Kitchen
Greendale, Wisconsin

2 cups pan juices

6 tablespoons all-purpose flour

2/3 cup cold water

Additional water *or* broth

Salt and pepper to taste

||| UltimateTIP

Leftover pan juices from whole roasted chicken or large cuts of beef make excellent gravy. They also add great flavor to soups and potpies. Here's an easy way to remove the fat: After the meat is cooked, pour the pan juices into a bowl. Refrigerate overnight. The next day, the fat will have hardened on the surface and can be lifted off the top with a spoon.

Pour pan juices into a saucepan or return to roasting pan. Combine flour and water until smooth; stir into pan juices. Bring to a boil; cook and stir for 2 minutes or until thickened, adding additional water or broth if necessary. Season with salt and pepper if desired. **Yield: about 3 cups.**

italian mixed vegetables

prep/cook: 25 minutes

Bottled salad dressing and herbs quickly dress up frozen vegetables in this easy and eye-catching recipe. It's a super side dish for busy weeknights.

Dawn Harvey
Danville, Pennsylvania

- 1 package (24 ounces) frozen California-blend vegetables
- 1/4 cup water
- 1/4 cup reduced-fat Italian salad dressing
- 1/4 teaspoon salt
- 1/4 teaspoon dried basil
- 1/8 teaspoon dried oregano

In a large nonstick skillet, bring vegetables and water to a boil. Cover and cook for 10-12 minutes or until vegetables are crisp-tender. Uncover; cook and stir until liquid is reduced. Add the salad dressing, salt, basil and oregano. Cook and stir until heated through. **Yield:** 6 servings.

cheese potato puff

prep: 35 minutes | **bake:** 30 minutes

These are the highest, fluffiest, tastiest potatoes I've ever had. They can be made a day ahead and refrigerated until ready to bake. This dish is Mom's specialty, and we all especially love the part along the edge of the casserole dish that gets golden brown.

Alyson Armstrong
Parkersburg, West Virginia

- 12 medium potatoes, peeled and cubed
- 2 cups (8 ounces) shredded cheddar *or* Swiss cheese, *divided*
- 1-1/4 cups milk
- 1/3 cup butter, softened
- 1 to 2 teaspoons salt
- 2 eggs, lightly beaten

Place potatoes in a large saucepan and cover with water. Bring to a boil. Reduce heat; cover and simmer for 15-20 minutes or until tender. Drain; mash potatoes. Add 1-3/4 cups cheese, milk, butter and salt; cook and stir over low heat until cheese and butter are melted. Fold in eggs.

Spread into a greased 13-in. x 9-in. baking dish. Bake, uncovered, at 350° for 25-30 minutes. Sprinkle with the remaining shredded cheese. Bake 5 minutes longer or until golden brown. **Yield:** 12-14 servings.

asparagus with blue cheese sauce

prep/cook: 20 minutes

My sister introduced me to this recipe several years ago because she knows I love blue cheese. This dish is a simple way to dress up asparagus, giving the sauce a tangy taste that is entirely unique. I make it every spring when we have fresh home-grown asparagus.

Leona Luecking
West Burlington, Iowa

1/2 **pound fresh asparagus spears**

2 **ounces cream cheese, softened**

3 **tablespoons evaporated milk *or* half-and-half cream**

1/8 **teaspoon salt**

1 **to 2 tablespoons crumbled blue cheese**

In a small saucepan, cook asparagus in a small amount of water until crisp-tender. Meanwhile, in another saucepan, whisk cream cheese, milk and salt over low heat until smooth. Stir in blue cheese and heat through. Drain asparagus and top with sauce. **Yield:** 2 servings.

perfect scalloped oysters

prep: 15 minutes | **bake:** 30 minutes

Creamy and delicious, this dish is a real treat with fresh or canned oysters.

Alice King
Nevada, Ohio

2 cups crushed butter-flavored crackers (about 50)

1/2 cup butter, melted

1/2 teaspoon salt

Dash pepper

1 pint shucked oysters *or* 2 cans (8 ounces *each*) whole oysters, drained

1 cup heavy whipping cream

1/4 teaspoon Worcestershire sauce

Combine the cracker crumbs, butter, salt and pepper; sprinkle a third into a greased 1-1/2-qt. baking dish. Arrange half of the oysters over crumbs. Top with another third of the crumb mixture and the remaining oysters.

Combine cream and Worcestershire sauce; pour over oysters. Top with remaining crumb mixture. Bake, uncovered, at 350° for 30-40 minutes or until top is golden brown. **Yield:** 8 servings.

beans with celery bacon sauce

prep/cook: 20 minutes

Bacon adds nice crunch and flavor to the sauce for the dressed-up green beans I serve for our Christmas ham dinner. Since this dish goes well with many other foods, too, it's a recipe I use often throughout the year.

Christine Eilerts
Tulsa, Oklahoma

6 cups fresh green beans

4 bacon strips, diced

1 cup finely chopped onion

1 can (10-3/4 ounces) condensed cream of celery soup, undiluted

1/2 cup milk

Place beans in a large saucepan and cover with water; bring to a boil. Cook, uncovered, for 8-10 minutes or until crisp-tender; drain and set aside.

In a skillet, cook bacon over medium heat until crisp. Remove to paper towels; drain, reserving 2 tablespoons drippings. Saute onion in drippings until tender. Stir in soup and milk until blended; heat through. Spoon over beans. Sprinkle bacon over top. **Yield:** 8 servings.

2-1/2 cups cubed peeled ripe pears
    (about 3 medium)
    1 cup water
  1/2 teaspoon ground ginger
    1 cinnamon stick (3 inches),
      broken in half
    1 package (12 ounces) fresh *or*
      frozen cranberries
    1 to 1-1/4 cups sugar

In a large saucepan, combine the peas, water, ginger and cinnamon. Bring to a boil. Reduce heat; simmer, uncovered, for 5 minutes. Stir in the cranberries and sugar. Bring to a boil. Reduce heat; simmer, uncovered, for 10-12 minutes or until the cranberries have popped and sauce is slightly thickened, stirring occasionally.

Discard cinnamon sticks. Mash sauce if desired. Cool. Cover and refrigerate until serving. **Yield:** about 2 cups.

pear cranberry sauce

prep: 10 minutes | **cook:** 20 minutes + chilling

We don't care for regular cranberry sauce, so I usually perk it up with other fruit. This version includes fresh pears, and is the one my family requests most often. It's sweet, tangy and a beautiful ruby-red color.

Joyce Bowman
Lady Lake, Florida

||| UltimateTIP

Purchase pears that are firm, fragrant and free of blemishes or soft spots. To ripen, place them in a paper bag at room temperature for several days. When the pears give in slightly to pressure, refrigerate. Pears used for cooking should be a little more firm. Before cooking, remove the skin, which turns dark and tough when exposed to heat.

---

creamy parmesan sauce

prep/cook: 10 minutes

This easy, cheesy sauce is great as a pasta sauce or over cooked broccoli or asparagus.

Maria Bacher
Westminster, South Carolina

    1 **package (8 ounces) cream cheese,
      cubed**
  3/4 **cup milk**
  1/2 **cup shredded Parmesan cheese**
Ground nutmeg and pepper to taste

In a 1-qt. microwave-safe dish, combine the cream cheese, milk and Parmesan cheese. Cover and microwave at 50% power for 2 to 2-1/2 minutes; stir. Cook 2-4 minutes longer or until cheeses are melted. Add nutmeg and pepper. Serve over vegetables. **Yield:** 2 cups.

Editor's Note: The shredded Parmesan cheese will give the sauce a creamier texture than grated Parmesan. This recipe was tested in a 1,100-watt microwave.

ballpark baked beans

prep: 5 minutes | **bake:** 1 hour

You'll taste a sweet hint of pineapple in every bite of this easy bean casserole. I asked my sister-in-law's mom for her recipe after she brought these delicious beans to a family gathering. They're always a big hit with the kids.

Sue Gronholz
Columbus, Wisconsin

2 cans (16 ounces *each*) baked beans

1/4 cup packed brown sugar

2 tablespoons ketchup

2 teaspoons prepared mustard

1 can (20 ounces) pineapple tidbits, drained

In a large bowl, combine the beans, brown sugar, ketchup and mustard. Transfer to a 2-qt. baking dish. Bake, uncovered, at 350° for 30 minutes. Stir in the pineapple; bake 30 minutes longer or until bubbly. **Yield:** 10 servings.

garlic brussels sprouts

prep/cook: 15 minutes

These tasty brussels sprouts are perfect for one person, but it's fine to double or triple the recipe (or more!) for extra dinner guests.

Chris Tucker
Portland, Oregon

5 brussels sprouts, halved

1 garlic clove, minced

1 teaspoon butter, melted

1 tablespoon shredded Parmesan cheese, optional

Place brussels sprouts and garlic in a small saucepan; add 1 in. of water. Bring to a boil; reduce heat. Cover and simmer for 6-8 minutes or until sprouts are crisp-tender; drain. Drizzle with butter. Sprinkle with Parmesan cheese if desired. **Yield:** 1 serving.

8 to 10 medium potatoes, peeled and cubed

1 can (10-3/4 ounces) condensed cream of chicken soup, undiluted

3 cups (12 ounces) shredded cheddar cheese, *divided*

1 cup (8 ounces) sour cream

3 green onions, chopped

Salt and pepper to taste

Place potatoes in a saucepan and cover with water. Bring to a boil; cover and cook until almost tender. Drain and cool.

In a large bowl, combine soup, 1-1/2 cups cheese, sour cream, onions, salt and pepper; stir in potatoes.

Place in a greased 13-in. x 9-in. baking dish. Sprinkle with remaining cheese. Bake, uncovered, at 350° for 25-30 minutes or until heated through. **Yield:** 8-10 servings.

potatoes supreme

prep: 35 minutes + cooling | **bake:** 25 minutes

Hailing from the state known for its potatoes, I thought I'd send in this recipe. Every time my grandson comes home from college, he asks me to make it. In fact, it's the whole family's favorite potato dish.

Mrs. Afton Johnson
Sugar City, Idaho

|||UltimateTIP

If you're watching your weight or just want to reduce the amount of calories in the Potatoes Supreme, plain yogurt can be substituted in equal amounts for sour cream in baking recipes as well as in casseroles, dips and sauces. You may notice dips and sauces might be thinner in consistency when using yogurt. Nonfat yogurt does not work well in recipes that are baked.

baked cranberry relish

prep: 5 minutes + chilling | **bake:** 1 hour

Orange marmalade and walnuts make this chilled cranberry sauce a delightful change from the ordinary. With just five ingredients, it's a simple dish that adds festive color to the table.

Anita Curtis
Camarillo, California

4-1/2 cups cranberries

1-1/2 cups sugar

1 cup chopped walnuts, toasted

1 cup orange marmalade

2 tablespoons lemon juice

Toss cranberries and sugar; place in a lightly greased 2-qt. baking dish. Cover and bake at 350° for 1 hour. Stir in walnuts, marmalade and lemon juice. Refrigerate. **Yield:** 6-8 servings.

cheesy hash brown bake

prep: 10 minutes | **bake:** 40 minutes

This creamy, comforting recipe was so popular at the morning meetings of our Mothers of Preschoolers group that we published it in our newsletter.

Karen Burns
Chandler, Texas

1 package (30 ounces) frozen shredded
   hash brown potatoes, thawed

2 cans (10-3/4 ounces *each*) condensed
   cream of potato soup, undiluted

2 cups (16 ounces) sour cream

2 cups (8 ounces) shredded cheddar
   cheese, *divided*

1 cup grated Parmesan cheese

In a large bowl, combine the potatoes, soup, sour cream, 1-3/4 cups of cheddar cheese and Parmesan cheese. Transfer to a greased 3-qt. baking dish. Sprinkle with remaining cheddar cheese.

Bake, uncovered, at 350° for 40-45 minutes or until bubbly and cheese is melted. Let stand for 5 minutes before serving. **Yield:** 10 servings.

skillet ranch vegetables

prep/cook: 15 minutes

Celebrate the last garden harvest with this satisfying side dish. Simply cook carrots, squash and zucchini in oil that's been spiced up with ranch dressing mix. You'll be able to dish out hot and hearty helpings in minutes!

Taste of Home Test Kitchen
Greendale, Wisconsin

1 tablespoon canola oil

1 envelope buttermilk ranch salad
   dressing mix

2 medium carrots, thinly sliced

2 medium yellow squash, sliced

2 medium zucchini, sliced

In a skillet, combine the oil and salad dressing mix. Add carrots; cook over medium heat for 4-5 minutes or until crisp-tender. Add squash and zucchini; cook 4-5 minutes longer or until all of the vegetables are tender. Remove with a slotted spoon to serving dish. **Yield:** 4 servings.

1-1/2 pounds fresh green beans, cut into 1-1/2-inch pieces

1 tablespoon olive oil

1 tablespoon minced fresh garlic

1/4 teaspoon salt

1/2 cup feta *or* part-skim mozzarella cheese

In a microwave-safe dish, combine the beans, oil, garlic and salt. Cover and microwave on high for 5-7 minutes or until tender, stirring twice. Stir in cheese. Serve immediately. **Yield:** 5 servings.

Editor's Note: This recipe was tested in a 1,100-watt microwave.

greek green beans

prep/cook: 15 minutes

In an effort to eat healthier, I'm trying to serve more vegetables. So I substituted green beans for the pasta in one of my favorite Greek dishes. It's even better than the original.

Kathleen Law
Pullman, Washington

||| Ultimate**TIP**

Buy fresh green beans with slender green pods that are free of bruises or brown spots. Store unwashed fresh green beans in a resealable plastic bag for up to 4 days. Wash just before using, removing strings and ends if necessary. For easy washing, use a salad spinner to remove moisture from the beans. It removes most of the water without all the work.

dill mustard

prep: 10 minutes + standing | **cook:** 10 minutes

I pick up small, decorative canning jars at rummage sales or in hardware stores. Then I fill them with the zesty mustard I make as gifts for my friends.

Sue Braunschweig
Delafield, Wisconsin

1 cup ground mustard

1 cup cider vinegar

3/4 cup sugar

1/4 cup water

2 teaspoons salt

1-1/2 teaspoons dill weed

2 eggs, lightly beaten

In the top of a double boiler, combine mustard, vinegar, sugar, water, salt and dill. Cover and let stand at room temperature for 4 hours. Bring water in bottom of double boiler to a boil. Add eggs to mustard mixture. Cook and stir until thickened, about 10 minutes. Cool. Store in refrigerator. **Yield:** 32 servings.

herbed corn on the cob

prep/cook: 5 minutes

People always ask what's in the butter after they taste my herb-speckled blend on fresh sweet corn. I'm more than happy to share the secret. Once you have tried this recipe, you won't want to eat corn plain again!

Priscilla Weaver
Hagerstown, Maryland

1/2 cup butter, softened

2 tablespoons minced fresh chives

2 tablespoons minced fresh parsley

1/2 teaspoon Salad Supreme Seasoning

8 medium ears sweet corn, cooked

Combine butter and seasonings; spread over hot cooked corn. **Yield:** 8 servings.

Editor's Note: This recipe was tested with McCormick's Salad Supreme Seasoning. Look for it in the spice aisle.

---

4 medium baking potatoes

1 can (18.8 ounces) ready-to-serve chunky savory vegetable soup

2 cups cooked fresh broccoli florets

1/8 teaspoon pepper

1 cup (4 ounces) shredded cheddar cheese

Chopped green onions, optional

savory soup spuds

prep/cook: 20 minutes

My family loves baked potatoes, but sometimes I just don't have the time to make them. With the help of a microwave and hearty canned soup, the potatoes get a delicious and quick makeover. Use vegetable beef soup to turn the baked potatoes into a hearty meal.

Joleen Jackson
Zumbrota, Minnesota

Scrub the baking potatoes, dry thoroughly and then pierce; place on a microwave-safe plate. Microwave, uncovered, on high for 7-9 minutes on each side or until tender.

Meanwhile, in a large saucepan, combine the soup, broccoli and pepper; cook until heated through. With a sharp knife, cut an X in the top of each potato; fluff pulp with a fork. Top with soup mixture, cheese and onions if desired. **Yield:** 4 servings.

Editor's Note: This recipe was tested in a 1,100-watt microwave.

sunday dinner
mashed potatoes

prep: 35 minutes | **bake:** 20 minutes

Sour cream and cream cheese add delicious flavors to these potatoes. They're special enough to serve guests and can be prepared in advance. Since I'm a busy mother, that's a convenience I appreciate.

Melody Mellinger
Myerstown, Pennsylvania

- 5 **pounds potatoes, peeled and cubed**
- 1 **cup (8 ounces) sour cream**
- 2 **packages (3 ounces *each*) cream cheese, softened**
- 3 **tablespoons butter, *divided***
- 1 **teaspoon salt**
- 1 **teaspoon onion salt**
- 1/4 **teaspoon pepper**

Place potatoes in a Dutch oven; cover with water. Cover and bring to a boil. Cook for 20-25 minutes or until very tender; drain well.

In a large bowl, mash the potatoes. Add the sour cream, softened cream cheese, 2 tablespoons butter, salt, onion salt and pepper; beat until fluffy.

Transfer to a greased 2-qt. baking dish. Dot with the remaining butter. Bake, uncovered, at 350° for 20-25 minutes or until heated through. **Yield:** 8 servings.

broccoli with mock hollandaise

prep/cook: 20 minutes

I dress up broccoli with a lemony sauce that complements the veggie flavor nicely. Even if you're not a fan of broccoli, this simple side dish will change your mind.

Roxanna Quarles
Ralph, Alabama

- 2 **packages (9 ounces *each*) frozen broccoli spears**
- 4 **ounces reduced-fat cream cheese, cubed**

- 1 **egg**
- 2 **tablespoons lemon juice**
- 1/4 **teaspoon salt**
- 1/4 **teaspoon pepper**

Place broccoli in a steamer basket; place in a saucepan over 1 in. of water. Bring to a boil; cover and steam for 5-7 minutes or until crisp-tender.

Meanwhile, in a small saucepan, combine the cream cheese, egg, lemon juice, salt and pepper. Cook and stir over low heat for 3-5 minutes or until sauce is thickened and reaches 160°. Serve with broccoli. **Yield:** 4 servings.

- 2 **medium zucchini, cut into 1/2-inch slices**
- 1/4 **cup water**
- 1 **can (15-1/2 ounces) hominy, drained**
- 1 **can (15-1/4 ounces) whole kernel corn, drained**
- 1 **jalapeno pepper, seeded and chopped**
- 1/2 **teaspoon salt**
- 1 **cup (4 ounces) shredded pepper Jack cheese**

In a 1-1/2-qt. microwave-safe dish, combine the zucchini and water. Cover and microwave on high for 1-1/2 minutes; drain. Stir in the hominy, corn, jalapeno and salt. Cover and microwave on high for 2-3 minutes.

Sprinkle with the cheese. Cook, uncovered, on high for 1-2 minutes until cheese is melted and vegetables are tender. Let stand for 2 minutes before serving. **Yield:** 6-8 servings.

Editor's Note: When cutting hot peppers, disposable gloves are recommended. Avoid touching your face. This recipe was tested in a 1,100-watt microwave.

zucchini corn medley

prep/cook: 25 minutes

One day when I was a girl, a neighbor brought over a dish similar to this one. I hadn't had it in 20 years but kept thinking about the fabulous flavor combination, so I decided to re-create it. I don't know if it's the same, but my family likes it today as much as I did back then.

Marian Quaid-Maltagliati
Nipomo, California

2 to 2-1/2 cups all-purpose flour, *divided*

1/2 teaspoon salt

3 eggs, lightly beaten

1 tablespoon cold water

1 tablespoon canola oil

Place 2 cups flour and salt on a pastry board or in a deep mixing bowl. Make a well in a center of the flour; add eggs and water. Gradually mix with hands or a wooden spoon until well blended.

Gather into a ball and knead on a floured surface until smooth, about 10 minutes. If necessary, add remaining flour to keep dough from sticking to surface or hands. Divide the dough into thirds. On a lightly floured surface, roll each section into a paper-thin rectangle. Dust top of dough with flour to prevent sticking while rolling. Trim the edges and flour both sides of dough.

Roll dough, jelly-roll style. Using a sharp knife, cut 1/4-in. slices. Unroll noodles and allow to dry on paper towels before cooking.

To cook, bring salted water to a rapid boil. Add 1 tablespoon oil to the water; drop noodles into water and cook until tender but not soft. **Yield: 10 servings.**

homemade noodles

prep: 30 minutes + standing | **cook:** 5 minutes

It's hard to beat homemade noodles in soups or as a side dish with meat and gravy. You can freeze serving-size portions to use as you need them.

Helen Heiland
Joliet, Illinois

spiced honey butter

prep/cook: 5 minutes

I like to give jars of this honey as gifts in the fall months. It tastes great on pancakes or biscuits.

Mary Bates
Cleveland, Ohio

1/2 cup butter, softened

1/4 cup honey

1 teaspoon grated orange peel

1/2 teaspoon ground cinnamon

Combine all of the ingredients; mix well. Refrigerate, covered, until ready to serve. Recipe may be doubled or tripled and packed into small jars or plastic containers for gifts. **Yield: 3/4 cup.**

spiced carrot strips

prep/cook: 20 minutes

Carrots are readily available year-round, but their beautiful harvest color is perfect this time of year. These lightly sweet strips get unique flavor from cinnamon, which enhances the fresh carrot taste. Give this special yet simple side dish a try!

Ruth Andrewson
Leavenworth, Washington

- 5 large carrots, julienned
- 2 tablespoons butter, melted
- 1 tablespoon sugar
- 1 teaspoon salt
- 1/4 teaspoon ground cinnamon

Place carrots in a saucepan; cover with water. Cook for 8-10 minutes or until crisp-tender; drain. Combine the butter, sugar, salt and cinnamon; add to carrots and toss to coat. **Yield:** 4-6 servings.

italian vegetable saute

prep/cook: 15 minutes

This speedy side dish is loaded with flavor. It's a wonderful way to use up vegetables from your garden. I like to top servings with a few seasoned croutons.

Kenda Nicholson
Honey Grove, Texas

- 2 medium green peppers, sliced
- 1 garlic clove, minced
- 1 teaspoon Italian seasoning
- 1 tablespoon butter
- 1 cup cherry tomatoes, halved

In a skillet, saute the peppers, garlic and Italian seasoning in butter until peppers are crisp-tender, about 5 minutes. Add tomatoes; cook for 1-2 minutes or until heated through. **Yield:** 4 servings.

1 cup uncooked long grain rice

2-1/4 cups water

2 to 3 tablespoons onion *or* vegetable soup mix

1/4 teaspoon salt

2 cups frozen corn, peas *or* mixed vegetables

In a saucepan, combine the rice, water, soup mix and salt; bring to a boil. Add the vegetables; return to a boil. Reduce heat; cover and simmer for 15 minutes. Cook until the rice and vegetables are tender. **Yield: 4-6 servings.**

vegetable rice medley

prep/cook: 20 minutes

The flavorful rice makes a great accompaniment to oodles of main dishes, but I like to serve it with chicken or beef to make a whole meal.

Coleen Martin
Brookfield, Wisconsin

|||UltimateTIP

Cooking with brown rice instead of white rice is a great way to add fiber to your diet. To cook brown rice, use a heavy pan with a tight-fitting lid and plenty of room above the rice. Once all the ingredients are combined and brought to a boil, cover and reduce the heat to a low simmer for 35-45 minutes. After 35 minutes, remove it from the heat and let stand, covered, for 10-15 minutes before serving.

cran-apple sauce

prep/cook: 5 minutes

I often fix this sweet-tart combination as a side dish with a turkey dinner. It's also delicious as a last-minute dessert topped with whipped cream.

Romaine Wetzel
Ronks, Pennsylvania

1 can (8 ounces) jellied cranberry sauce

1 jar (24 ounces) applesauce

Whipped topping, optional

In a bowl, break apart cranberry sauce with a fork. Stir in applesauce. Refrigerate until serving. Garnish with whipped topping if desired. **Yield: 4-6 servings.**

spiced pineapple

prep/cook: 25 minutes

This aromatic pineapple mixture is a lot like a chutney and can be paired with meat. I think it turns ordinary grilled pork chops into something special.

Chris Nash
Berthoud, Colorado

- 2 **cans (one 20 ounces, one 8 ounces) pineapple chunks**
- 1-1/4 **cups sugar**
- 1/2 **cup cider vinegar**
- 1 **cinnamon stick (3 inches)**
- 6 **to 8 whole cloves**

Dash salt

Drain the pineapple, reserving 1 cup juice. In a saucepan, combine the sugar, vinegar, cinnamon stick, cloves, salt and reserved pineapple juice. Bring to a boil. Reduce heat; cover and simmer for 10 minutes.

Discard cinnamon and cloves. Add pineapple chunks. Return to a boil; cook and stir for 2-3 minutes. Serve warm with a slotted spoon. **Yield: 4-6 servings.**

basil cherry tomatoes

prep/cook: 10 minutes

These tomatoes are a quick and delicious side dish that add Italian flair to any dinner. Basil and olive oil are simple additions to sweet cherry tomatoes, but the flavors are wonderful together.

Melissa Stevens
Elk River, Minnesota

- 3 **pints cherry tomatoes, halved**
- 1/2 **cup chopped fresh basil**
- 1-1/2 **teaspoons olive oil**

Salt and pepper to taste

Lettuce leaves, optional

In a large bowl, combine the tomatoes, basil, oil, salt and pepper. Cover and refrigerate until serving. Serve on lettuce if desired. **Yield: 4-6 servings.**

broccoli with orange sauce

prep/cook: 15 minutes

As a busy working mother, I was looking for a good broccoli recipe that didn't take very long to make. This one, adapted from an old cookbook, can be whipped up in a hurry. I think you'll find it complements the rest of my favorite meal.

Edie DeSpain
Logan, Utah

2 **packages (10 ounces *each*) frozen broccoli spears**

1/4 **cup butter, cubed**
1 **teaspoon cornstarch**
1/2 **cup orange juice**
1 **tablespoon grated orange peel**

Cook broccoli according to package directions. Meanwhile, in a small saucepan, melt the butter. Whisk in the cornstarch until smooth. Gradually stir in orange juice; add orange peel. Bring to a boil; cook and stir for 2 minutes or until thickened. Drain broccoli; drizzle with sauce. **Yield:** 4 servings.

seasoned fries

prep/cook: 15 minutes

It's easy to make French fries at home by using frozen shoestring potatoes. It satisfies my craving, and it's a lot healthier, too!

Maribeth Edwards
Follansbee, West Virginia

6 **cups frozen shoestring potatoes**

1/2 **cup grated Parmesan cheese**

2 **teaspoons Italian seasoning**

1/2 **teaspoon salt**

Place potatoes on a foil-lined baking sheet. Bake at 450° for 8 minutes. Combine remaining ingredients; sprinkle over potatoes and mix gently. Bake 4-5 minutes longer or until the potatoes are browned and crisp. **Yield:** 4-6 servings.

1 **pound fresh sugar snap** *or* **snow peas**

1/2 **cup sliced fresh mushrooms**

2 **tablespoons sliced green onions**

1 **tablespoon snipped fresh dill**
   or 1 **teaspoon dill weed**

2 **tablespoons butter**

Salt and pepper to taste

Place the peas and mushrooms on a piece of double-layer heavy-duty foil (about 18 in. square). Sprinkle with onions and dill; dot with butter. Fold foil around the mixture and seal tightly.

Grill, covered, over medium-hot heat for 5 minutes. Turn; grill 5-8 minutes longer or until the vegetables are tender. Season with salt and pepper. **Yield:** 8-10 servings.

snappy peas 'n' mushrooms

prep/cook: 20 minutes

Seasoned with dill, this versatile side dish can be on the buffet table in mere minutes. Just wrap the fresh vegetables in foil, seal tightly and grill until tender. It's that easy!

Laura Mahaffey
Annapolis, Maryland

sweet-and-sour mustard

prep/cook: 15 minutes

In addition to using my mustard as gifts for friends, I give it to my father each Christmas. One year, I absentmindedly left it behind in my refrigerator—and he was so disappointed when he didn't find it under the tree that I had to send him some as soon as I got back home! Of course, I like using this mustard in everything from honey-mustard chicken to sandwiches.

Cheri White
Richland, Michigan

1 **cup packed brown sugar**
1 **cup cider vinegar**
1/3 **cup ground mustard**
2 **tablespoons water**
2 **eggs, lightly beaten**

In a large saucepan, whisk together all ingredients. Cook over low heat, stirring constantly, until thickened. Pour into small jars. Cover and refrigerate. **Yield:** 1-1/2 cups.

brussels sprouts with pecans

prep/cook: 10 minutes

No one in our family enjoyed brussels sprouts until I served this simply delicious saute. Now it's a favorite at our holiday get-togethers. For a fun alternative, if you can find them at your grocery store, substitute chestnuts for the pecans.

Juanita Haugen
Pleasanton, California

1 **pound brussels sprouts, halved**
1/2 **pound pecan halves**
2 **tablespoons butter**
1/2 **teaspoon salt**
1/4 **teaspoon pepper**

In a large skillet, saute brussels sprouts and pecans in butter for 5-7 minutes or until crisp-tender. Sprinkle with salt and pepper. **Yield:** 6 servings.

buttery peas and carrots

prep/cook: 20 minutes

This simple side dish is one you'll rely on often to serve with a variety of main courses.

Taste of Home Test Kitchen
Greendale, Wisconsin

2-1/2 **cups baby carrots, halved lengthwise**
   2 **tablespoons butter**
1-1/2 **cups frozen peas**
   2 **tablespoons water**
   1 **teaspoon sugar**
Salt and pepper to taste

In a skillet, saute carrots in butter for 5 minutes. Stir in the remaining ingredients. Cover and simmer for 10-12 minutes or until the vegetables are tender. **Yield:** 4 servings.

|||Ultimate**TIP**

Here are some suggestions to help you decide which side dishes to serve with your entree. Have an assortment of hot and cold foods and offer vegetables along with grains and pasta. For kids and older guests, provide at least one simple, lightly seasoned side dish. If your entree has an intense flavor, pair it with milder side dishes and vice versa.

---

parmesan noodles

prep/cook: 20 minutes

This is an excellent side dish that even kids love. It's a perfect quick side dish when you don't have time to peel potatoes...and oh-so-flavorful!

Ruth Dirks
Ravensdale, Washington

1 **package (8 ounces) medium egg noodles**
3 **tablespoons chopped green onions**
2 **tablespoons butter**
1/2 **cup grated Parmesan cheese**
Garlic salt and pepper to taste

Cook noodles according to package directions; drain. Toss with onions, butter, Parmesan cheese, garlic salt and pepper. **Yield:** 4 servings.

breads, biscuits & baked goods

pg. 174

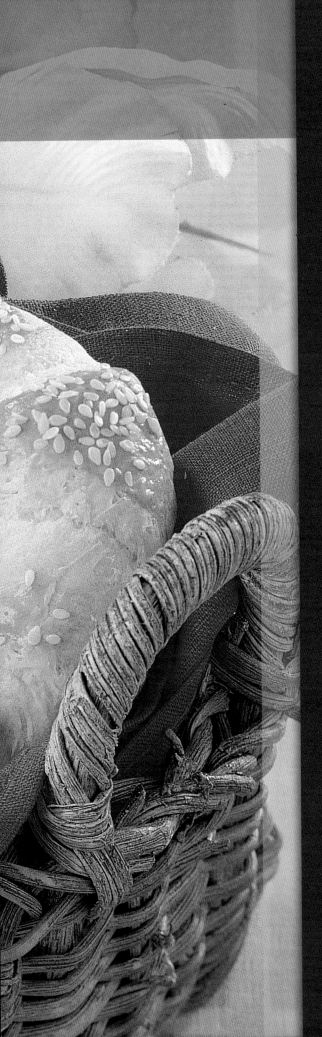

lemon poppy seed bread 154
honey oatmeal bread 155
cherry danish 155
ranch garlic bread 156
mozzarella pepperoni bread 156
garlic bread .157
maple oatmeal bread 157
country white bread 158
baked bean corn bread 158
chive corn bread 159
mushroom bread wedges 159
sour cream blueberry muffins 160
beer 'n' brat biscuits 161
fluffy biscuit muffins 161
overnight rolls 162
buttery french bread 162
monkey bread 163
kid's favorite biscuits 163
tomato pizza bread 164
poppy seed french bread 164
cheese crisps .165
biscuit bites .165
cheddar chili braid 166
pizza sticks 166
apple pinwheels 167
cheese toast .167
apple cinnamon bismarcks 168
basil-buttered french bread 168
paprika cheese biscuits 169
beefy biscuit cups 169
french onion bread 170
cheddar-salsa biscuit strips 171
simple pecan rolls 171
mini blue cheese rolls 172
cheddar bacon toasts 172
crunchy cheese toasts 173
popovers 173
garlic crescent rolls 174
bread bowls .175
cheese danish dessert 175
crusty french bread 176
cheese bread .176
crispy garlic breadsticks 177
parmesan cheese straws 177

lemon poppy seed bread

prep: 10 minutes | **bake:** 35 minutes + cooling

If the days that you have time for baking are few and far between, try this extra-quick bread. You'll love the ease of preparation and delicious flavor.

Karen Dougherty
Freeport, Illinois

1 **package (18-1/4 ounces) white cake mix**

1 **package (3.4 ounces) instant lemon pudding mix**

1 **cup warm water**

4 **eggs**

1/2 **cup vegetable oil**

4 **teaspoons poppy seeds**

In a large bowl, combine the cake mix, pudding mix, water, eggs and oil; beat on low speed for 30 seconds. Beat on medium for 2 minutes. Fold in poppy seeds.

Pour the batter into two greased 9-in. x 5-in. loaf pans. Bake at 350° for 35-40 minutes or until a toothpick inserted near the center comes out clean. Cool in pans for 10 minutes before removing to a wire rack. **Yield:** 2 loaves (16 slices each).

honey oatmeal bread

prep: 5 minutes | **bake:** 3-4 hours

My mother served this honey-flavored loaf at a family gathering, and I just had to have the recipe.

Megan Schwartz
Burbank, Ohio

1-1/4 cups water (70° to 80°)
  1/2 cup honey
    2 tablespoons canola oil
    1 cup quick-cooking oats
1-1/2 teaspoons salt
    3 cups plus 2 tablespoons bread flour
2-1/4 teaspoons active dry yeast

In bread machine pan, place all ingredients in order suggested by manufacturer. Select basic bread setting. Choose the crust color and loaf size if available. Bake according to bread machine directions (check dough after 5 minutes; add 1 to 2 tablespoons of water or flour if needed). **Yield:** 1 loaf (1-1/2 pounds).

||| Ultimate**TIP**

In general, lighter-colored honey is milder in flavor, whereas darker styles of honey are stronger in flavor. If your honey has crystallized, simply place the honey jar in warm water and stir it until the crystals dissolve. Or place the honey in a microwave-safe container and with the lid off, microwave it, stirring every 30 seconds. Be sure not to burn the honey.

---

    2 tubes (11 ounces *each*) refrigerated breadsticks
  1/3 cup butter, melted
    1 tablespoon sugar
    1 cup cherry pie filling
    1 cup confectioners' sugar
1-1/2 teaspoons water

Separate each tube of breadsticks into six sections but leave coiled. Place in a greased 15-in. x 10-in. x 1-in. baking pan. Brush generously with butter; sprinkle with sugar.

Make an indentation in the top of each coil; fill with about 1 tablespoon of pie filling. Bake at 400° for 15-20 minutes or until golden brown. Combine confectioners' sugar and water; drizzle over warm rolls. **Yield:** 1 dozen.

Editor's Note: This recipe was tested with Pillsbury refrigerated breadsticks.

cherry danish

prep/cook: 30 minutes

These delightful Danish are so quick to fix, you don't even have to uncoil the refrigerated breadsticks. We prefer them with cherry pie filling, but you can use peach, blueberry or your favorite one instead.

Margaret McNeil
Germantown, Tennessee

mozzarella pepperoni bread

prep/cook: 30 minutes

My family enjoys this tempting bread as an appetizer when we have company...and as a quick meal on hectic evenings.

Terri Toti
San Antonio, Texas

- **1 loaf (1 pound) French bread**
- **3 tablespoons butter, melted**
- **3 ounces sliced turkey pepperoni**
- **1-1/2 cups (6 ounces) shredded part-skim mozzarella cheese**
- **3 tablespoons minced fresh parsley**

Cut loaf of bread in half widthwise; cut into 1-in. slices, leaving slices attached at bottom. Brush butter on both sides of each slice. Arrange pepperoni between slices; sprinkle with cheese and parsley.

Place the bread on an ungreased baking sheet. Bake at 350° for 12-15 minutes or until cheese is melted. **Yield:** 24 slices.

ranch garlic bread

prep/cook: 10 minutes

I've worked as a manager of a fast-food restaurant for 12 years, but I still like to cook up different things at home using everyday ingredients. This buttery loaf of French bread gets plenty of flavor from a salad dressing mix and garlic powder.

John Palmer
Cottonwood, California

- **1 cup butter, softened**
- **2 to 3 tablespoons ranch salad dressing mix**
- **2 teaspoons garlic powder**
- **1 loaf (1 pound) French bread, halved lengthwise**

In a small bowl, combine butter, dressing mix and garlic powder; beat until combined. Spread the mixture over cut sides of bread. Place on a baking sheet. Broil 4-6 in. from the heat for 3-4 minutes or until golden brown. **Yield:** 8 servings.

Editor's Note: Italian salad dressing mix, taco seasoning or onion soup mix may be substituted for the ranch dressing mix.

garlic bread

prep/cook: 20 minutes

This wonderful accompaniment could not be tastier or simpler to make. Minced fresh garlic is key to these flavor-packed crusty slices, which our big family would snap up before they even had a chance to cool.

Grace Yaskovic
Lake Hiawatha, New Jersey

1/2   **cup butter, melted**

3   **to 4 garlic cloves, minced**

1   **loaf (1 pound) French bread, halved lengthwise**

2   **tablespoons minced fresh parsley**

In a small bowl, combine butter and garlic. Brush over cut sides of bread; sprinkle with parsley. Place, cut side up, on a baking sheet.

Bake at 350° for 8 minutes. Broil 4-6 in. from the heat for 2 minutes or until golden brown. Cut into 2-in. slices. Serve warm. **Yield:** 8 servings.

maple oatmeal bread

prep: 10 minutes | **bake:** 3 hours + cooling

Maple syrup gives this soft, tender bread its delicate flavor and golden color. The pleasantly sweet slices taste terrific when toasted.

Kathy Morin
Haverhill, Massachusetts

3/4   **cup plus 2 tablespoons water**

1/3   **cup maple syrup**

1   **tablespoon canola oil**

1   **teaspoon salt**

3/4   **cup quick-cooking oats**

2-1/2   **cups bread flour**

2-1/4   **teaspoons active dry yeast**

In the bread machine pan, place all ingredients in order suggested by manufacturer. Select basic bread setting. Choose the crust color and loaf size if available.

Bake according to bread machine directions (check dough after 5 minutes of mixing; add 1 to 2 tablespoons of water or flour if needed). **Yield:** 1 loaf (1-1/2 pounds, 16 slices).

country white bread

prep: 15 minutes + rising | **bake:** 25 minutes

Anytime is the right time for a comforting slice of homemade bread. These loaves are especially nice since the crust stays so tender. This recipe is my husband Nick's favorite. Best of all, it makes two loaves!

Joanne Shew Chuk
St. Benedict, Saskatchewan

2 packages (1/4 ounce *each*) active dry yeast
2 cups warm water (110° to 115°)
1/2 cup sugar
1 tablespoon salt
2 eggs, beaten
1/4 cup canola oil
6-1/2 to 7 cups all-purpose flour

In a large bowl, dissolve the yeast in water. Add sugar, salt, eggs, oil and 3 cups of flour; beat until smooth. Stir in enough remaining flour to form a soft dough.

Turn onto a floured surface; knead until smooth and elastic, about 6 to 8 minutes. Place in a greased bowl, turning once to grease top. Cover and let rise in a warm place until doubled, about 1 hour.

Punch the dough down. Divide in half and shape into two loaves. Place each in a greased 9-in. x 5-in. loaf pan. Cover and let rise until doubled, about 1 hour.

Bake at 375° for 25 to 30 minutes or until golden brown. Remove loaves from pans to cool on wire racks. **Yield:** 2 loaves.

baked bean corn bread

prep: 15 minutes | **bake:** 25 minutes

My daughter created this moist bread, and she loves to fix it for our family along with hot dogs and a salad. It's quick, simple, delicious and kid-friendly.

Lauren McBride
Houston, Texas

2 packages (8-1/2 ounces *each*) corn bread/muffin mix
2/3 cup milk
2 eggs, lightly beaten
1 can (10 ounces) baked beans

In a large bowl, combine the corn bread mixes, milk and lightly beaten eggs. Pour 1-1/2 cups batter into a greased 9-in. pie plate. Spread with baked beans. Spread with the remaining batter.

Bake, uncovered, at 400° for 25-30 minutes or until a toothpick inserted into the corn bread comes out clean. Serve warm. **Yield:** 4-6 servings.

chive corn bread

prep/cook: 30 minutes

"Busy" is my middle name, so I use this incredibly quick corn bread to simplify meals. Easy recipes like this help me to get back to working and keep up with my family's fast-paced schedule.

Terri Keeney
Greeley, Colorado

- 1 **package (8-1/2 ounces) corn bread/muffin mix**
- 1/2 **cup shredded cheddar cheese**
- 1 **tablespoon minced chives**

Prepare corn bread batter according to package directions. Stir in cheese and chives. Pour into a greased 8-in. square baking dish. Bake at 400° for 20-25 minutes or until lightly browned. Serve warm. **Yield:** 9 servings.

mushroom bread wedges

prep/cook: 25 minutes

Tender sliced mushrooms and a sprinkling of Parmesan cheese dot my crisp bread wedges. You can serve them with soup, chili or a main-dish salad.

Patricia Mele
Apollo, Pennsylvania

- 1 **tube (8 ounces) refrigerated crescent rolls**
- 1/2 **pound fresh mushrooms, sliced**
- 3 **tablespoons butter, melted**
- 1/4 **cup grated Parmesan cheese**
- 1/4 **teaspoon Italian seasoning**

Separate crescent dough into eight triangles and place on a greased 12-in. round pizza pan with points toward the center; seal perforations.

In a small bowl, combine the mushrooms and butter; toss to coat. Spoon mushroom mixture over the dough. Sprinkle with Parmesan cheese and Italian seasoning.

Bake at 375° for 15-20 minutes or until crust is golden brown and mushrooms are tender, **Yield:** 8 servings.

sour cream blueberry muffins

prep: 15 minutes | **bake:** 20 minutes

When I was growing up, my mom made these warm, delicious muffins on chilly mornings. I'm now in college and enjoy baking them for friends. This is one recipe that never goes out of style!

Tory Ross
Cincinnati, Ohio

2 cups biscuit/baking mix

3/4 cup plus 2 tablespoons sugar, *divided*

2 eggs

1 cup (8 ounces) sour cream

1 cup fresh *or* frozen blueberries

In a large bowl, combine the biscuit mix and 3/4 cup sugar. In a small bowl, combine eggs and sour cream; stir into the dry ingredients just until combined. Fold in blueberries.

Fill greased muffin cups three-fourths full. Sprinkle with remaining sugar. Bake at 375° for 20-25 minutes or until a toothpick comes out clean. Cool for 5 minutes before removing from pan to a wire rack. **Yield:** 1 dozen.

Editor's Note: If using frozen blueberries, do not thaw before adding to batter.

beer 'n' brat biscuits

prep/cook: 30 minutes

My husband, our three girls and I all love to cook, so we're always coming up with something new to try. These yummy biscuits require just four ingredients, including leftover brats. Serve them with mustard and a big bowl of rice and beans or bean soup.

Nancy Bourget
Round Rock, Texas

- 2 **fully cooked bratwurst links, casings removed**
- 4 **cups biscuit/baking mix**
- 2 **to 3 teaspoons caraway seeds**
- 1 **can (12 ounces) beer** *or* **nonalcoholic beer**

Cut bratwurst into bite-size pieces. In a bowl, combine the biscuit mix, caraway seeds and bratwurst; stir in beer just until moistened. Fill greased muffin cups two-thirds full.

Bake at 400° for 18-20 minutes or until golden brown. Cool for 5 minutes before removing from pans to wire racks. Serve warm. Refrigerate leftovers. **Yield:** 16 biscuits.

fluffy biscuit muffins

prep/cook: 20 minutes

These biscuits are simple to make and have a wonderful aroma when baking! This particular recipe is one of my husband's favorites. Biscuits were a steady diet in the Southern household where he grew up. The muffin shape makes them a bit different.

Virginia Foster
Paducah, Kentucky

- 1 **cup self-rising flour**
- 2 **tablespoons mayonnaise**
- 1/2 **cup milk**

In a bowl, cut flour and mayonnaise together until mixture resembles coarse crumbs. Add milk; stir just until mixed. Spoon into four greased muffin cups. Bake at 425° for 14-16 minutes or until lightly browned. **Yield:** 4 biscuits.

Editor's Note: As a substitute for 1 cup of self-rising flour, place 1-1/2 teaspoons baking powder and 1/2 teaspoon salt in a measuring cup. Add all-purpose flour to measure 1 cup.

1 package (1/4 ounces) active dry yeast
1/2 cup plus 3/4 teaspoon sugar, *divided*
1-1/3 cups plus 3 tablespoons warm water (110° to 115°), *divided*
1/3 cup canola oil
1 egg
1 teaspoon salt
4-3/4 to 5-1/4 cups all-purpose flour

overnight rolls

prep: 25 minutes + chilling | **bake:** 15 minutes

I'm pleased to share the recipe for these light and tender rolls, which I've made for 25 years. I once served them to a woman who'd been in the restaurant business for half a century. She said they were the best rolls she'd ever tasted.

Dorothy Yagodich
Charlerio, Pennsylvania

In a bowl, dissolve yeast and 3/4 teaspoon sugar in 3 tablespoons water. Add remaining sugar and water, oil, egg, salt and 2 cups flour; mix well. Add enough remaining flour to form a soft dough.

Turn onto a floured surface; knead the dough until smooth and elastic, about 6-8 minutes. Place in a greased bowl, turning once to grease top. Cover and let rise in a warm place until doubled, about 1 hour.

Punch the dough down. Shape into 20 rolls. Place on a greased baking sheet; cover and refrigerate overnight. Allow rolls to sit at room temperature for 15 minutes before baking.

Bake at 375° for 12-15 minutes or until lightly browned. Remove to wire racks to cool. **Yield: 20 rolls.**

buttery french bread

prep/cook: 25 minutes

Mom dressed up plain French bread with this deliciously different recipe. The combination of paprika, celery seed and butter makes for a full-flavored bread. It also looks lovely when it bakes to a golden brown.

Sally Holbrook
Pasadena, California

1/2 cup butter, softened
1/4 teaspoon paprika
1/4 teaspoon celery seed
1 loaf (1 pound, 20 inches) French bread, sliced

In a small bowl, combine butter, paprika and celery seed; spread between bread slices and over top. Wrap bread tightly in foil. Bake at 375° for 15 minutes. Open the foil and bake 5 minutes longer. **Yield: 6-8 servings.**

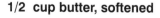

monkey bread

prep: 15 minutes | **bake:** 30 minutes + cooling

Both of my boys really enjoyed helping me make Monkey Bread when they were young. It seemed to taste twice as good when they helped fix it. Try tossing some chopped pecans in the resealable bag with the cinnamon and sugar for extra flair.

Carol Allen
McLeansboro, Illinois

- **1 package (3-1/2 ounces) cook-and-serve butterscotch pudding mix**
- **3/4 cup sugar**
- **3 teaspoons ground cinnamon**
- **1/2 cup butter, melted**
- **3 tubes (10 ounces *each*) refrigerated biscuits**

In a large resealable plastic bag, combine the pudding mix, sugar and cinnamon. Pour the butter into a shallow bowl. Cut the biscuits into quarters. Dip several pieces into the butter, then place in bag and shake to coat.

Arrange in a greased 10-in. fluted tube pan. Repeat until all the biscuit pieces are coated. Bake at 350° for 30-35 minutes or until browned. Cool for 30 minutes before inverting onto a serving plate. **Yield:** 10-12 servings.

||| Ultimate**TIP**

Aluminum baking pans with dull finishes give the best overall baking results. Pans with dark finishes often cook and brown foods more quickly. If you use pans with dark finishes, you may need to adjust the baking time and cover the tops of baked goods with foil to prevent overbrowning. Insulated pans generally take longer to bake and brown foods.

---

kid's favorite biscuits

prep/cook: 15 minutes

When I was 6 years old, I combined two of my favorite flavors—peanut butter and jelly—in a new way. Refrigerated biscuits with a warm, gooey filling make these a yummy lunch or snack.

Dustin Chasteen
Weaverville, North Carolina

- **1 tube (12 ounces) refrigerated flaky buttermilk biscuits**
- **1/2 cup peanut butter**
- **1/2 cup jelly**

Separate the biscuits; pat onto the bottom and up the sides of greased muffin cups. Bake at 450° for 8-10 minutes or until golden brown. Remove to a wire rack.

Place a scant tablespoonful of peanut butter in each warm biscuit cup; top each with a scant tablespoonful of jelly. Serve immediately. **Yield:** 10 servings.

1 tube (13.8 ounces) refrigerated pizza crust

2 garlic cloves, minced

1/2 teaspoon dried oregano

1 cup (4 ounces) shredded part-skim mozzarella cheese, *divided*

1 plum tomato, halved lengthwise and thinly sliced

1/2 teaspoon Italian seasoning, optional

On a greased baking sheet, roll pizza crust into a 12-in. x 8-in. rectangle. Bake at 425° for 6-8 minutes or until the edges are lightly browned. Sprinkle with the garlic, oregano and half of the cheese.

Arrange tomato slices in a single layer over cheese. Top with remaining cheese and Italian seasoning if desired. Bake 6-8 minutes longer or until cheese is melted and crust is lightly browned. **Yield:** 8 servings.

tomato pizza bread

prep/cook: 30 minutes

Refrigerated pizza crust dough gets a tasty treatment from pleasant seasonings and easy cheese and tomato toppings. This basic recipe can be modified to suit individual tastes. My husband loves to add sliced ripe olives just before baking. We think it's best when served fresh out of the oven.

Kimberly McFarland
Broken Arrow, Oklahoma

||UltimateTIP

Use the blade of a chef's knife to crush garlic cloves and peel away their skin. Mince as directed. If you don't have any fresh garlic bulbs available, substitute 1/4 teaspoon of garlic powder for each clove. Or, next time you're shopping, look for convenient jars of fresh minced garlic in the produce section. Use 1/2 teaspoon of minced garlic for each clove.

poppy seed french bread

prep/cook: 25 minutes

The flavor of Parmesan cheese comes through nicely in my recipe. Feel free to dash your favorite dried herb over the slices before baking.

Ruth Andrewson,
Leavenworth, Washington

1/4 cup butter, softened

1/2 cup grated Parmesan cheese

1-1/2 tablespoons poppy seeds

8 slices French bread (1 inch thick)

Combine butter, Parmesan cheese, and poppy seeds; spread on both sides of each piece of bread. Place on baking sheet. Bake at 350° for 12-16 minutes, turning once. **Yield:** 6-8 servings.

cheese crisps

prep/cook: 25 minutes

The surprising crunch of these fun snacks makes them great for parties or anytime of day. I like them for a simple, late-night snack.

Janelle Lee
Sulphur, Louisiana

- 1 cup butter, softened
- 2 cups all-purpose flour
- 1/2 teaspoon salt
- 1/4 teaspoon cayenne pepper
- 2 cups (8 ounces) shredded sharp cheddar cheese
- 3 cups crisp rice cereal

In a bowl, cream the butter until fluffy. Slowly mix in the flour, salt and cayenne pepper. Stir in cheese and cereal. Shape into 1-1/2-in. balls and place on ungreased baking sheets. Bake at 350° for 15-17 minutes or until lightly browned. Serve warm or cold. **Yield:** 32 servings.

biscuit bites

prep/cook: 20 minutes

My tasty bites couldn't be easier. Convenient refrigerated biscuits are simply sprinkled with Parmesan cheese and onion powder, then baked. The savory biscuits are wonderful with soup, alongside a main dish or even as a snack. In fact, we like to munch on them instead of popcorn while watching television.

Joy Beck
Cincinnati, Ohio

- 1 tube (12 ounces) refrigerated buttermilk biscuits
- 2 tablespoons grated Parmesan cheese
- 1 teaspoon onion powder

Cut each biscuit into thirds; place on a greased baking sheet. Combine the Parmesan cheese and onion powder; sprinkle over the biscuits. Bake at 400° for 7-8 minutes or until golden brown. **Yield:** 5 servings.

cheddar chili braid

prep: 20 minutes + rising | **bake:** 30 minutes

Hot roll mix gives me a good head start when preparing this savory bread. I usually make it with a big pot of chili and serve thick warm slices for dunking. What a great way to warm up a cold winter night!

Katie Dreibelbis
State College, Pennsylvania

1 package (16 ounces) hot roll mix

1 cup warm water (120° to 130°)

2 eggs

2 cups (8 ounces) shredded cheddar cheese

2 tablespoons canned chopped green chilies, drained

2 tablespoons grated Parmesan cheese

In a large bowl, combine the contents of the roll mix and yeast packets; stir in water, one egg, cheddar cheese and chilies. Turn onto a floured surface; knead dough until smooth and elastic, about 5 minutes. Cover and let rest for 5 minutes.

Divide into thirds. Shape each into a 14-in. rope. Place ropes on a greased baking sheet and braid; pinch ends to seal and tuck under. Cover and let rise in a warm place until doubled, about 30 minutes.

Beat remaining egg; brush over dough. Sprinkle with Parmesan cheese. Bake at 375° for 30 minutes or until golden brown. Remove from pan to a wire rack. **Yield:** 1 loaf.

pizza sticks

prep/cook: 30 minutes

Everyone likes pepperoni pizza, so these delicious sticks are a hit with just about anyone who tries them. They're super easy to make with refrigerated dough, pizza sauce and packaged deli meats. These breadsticks make for a savory addition to any casual dinner.

Martha Riggs
Upton, Kentucky

1 tube (11 ounces) refrigerated breadsticks

1/2 cup pizza sauce

12 slices pepperoni, chopped

12 slices Canadian bacon, chopped

1 cup (4 ounces) shredded Italian cheese blend *or* part-skim mozzarella cheese

Arrange breadsticks with long sides touching on a greased baking sheet. Top with the pizza sauce, pepperoni, Canadian bacon and cheese. Bake at 375° for 18-22 minutes or until the breadsticks are golden. Cut apart into sticks. **Yield:** 1 dozen.

Editor's Note: This recipe was tested with Pillsbury refrigerated breadsticks.

apple pinwheels

prep: 20 minutes | **bake:** 40 minutes

I swirl convenient crescent roll dough with a spiced apple filling for homemade appeal. The apple flavor is simply wonderful. When I have extra time, I drizzle the rolls with a confectioners' sugar glaze.

Christine Campos
Scottsdale, Arizona

1/3 **cup water**

1/3 **cup butter**

1-1/3 **cups sugar,** *divided*

2 **tubes (8 ounces** *each***) refrigerated crescent rolls**

3 **cups finely chopped peeled tart apples**

1 **teaspoon apple pie spice**

In a saucepan, combine water, butter and 1 cup sugar; cook over medium heat until butter is melted and sugar is dissolved. Set aside.

Unroll the crescent dough into one long rectangle; seal seams and perforations. Combine the apples, apple pie spice and remaining sugar; sprinkle over the dough to within 1 in. of edges. Roll up, jelly-roll style, starting with a long side. Cut into 1-in. rolls; place in a greased 15-in. x 10-in. x 1-in. baking pan.

Pour reserved syrup over rolls. Bake at 350° for 40-45 minutes or until golden brown. Serve warm. **Yield:** 2 dozen.

||| Ultimate**TIP**

Our home economists found that both reduced-fat and fat-free mayonnaise can break down when heated, leaving an unpleasant texture. Also, in recipes for baked goods, the eggs in mayonnaise may be needed as a leavener—and reduced-fat and fat-free mayonnaise may not contain eggs. If whipped salad dressing contains eggs and fat, it can be used in place of mayonnaise.

---

cheese toast

prep/cook: 15 minutes

My mom came up with this fabulous no-fuss recipe when I was growing up. The tangy triangles broil to a pretty golden color in just minutes.

Eve Gauger Vargas
Prairie Village, Kansas

2 **tablespoons mayonnaise**

2 **teaspoons prepared mustard**

6 **to 8 slices bread, crusts removed**

1/3 **cup grated Parmesan cheese**

Combine mayonnaise and mustard; spread on one side of each slice of bread. Cut each slice into four triangles; place with plain side down on a lightly greased baking sheet. Sprinkle with cheese. Broil 4 in. from the heat for 1-2 minutes or until lightly browned. **Yield:** 4-6 servings.

1 tube (16.3 ounces) large
   refrigerated flaky biscuits
1/2 cup sugar
1/2 teaspoon ground cinnamon
1/4 cup butter, melted
1 cup apple pie filling

Bake biscuits according to package directions. In a shallow bowl, combine the sugar and cinnamon. Brush warm biscuits with butter, then roll in cinnamon-sugar.

In a small bowl, beat pie filling until smooth. Cut a small hole in the corner of a pastry bag; insert a large round tip. Fill bag with pie filling. Push the tip through the top of each biscuit to fill. **Yield:** 8 servings.

apple cinnamon bismarcks

prep/cook: 30 minutes

I use convenience items to speed the preparation of these down-home treats. For a simple snack, it's a breeze to pipe a bit of apple pie filling into the baked biscuits topped with a comforting combination of sugar and cinnamon.

Leigh Ann Baird
Knoxville, Tennessee

basil-buttered french bread

prep/cook: 15 minutes

I make this warm bread when I want to round out quick dinners. Just pop it in a hot oven for a few minutes to have it ready when the rest of your meal is served. What could be easier?

Dixie Terry
Goreville, Illinois

2 tablespoons butter, melted
1/2 teaspoon dried basil
4 slices French bread (1 inch thick)

In a small bowl, combine butter and basil. Brush butter mixture over one side of each bread slice. Place buttered side up on an ungreased baking sheet. Bake, uncovered, at 400° for 5 minutes or until golden brown. **Yield:** 4 servings.

paprika cheese biscuits

prep/cook: 20 minutes

It's so nice to offer warm biscuits with dinner. Thanks to biscuit mix, I can serve up these cheesy bites any time. Stir in a dash of your favorite herb if you'd like.

Melody Smaller
Fowler, Colorado

- 2-1/4 **cups biscuit/baking mix**
- 1/2 **cup shredded cheddar cheese**
- 2/3 **cup milk**
- 1 **tablespoon butter, melted**
- 1/2 **teaspoon paprika**

In a large bowl, combine the biscuit mix and cheese. With a fork, stir in the milk just until moistened. Turn onto a floured surface; knead 10 times. Roll dough to 1/2-in. thickness; cut with a 2-1/2-in. biscuit cutter.

Place on an ungreased baking sheet. Brush with butter; sprinkle with paprika. Bake at 450° for 8-10 minutes or until golden brown. **Yield:** 8 biscuits.

beefy biscuit cups

prep/cook: 30 minutes

On-the-go families will love my handheld pizzas. They're made in a wink with ground beef, convenient refrigerated biscuits and a jar of prepared spaghetti sauce. They're great for lunches and even make great after-school snacks for teenagers.

Kimberly Ledon
St. Marys, Georgia

- 1 **pound ground beef**
- 1 **jar (14 ounces) spaghetti sauce**
- 2 **tubes (8 ounces *each*) large refrigerated biscuits**
- 1 **cup (4 ounces) shredded cheddar cheese**

In a large skillet, cook beef over medium heat until no longer pink; drain. Stir in the spaghetti sauce; cook over medium heat for 5-10 minutes or until heated through.

Press biscuits onto the bottom and up the sides of greased muffin cups. Spoon 2 tablespoons beef mixture into the center of each cup.

Bake at 375° for 15-17 minutes or until golden brown. Sprinkle with cheese; bake 3 minutes longer or until cheese is melted. **Yield:** 8 servings.

french onion bread

prep: 25 minutes + rising | **bake:** 30 minutes

I make this savory bread every week. My family never tires of it. I've shared it with friends and have received many compliments.

Dorothy Jorgensen
Fort Dodge, Iowa

2 **packages (1/4 ounce *each*) active dry yeast**

1 **cup warm water (110° to 115°)**

5-1/4 **to 5-3/4 cups all-purpose flour, *divided***

4 **tablespoons sugar, *divided***

3/4 **teaspoon salt**

1-1/4 **cups hot water (120° to 130°)**

1 **envelope onion soup mix**

3 **tablespoons shortening**

In a bowl, dissolve the yeast in warm water. Add 1/2 cup flour, 2 tablespoons sugar and salt; beat until smooth, about 1 minute. Cover and let rise in a warm place for 20 minutes.

In a small bowl, combine hot water, soup mix, shortening and remaining sugar. Cool to 115°. Add to yeast mixture with 2 cups flour; mix for 1-2 minutes. Stir in enough remaining flour to form a soft dough.

Turn onto a floured surface; knead until smooth and elastic, about 6-8 minutes. Place in a greased bowl, turning once to grease top. Cover and let rise in a warm place until doubled, about 1 hour.

Punch the dough down; divide into thirds. Shape into loaves; place in three greased 8-in. x 4-in. loaf pans. Cover and let rise until doubled, about 30 minutes.

Bake at 375° for 30 minutes or until golden brown. Remove from pans to cool on wire racks. **Yield:** 3 loaves.

cheddar-salsa biscuit strips

prep/cook: 30 minutes

A half hour is all you'll need for these tender breadsticks that get their kick from salsa. I brought them to a wedding shower and got rave reviews. They're an excellent finger food for parties and equally good alongside soup or chili.

Peggy Key
Grant, Alabama

1-2/3 **cups self-rising flour**

   1 **cup (4 ounces) shredded cheddar cheese**

1/2 **cup salsa**

1/4 **cup butter, melted**

1/4 **cup water**

Additional melted butter, optional

In a large bowl, combine the flour and cheese. Stir in the salsa, butter and water just until combined. Turn dough onto a floured surface; knead gently 6-8 times or until smooth.

Roll out into a 12-in. x 6-in. rectangle. Cut into 2-in. x 1-in. strips. Place 1 in. apart on a greased baking sheet.

Bake at 425° for 6-8 minutes or until golden brown. Brush with the butter if desired. Remove from the pan to wire racks. Serve warm. **Yield: about 3 dozen.**

Editor's Note: As a substitute for each cup of self-rising flour, place 1-1/2 teaspoons baking powder and 1/2 teaspoon salt in a measuring cup. Add all-purpose flour to measure 1 cup.

||| Ultimate**TIP**

If you use lots of nuts while cooking and baking, it can be frustrating to run out of them while in the middle of making a recipe. To prevent this from happening, buy large bags of walnuts, pecans and other nuts from wholesale stores, pour them into freezer bags, label them and store them in the freezer. When fixing a recipe, just use the amount of nuts needed straight from the freezer.

simple pecan rolls

prep/cook: 20 minutes

There's no letting the dough rise overnight with these delightful cinnamon pecan rolls...all you need is a package of ready-made rolls. It can stay your secret that these sticky treats weren't made from scratch!

Taste of Home Test Kitchen
Greendale, Wisconsin

1/2 **cup butter, softened**

1/2 **cup packed brown sugar**

1/2 **teaspoon ground cinnamon**

3/4 **cup pecan halves**

   1 **package (12 count) brown-and-serve rolls**

In a bowl, beat the butter, brown sugar and cinnamon until well blended. Spread in the bottom of a 9-in. round baking pan. Top with pecans. Place rolls upside down over pecans.

Bake at 450° for 8-10 minutes or until golden. Immediately turn onto a serving platter. Serve warm. **Yield: 4-6 servings.**

mini blue cheese rolls

prep/cook: 25 minutes

Here's a fun, easy way to dress up refrigerated breadsticks. Serve them with pasta or on the side of a green salad. The blue cheese offers a great flavor surprise.

Myrtle Albrecht
Shingle Springs, California

- **1/4 cup butter, cubed**
- **1/2 cup crumbled blue cheese**
- **1 tube (11 ounces) refrigerated breadsticks**

In a saucepan, melt butter and blue cheese over low heat. Unroll dough. Separate into six sections. Cut each double breadstick into six pieces; place in a foil-lined 11-in. x 7-in. baking pan. Pour the cheese mixture over dough.

Bake at 400° for 20 minutes or until butter is absorbed and rolls are lightly browned. Carefully lift foil out of pan; transfer rolls to a serving plate. Serve warm. **Yield:** 4-6 servings.

Editor's Note: This recipe was tested with Pillsbury refrigerated breadsticks.

cheddar bacon toasts

prep/cook: 20 minutes

Four ingredients are all you need to bake up these golden appetizers. They go great with a bowl of soup or can be served as an after-school snack.

Mary Martin
Columbus, Kansas

- **2 cups (8 ounces) finely shredded cheddar cheese**
- **3/4 cup mayonnaise**
- **1/3 cup crumbled cooked bacon**
- **1 loaf unsliced French bread (1 pound)**

In a large bowl, combine the cheese, mayonnaise and bacon. Cut the bread into 24 slices, about 1/2 in. each. Spread the cheese mixture on one side of each slice.

Place plain side down on an ungreased baking sheet. Bake at 425° for 8-10 minutes or until golden brown. **Yield:** 2 dozen.

crunchy cheese toasts

prep/cook: 30 minutes

Cayenne pepper lends a little zip to these crisp and cheesy treats. They look and taste like they're a lot of trouble to make, but with only five ingredients needed to make them, they're not. That's my favorite kind of recipe!

Camille Langford
Branson, Missouri

- 1 loaf (1 pound) French bread
- 1/2 cup olive oil
- 1 teaspoon dried thyme
- 1/4 to 1/2 teaspoon cayenne pepper
- 2 cups (8 ounces) shredded Mexican cheese blend

Cut French bread into 54 slices, about 1/4 in. thick. Place on ungreased baking sheets.

In a small bowl, whisk the oil, thyme and cayenne until blended. Brush over bread slices. Sprinkle with cheese.

Bake at 300° for 12-15 minutes or until bread is golden brown and cheese is bubbly. Serve warm. **Yield:** 4-1/2 dozen.

popovers

prep: 10 minutes | **bake:** 35 minutes

A popular restaurant was noted for the giant popovers they served with their meals. I decided to do the same for special birthdays and other occasions. These popovers soon became family favorites, and they've been one of my specialties for 40 years.

Emma Magielda
Amsterdam, New York

- 1/2 cup milk, room temperature
- 1 egg, room temperature
- 1/2 cup all-purpose flour
- 1/4 teaspoon salt

In a bowl, beat all ingredients just until smooth. Pour into four greased muffin cups. Fill the remaining muffin cups two thirds full with water.

Bake at 450° for 15 minutes. Reduce heat to 350° (do not open door). Bake 20 minutes longer or until deep golden brown (do not underbake). **Yield:** 2 servings.

garlic crescent rolls

prep/cook: 20 minutes

Delicious rolls can embellish a dinner, and it only takes a few minutes using convenient refrigerator rolls. With a little imagination, you can create several flavor combinations to complement your menu. I experimented and came up with a few touches that make these rolls a conversation piece!

Pat Habiger
Spearville, Kansas

1 **package (4 ounces) refrigerated crescent rolls**

2 **teaspoons grated Parmesan cheese**

1/4 **to 1/2 teaspoon garlic powder**

1 **egg, beaten**

1/2 **teaspoon sesame *and*/*or* poppy seeds**

Separate crescent dough into four triangles. Sprinkle with Parmesan cheese and garlic powder. Beginning at the wide end, roll up the dough. Place with points down on a greased baking sheet.

Brush with egg; sprinkle with sesame and/or poppy seeds. Bake at 375° for 11-13 minutes or until golden brown. Serve warm. **Yield:** 2 servings.

bread bowls

prep: 15 minutes + rising | **bake:** 15 minutes + cooling

I never thought it could be this easy to make bread bowls at home. While the dough is mixing and rising, you have time to stir up a thick soup or chili to fill the bowls.

Renee Keller
Dodgeville, Wisconsin

- 1 **cup plus 3 tablespoons water (70° to 80°)**
- 2 **tablespoons olive oil**
- 1/4 **cup grated Parmesan cheese**
- 1 **teaspoon sugar**
- 1 **teaspoon salt**
- 3 **cups bread flour**
- 2-1/2 **teaspoons active dry yeast**

In bread machine pan, place all ingredients in order suggested by manufacturer. Select dough setting (check after 5 minutes of mixing; add 1 to 2 tablespoons of water or flour if needed).

When the cycle is completed, turn dough onto a lightly floured surface. Divide into fourths; shape each into a ball. Place on a greased baking sheet. Cover and let rise in a warm place until doubled, about 30 minutes.

Bake at 400° for 15-20 minutes or until golden brown. Cool. Cut the top fourth off each roll; carefully hollow out bottom, leaving a 1/4-in. shell (discard removed bread or save for another use). Fill with chili, chowder or stew. **Yield:** 4 servings.

‖Ultimate**TIP**

To make sure active dry yeast (not quick-rise yeast) is alive and active, you may first want to proof it. Here's how: Dissolve one package of yeast and 1 teaspoon sugar in 1/4 cup warm water (110° to 115°). Let stand for 5 to 10 minutes. If the mixture foams up, the yeast mixture can be used because the yeast is active. If it does not foam, the yeast should be discarded.

- 1 **tube (4 ounces) refrigerated crescent rolls**
- 1 **package (3 ounces) cream cheese, softened**
- 1/4 **cup sugar**
- 1/4 **teaspoon vanilla extract**
- 1 **teaspoon butter, melted**

Unroll crescent roll dough and separate into two rectangles; place on an ungreased baking sheet and press the perforations together.

In a small bowl, beat cream cheese, sugar and vanilla until smooth. Spread over half of each rectangle; fold dough over filling and pinch to seal. Brush with butter. Bake at 350° for 15-20 minutes or until golden brown. **Yield:** 2 servings.

cheese danish dessert

prep/cook: 30 minutes

Crescent roll dough makes it a snap to whip up these Danishes. I sprinkle them with a topping of 1/4 cup sugar and 2 teaspoons cinnamon before setting them in the oven.

Mary Margaret Merritt
Washington Court House, Ohio

1 package (1/4 ounce) active dry yeast

1-1/2 cups warm water (110° to 115°), *divided*

1 tablespoon sugar

2 teaspoons salt

1 tablespoon shortening, melted

4 cups all-purpose flour

Cornmeal

In a large bowl, dissolve yeast in 1/2 cup water. Add the sugar, salt, shortening and remaining water; stir until blended. Stir in flour until smooth. Do not knead. Cover and let rise in a warm place for 1 hour or until doubled.

Turn onto a floured surface. Divide in half; let rest for 10 minutes. Roll each half into a 10-in. x 8-in. rectangle. Roll up from a long side; pinch to seal. Place seam side down on greased baking sheets sprinkled with cornmeal. Sprinkle the tops with cornmeal. Cover and let rise until doubled, about 45 minutes.

With a very sharp knife, make five diagonal cuts across the top of each loaf. Bake at 400° for 20-30 minutes or until lightly browned. Remove from the pans to wire rack to cool. **Yield:** 2 loaves (10 slices each).

crusty french bread

prep: 30 minutes + rising | **bake:** 20 minutes + cooling

What we think of as French bread in America is actually called a baguette in France. It has a lighter texture than Italian bread and is shaped into a long, narrow loaf.

Christy Freeman
Central Point, Oregon

cheese bread

prep: 5 minutes | **bake:** 25 minutes

For a slightly different flavor, I'll replace half the mozzarella in this bread recipe with cheddar...or whatever cheese I have in the fridge.

Donna Britsch
Tega Cay, South Carolina

1 **unsliced loaf (1/2 pound) French bread**

2 **tablespoons butter, softened**

1/2 **teaspoon Italian seasoning**

1/2 **cup shredded part-skim mozzarella cheese**

1/4 **cup grated Parmesan cheese**

Slice bread lengthwise; place cut side up on a baking sheet. Spread butter on cut surfaces; sprinkle with half of the Italian seasoning. Top with cheeses and remaining Italian seasoning.

Bake at 350° for 20-25 minutes or until the cheese is melted. Cut widthwise into 1-in. pieces. **Yield:** 4 servings.

crispy garlic breadsticks

prep/cook: 30 minutes

This is a surprisingly tasty way to use day-old hot dog buns. Thanks to the garlic flavor, they're a nice accompaniment to a hearty pasta dinner or simply as a crunchy snack. For a kid-pleasing treat, substitute cinnamon and sugar for the garlic powder.

Linda Rainey
Monahans, Texas

4 day-old hot dog buns
1/2 cup butter, melted
1/2 teaspoon garlic powder

Split buns in half; cut each half length-wise. Combine butter and garlic; brush over breadsticks. Place on a greased 15-in. x 10-in. x 1-in. baking pan. Bake at 325° for 25-30 minutes or until golden brown. **Yield:** 8-10 servings.

Editor's Note: Breadsticks may also be baked at 250° for 60-70 minutes.

parmesan cheese straws

prep/cook: 30 minutes

These rich and buttery breadsticks are a fun change from regular dinner rolls and are fairly easy to make. They're great alongside salads and soups.

Mitzi Sentiff
Alexandria, Virginia

1/2 cup butter, softened
2/3 cup grated Parmesan cheese
1 cup all-purpose flour
1/4 teaspoon salt
1/8 teaspoon cayenne pepper
1/4 cup milk

In a small bowl, beat butter and cheese until well blended. Add the flour, salt and cayenne; mix well. Divide dough in half. On a lightly floured surface; roll each portion into an 18-in. x 3-in. rectangle. Cut into 3-in. x 1/2-in. strips.

Place 1 in. apart on greased baking sheets; brush with milk. Bake at 350° for 8-10 minutes or until lightly browned. Remove to wire racks to cool. Store in an airtight container. **Yield:** 6 dozen.

cookies, bars & candy

pg. 192

peanut butter kiss cookies 180

crisp peanut candies 181

chocolate chip cheese bars 181

chocolate truffles 182

butterscotch peanut candy 182

buttery yeast spritz 183

caramel corn chocolate bars 183

angel wings 184

cherry almond bark 185

peanut butter fudge 185

chocolate-covered peanut butter bars 186

chewy walnut bars 186

peanut butter chocolate cups 187

holiday wreath cookies 187

layered mint candies 188

apricot cashew clusters 189

old-time butter crunch candy 189

crispy kiss squares 190

cherry squares 190

sugar cookie slices 191

white chocolate cereal bars 191

marshmallow fudge 192

quick elephant ears 193

cinnamon stars 193

italian horn cookies 194

chocolate mousse balls 194

salted nut squares 195

chewy macaroons 195

terrific toffee 196

gooey chip bars 197

truffle cups .197

dairy state fudge 198

honey cereal bars 198

crunchy chocolate cups 199

microwave oatmeal bars 199

chocolate pudding sandwiches 200

s'mores crumb bars 201

flourless peanut butter cookies 201

holiday shortbread cookies 202

strawberry cookies 202

butterscotch taffy 203

nuts-about-you cookie sticks 203

christmas candies 204

lemon snowflakes 205

german chocolate bars 205

chocolate marshmallow squares 206

sweet graham snacks 206

toffee crunch grahams 207

sweetheart cookies 207

no-bake cereal bars 208

quick toffee bars 209

black walnut butter cookies 209

peanut butter kiss cookies

prep: 20 minutes | **bake:** 10 minutes + cooling

Here's an all-time classic. These cookies are great for little ones, and they keep adults guessing as to how they can be made with only five ingredients.

Dee Davis
Sun City, Arizona

1 cup peanut butter
1 cup sugar
1 egg
1 teaspoon vanilla extract
24 milk chocolate kisses

In a large bowl, cream the peanut butter and the sugar. Add the egg and vanilla; beat until blended.

Roll into 1-1/4-in. balls. Place 2 in. apart on ungreased baking sheets. Bake at 350° for 10-12 minutes or until tops are slightly cracked. Immediately press one chocolate kiss into the center of each cookie. Cool for 5 minutes before removing from pans to wire racks. **Yield:** 2 dozen.

Editor's Note: This recipe does not contain any type of flour. Reduced-fat or generic brands of peanut butter are not recommended for this recipe.

crisp peanut candies

prep: 15 minutes + standing

My sister gave me this fun-to-make recipe one year when I was tired of making the same old cookies. My husband absolutely loves the no-bake treats.

Christine Kehler
Nebo, North Carolina

2-2/3   **cups vanilla *or* white chips**
1/4   **cup peanut butter**
3   **cups crisp rice cereal**
1   **cup peanuts**

In a heavy saucepan, heat vanilla chips and peanut butter over low until melted; stir until smooth. Add cereal and peanuts; stir to coat. Crop by tablespoonfuls onto waxed paper; let stand until set. Store in an airtight container at room temperature. **Yield:** about 4-1/2 dozen.

|||Ultimate**TIP**

A simple way to measure solid vegetable shortening and peanut butter is to use the water-displacement method. If you want to measure 1/4 cup peanut butter, fill a measuring cup with 3/4 cup cold water. Add enough peanut butter to raise the water level to the 1-cup measure, making sure the peanut butter is completely immersed, then pour off all of the water.

---

1   **tube (18 ounces) refrigerated chocolate chip cookie dough**
1   **package (8 ounces) cream cheese, softened**
1/2   **cup sugar**
1   **egg**

Cut cookie dough in half. For crust, press half of the dough onto the bottom of a greased 8-in. square baking pan.

In a large bowl, beat the cream cheese, sugar and egg until smooth. Spread over the crust. Crumble the remaining dough over top.

Bake at 350° for 35-40 minutes or until a toothpick inserted near the center comes out clean. Cool bars on a wire rack. Refrigerate leftovers. **Yield:** 12-16 servings.

Editor's Note: 2 cups of your favorite chocolate chip cookie dough can be substituted for the refrigerated dough called for in the recipe.

chocolate chip cheese bars

prep: 15 minutes | **bake:** 35 minutes

This is my most requested dessert recipe. Everyone loves the yummy bars with their soft cream cheese filling. Making them couldn't be easier.

Teri Lindquist
Gurnee, Illinois

14 squares (1 ounce *each*)
    semisweet chocolate, *divided*
 1 cup heavy whipping cream
1/3 cup butter, softened
 1 teaspoon rum extract *or*
    vanilla extract
1/2 cup finely chopped pecans *or*
    walnuts, toasted

Coarsely chop 12 squares of chocolate; set aside. In a saucepan, heat the cream over low heat until bubbles form around the side of the pan. Remove from the heat; add chopped chocolate, stirring until melted and smooth.

Cool to room temperature. Stir in the butter and extract. Cover tightly and refrigerate for at least 6 hours or until firm.

Grate the remaining chocolate; place in a shallow dish. Add the nuts; set aside. Shape tablespoonfuls of chilled chocolate mixture into balls. Place on waxed paper-lined baking sheets. (If truffles are soft, refrigerate until easy to handle.) Roll truffles in the chocolate-nut mixture. Store in an airtight container in the refrigerator. **Yield:** 3 dozen.

chocolate truffles

prep: 25 minutes + chilling

It's hard to eat just one of these silky chocolate candies. I like to keep some on hand for a quick and sweet snack.

Deann Aleva
Hudson, Wisconsin

butterscotch peanut candy

prep: 10 minutes + chilling

What's not to love about these yummy bites that feature milk chocolate, butterscotch and peanuts? I adore the four-ingredient treats.

Callie Gregg
St. Lawrence, South Dakota

 1 package (11-1/2 ounces) milk
    chocolate chips
 1 package (10 ounces) butterscotch chips
 1 teaspoon butter-flavored
    shortening
 3 cups salted peanuts

In a microwave, heat chips and shortening, uncovered, at 50% power for 2 to 2-1/2 minutes or until melted. Stir until smooth. Add peanuts. Drop by tablespoonfuls onto waxed paper-lined baking sheets. Refrigerate until firm, about 45 minutes. **Yield:** 2-1/4 pounds (3-1/2 to 4 dozen).

Editor's Note: This recipe was tested in a 1,100-watt microwave.

buttery yeast spritz

prep: 15 minutes | **bake:** 10 min./batch

Yeast may seem like an unusual ingredient for cookies, but it adds to the buttery flavor of these fabulous treats. These were my mother's favorite...now I make them for my children and grandchildren.

Janet Stucky
Sterling, Illinois

- 1 **package (1/4 ounce) active dry yeast**
- 2 **tablespoons warm water (110° to 115°)**
- 2 **cups butter, softened**
- 1 **cup sugar**
- 2 **egg yolks**
- 4 **cups all-purpose flour**

In a small bowl, dissolve yeast in water; set aside. In another bowl, cream butter and sugar until light and fluffy. Beat in egg yolks and yeast mixture. Gradually add flour and mix well.

Using a cookie press fitted with disk of your choice, press dough into desired shapes 1 in. apart onto ungreased baking sheets. Bake at 400° for 7-9 minutes or until lightly browned. Remove to wire racks to cool. **Yield:** 13 dozen.

caramel corn chocolate bars

prep: 10 minutes | **cook:** 10 minutes + cooling

If you love caramel corn and chocolate, you've got to try these wonderful bars. They're a perfect combination of salty and sweet.

Jean Roczniak
Rochester, Minnesota

- 5 **cups caramel corn**
- 1 **cup chopped pecans**
- 1 **package (10-1/2 ounces) miniature marshmallows, *divided***
- 1/4 **cup butter, cubed**
- 1/2 **cup semisweet chocolate chips**

In a large bowl, combine the caramel corn, chopped pecans and 1 cup marshmallows. In a small heavy saucepan, melt the butter over low heat. Add the chips and remaining marshmallows; cook and stir until smooth.

Pour over the caramel corn mixture; toss to coat. With buttered hands, press into a greased 13-in. x 9-in. pan. Cool. Cut the bars with a serrated knife. **Yield:** 2 dozen.

angel wings

prep: 30 minutes + chilling | **bake:** 20 minutes

I knew I'd hit a winner with these crisp roll-ups when my sister first sampled them. After she tasted them, she was so impressed with the flavor she asked me to bake her wedding cake! I like to color the sugar for extra appeal.

R. Lane
Tenafly, New Jersey

   1 **cup cold butter, cubed**
1-1/2 **cups all-purpose flour**
   1/2 **cup sour cream**
   10 **tablespoons sugar, *divided***
   1 **tablespoon ground cinnamon, *divided***

In a bowl, cut butter into flour until the mixture resembles coarse crumbs. Stir in the sour cream. Turn onto a lightly floured surface; knead 6-8 times or until mixture holds together. Shape into four balls; flatten slightly. Wrap in plastic wrap; refrigerate for 4 hours or overnight.

Unwrap one ball. Sprinkle 2 tablespoons sugar on waxed paper; coat all sides of ball with sugar. Roll into a 12-in. x 5-in. rectangle between two sheets of waxed paper. Remove top sheet of waxed paper. Sprinkle dough with 3/4 teaspoon cinnamon. Lightly mark a line down the center of the dough, making two 6-in. x 5-in. rectangles.

Starting with a short side, roll up jelly-roll style to the center mark; peel waxed paper away while rolling. Repeat with other short side. Wrap in plastic wrap; freeze for 30 minutes. Repeat three times. Place remaining sugar (or colored sugar if desired) on waxed paper. Unwrap one roll. Cut into 1/2-in. slices; dip each side into sugar. Place 2 in. apart on ungreased baking sheets.

Bake at 375° for 12 minutes or until golden brown. Turn the cookies; bake 5-8 minutes longer. Remove to wire racks to cool. **Yield: about 3 dozen.**

cherry almond bark

prep/cook: 25 minutes + chilling

Chock-full of colorful cherries and almonds, this fast-to-fix candy is a Christmas tradition at our home. It's one of my family's favorite munchies while decorating the Christmas tree and wrapping presents.

Rita Goshaw
Milwaukee, Wisconsin

1 pound white confectionery coating, broken into pieces

3/4 cup chopped candied cherries

1/2 cup unblanched whole almonds

In a saucepan over medium-low heat, melt coating, stirring until smooth. Add cherries and almonds; mix well. Spread onto a foil-lined baking sheet. Refrigerate until firm. Break into pieces. **Yield:** about 1 pound.

|||Ultimate**TIP**

When making fudge, lining the baking pan with foil first makes for easy cutting later. To prepare a foil-lined pan, line the pan with foil extending over the sides of the pan. Grease the foil with butter or coat with nonstick cooking spray. When the fudge is firm, grasp the foil on opposite sides and lift the fudge out of the pan. Place it on a cutting board, remove the foil and cut.

peanut butter fudge

prep: 15 minutes + chilling

My sister shared the recipe for this unbelievably easy confection. I prefer using creamy peanut butter, but the chunky style works just as well.

Mrs. Kenneth Rummel
Linglestown, Pennsylvania

2 cups sugar

1/2 cup milk

1-1/3 cups peanut butter

1 jar (7 ounces) marshmallow creme

In a saucepan, bring sugar and milk to a boil; boil for 3 minutes. Add peanut butter and marshmallow creme; mix well. Quickly pour into a buttered 8-in. square pan; chill until set. Cut into squares. **Yield:** 3-4 dozen.

chocolate-covered peanut butter bars

prep: 30 minutes + cooling

My daughter won first place in a contest with this candy, which I make at Christmastime. It melts in your mouth.

Mary Esther Holloway
Bowerston, Ohio

3 cups sugar

1 cup light corn syrup

1/2 cup water

1 jar (18 ounces) creamy peanut butter, melted

1-1/2 pounds milk chocolate confectionery coating

In a large heavy saucepan, combine sugar, corn syrup and water. Cook and stir over low heat until sugar is dissolved; bring to a full rolling boil. Boil, stirring constantly, until a candy thermometer reads 290° (soft-crack stage).

Meanwhile, place melted peanut butter in a large greased heatproof bowl. Pour hot syrup over peanut butter; stir quickly until blended. Pour onto a well-buttered baking sheet; cover with a piece of buttered waxed paper. Roll mixture into a 14-in. x 12-in. rectangle. While warm, cut into 1-1/2-in. x 1-in. bars using a buttered pizza cutter or knife. Cool bars completely.

Melt confectionery coating; dip bars and place on waxed paper to harden. **Yield:** 6 dozen.

chewy walnut bars

prep: 10 minutes | **bake:** 30 minutes + cooling

Since they need just four ingredients and one bowl, I whip up a batch of these family-favorite bars all the time. I'm thanked "mmmm-many" times over!

Nancy Tuschak
Vacaville, California

2-1/3 cups packed brown sugar

2 cups biscuit/baking mix

4 eggs

2 cups chopped walnuts

||| Ultimate**TIP**

Both light and dark brown sugars are a mixture of granulated sugar and molasses, with dark brown sugar containing more molasses than light brown sugar. Light brown sugar has a delicate flavor while dark brown sugar has a stronger, more intense molasses flavor. They can be used interchangeably depending on your personal preference.

In a large bowl, combine brown sugar and biscuit mix. Beat in eggs until well blended. Fold in walnuts.

Pour into a greased 13-in. x 9-in. baking pan. Bake at 350° for 30-35 minutes or until golden brown. Cool on wire rack. Cut into bars. **Yield:** about 3 dozen.

peanut butter chocolate cups

prep: 20 minutes + chilling

Our children love these rich, creamy candies. Try them with your favorite chocolate bar.

Aljene Wendling
Seattle, Washington

1 milk chocolate candy bar (7 ounces)

1/4 cup butter

1 tablespoon shortening

1/4 cup creamy peanut butter

In a microwave or heavy saucepan, melt chocolate, butter and shortening; stir until smooth. Place foil or paper miniature baking cups in a miniature muffin tin. Place 1 tablespoon of chocolate mixture in each cup.

In a microwave or saucepan, heat peanut butter until melted. Spoon into cups. Top with remaining chocolate mixture. Refrigerate for 30 minutes or until firm. **Yield:** 1 dozen.

---

1 cup plus 2 tablespoons confectioners' sugar, *divided*

2 tablespoons light corn syrup

1 to 2 tablespoons water

Red and green gel food coloring

1 package (16 ounces) cutout butter cookies

Snowflake sprinkles and red decorating candies

In a small bowl, combine 1 cup confectioners' sugar, corn syrup and enough water to achieve a smooth consistency. Remove 2 tablespoons glaze to another bowl; tint red. Cover and set aside.

Tint remaining glaze green. Dip the tops of half of the cookies in green glaze. (Save remaining cookies for another use.) Decorate with sprinkles and candies.

Stir enough remaining confectioners' sugar into the red glaze to achieve piping consistency. Using a #3 round pastry tip, pipe small bows and ribbons onto cookies. Serve immediately or let stand until set. **Yield:** about 3-1/2 dozen.

holiday wreath cookies

prep/cook: 30 minutes

Time-crunched cooks will cheer for these cute Christmas nibbles. Simply dip store-bought butter cookies into a bright green glaze, then add decorated candies to form festive wreaths.

Taste of Home Test Kitchen
Greendale, Wisconsin

layered mint candies

prep: 15 minutes + chilling

These incredible melt-in-your-mouth candies have the perfect amount of mint nestled between layers of milk chocolate. Even when I make a double batch for everyone to enjoy, the supply never lasts long. Stir in some green food coloring with the peppermint extract if you'd like.

Rhonda Vauble
Sac City, Iowa

- 1 **tablespoon butter**
- 1-1/2 **pounds white candy coating, *divided***
- 1 **cup (6 ounces) semisweet chocolate chips**
- 1 **teaspoon peppermint extract**
- 3 **tablespoons heavy whipping cream**

Line a 13-in. x 9-in. baking pan with foil. Grease the foil with 1 tablespoon butter; set pan aside.

In a microwave or heavy saucepan, melt 1 pound candy coating and chocolate chips. Spread half into prepared pan; set remaining mixture aside. Melt remaining candy coating; stir in extract. Stir in cream until smooth (mixture will be stiff). Spread over first layer; refrigerate for 10 minutes or until firm.

Warm the reserved chocolate mixture if necessary; spread over mint layer. Refrigerate for 1 hour or until firm. Lift out of the pan with foil and remove the foil. Cut into 1-in. squares. Store in an airtight container in the refrigerator. **Yield:** about 2 pounds (about 9-1/2 dozen).

apricot cashew clusters

prep/cook: 30 minutes

Guests will enjoy the fruity surprise they find in these scrumptious nut candies. I make them often because they can be whipped up in no time.

Pamela Wagner
Madison, Wisconsin

1 package (11-1/2 ounces) milk chocolate chips
1 cup chopped dried apricots
1 cup chopped salted cashews

In a microwave or double boiler, melt the chocolate chips; stir until smooth. Stir in apricots and cashews. Drop by rounded tablespoonfuls onto waxed paper-lined baking sheets. Chill until set, about 15 minutes. Store in an airtight container. **Yield:** 2-1/2 dozen.

1 cup butter
1-1/4 cups sugar
2 tablespoons light corn syrup
2 tablespoons water
2 cups finely chopped toasted almonds
8 milk chocolate candy bars (1.55 ounces *each*)

Line a 13-in. x 9-in. baking pan with foil; set aside. Using part of the butter, grease the sides of a large heavy saucepan. Add remaining butter to saucepan; melt over low heat. Add sugar, corn syrup and water. Cook and stir over medium heat until a candy thermometer reads 300° (hard-crack stage).

Remove from the heat and stir in almonds. Quickly pour into the prepared pan, spreading to cover bottom of pan. Cool completely. Carefully invert pan to remove candy in one piece; remove foil.

Melt half of the chocolate in a double boiler or microwave-safe bowl; spread over top of candy. Let cool. Turn candy over and repeat with remaining chocolate; cool. Break into 2-in. pieces. Store in an airtight container. **Yield:** about 2 pounds.

old-time butter crunch candy

prep: 15 minutes + cooling | **cook:** 25 minutes

Both my children and my grandchildren say the holiday season wouldn't be the same without the big tray of candies and cookies I prepare. This one's the popular part of that collection. We love the nutty pieces draped in chocolate.

Mildred Duffy
Bella Vista, Arkansas

6 cups Cocoa Puffs
1/4 cup butter
40 large marshmallows
1 package (11-1/2 ounces) milk chocolate chips
24 striped chocolate *or* milk chocolate kisses

Place cereal in a large bowl; set aside. In a microwave-safe bowl, combine the butter and marshmallows. Microwave, uncovered, on high for 2 minutes; stir. Continue cooking until smooth, stirring every minute. Add chocolate chips and stir until melted.

Pour over cereal; stir until well coated. Spread evenly in a greased 13-in. x 9-in. pan. Arrange kisses in rows over the top. Cool before cutting. **Yield:** 2 dozen.

Editor's Note: This recipe was tested in a 1,100-watt microwave.

crispy kiss squares

prep: 20 minutes + cooling

White or milk chocolate kisses add the fun final touch to these chocolaty treats. Since you need just four other items, you can stir up a pan of the sweet squares in a jiffy.

Chris Budd
Lewiston, Idaho

cherry squares

prep: 15 minutes | **bake:** 40 minutes

A scrumptious coconut crust complements cherry pie filling in these quick-to-fix squares. Try them the next time you're entertaining a friend or two for coffee.

Mildred Schwartzentruber
Tavistock, Ontario

1-3/4 cups flaked coconut
1/2 cup butter, softened
1/2 cup sugar

1-1/2 cups all-purpose flour
1 can (21 ounces) cherry pie filling

In a bowl, combine first four ingredients. Press half the mixture into a greased 9-in. square baking pan. Top with the pie filling and sprinkle with remaining crumbs. Bake at 375° for 35-40 minutes or until golden brown. **Yield:** 9 servings.

sugar cookie slices

prep: 10 minutes + chilling | **bake:** 15 min./batch

I was fortunate to inherit this recipe from my husband's great-aunt. They slice nicely and are easier to make than traditional cutout sugar cookies.

Lonna Peterman
New Port Richey, Florida

1-1/2 **cups butter, softened**
1-1/2 **cups sugar**
  1/2 **teaspoon vanilla extract**
   3 **cups all-purpose flour**

   1 **teaspoon baking soda**
  1/2 **teaspoon salt**

In a large bowl, cream butter and sugar until light and fluffy. Beat in vanilla. Combine the flour, baking soda and salt; gradually add to the creamed mixture and mix well.

Shape into two 8-in. rolls; wrap each in plastic wrap. Refrigerate for 4 hours or until firm.

Unwrap and cut into 1/4-in. slices. Place 2 in. apart on ungreased baking sheets. Bake at 350° for 12-14 minutes or until set (do not brown). Remove to wire racks to cool. **Yield:** 5 dozen.

white chocolate cereal bars

prep/cook: 15 minutes

A friend gave me this recipe that's a different take on the traditional crispy rice treats. My husband loves them. I like them because they're so quick to make, you can prepare them during a TV commercial and you won't miss much of your program.

Anne Powers
Munford, Alabama

   4 **cups miniature marshmallows**
   8 **ounces white candy coating,**
     broken into pieces
  1/4 **cup butter, cubed**
   6 **cups crisp rice cereal**

In a microwave-safe bowl, combine the marshmallows, candy coating and cubed butter. Microwave, uncovered, on high for 2 minutes or until melted, stirring every minute. Add cereal; stir to coat. Transfer to a greased 13-in. x 9-in. pan and gently press mixture evenly into pan. Cut into squares. **Yield:** about 3 dozen.

Editor's Note: This recipe was tested in a 1,100-watt microwave.

marshmallow fudge

prep: 15 minutes + chilling

It's nearly impossible to resist this rich chocolate delight. Chock-full of marshmallows and graham crackers, no one will believe that this tantalizing treat is actually low in fat.

Holly Mann
Temple, New Hampshire

1-1/3 **cups semisweet chocolate chips**

2/3 **cup fat-free sweetened condensed milk**

1 **teaspoon vanilla extract**

1-1/3 **cups miniature marshmallows**

2 **whole reduced-fat graham crackers, broken into bite-size pieces**

Line an 8-in. square pan with foil and coat with cooking spray; set aside. In a heavy saucepan over low heat, melt chocolate chips with milk; stir until smooth. Remove from the heat; cool for 2 minutes. Stir in vanilla. Fold in the marshmallows and graham crackers.

Pour into the prepared pan. Refrigerate for 1 hour or until firm. Lift out pan and remove foil; cut into 48 pieces. **Yield:** 4 dozen.

quick elephant ears

prep/cook: 15 minutes

Our eight children love helping make these sweet crunchy treats. We fry flour tortillas for a few seconds in oil, then sprinkle with cinnamon and sugar. I usually do the frying, then have one of the older kids add the coating.

Terry Lynn Ayers
Anderson, Indiana

1-1/2 **cups sugar**
   2 **teaspoons ground cinnamon**
Oil for frying
  10 **flour tortillas (6 inches)**

Combine sugar and cinnamon in a shallow bowl or large plate; set aside. In a skillet, heat 1/2 in. of oil. Place one tortilla at a time in skillet, cook for 5 seconds; turn and cook 10 seconds longer or until browned. Place in sugar mixture and turn to coat. Serve immediately. **Yield: 10 servings.**

  1 **cup butter, softened**
  2 **cups sugar**
  2 **eggs**
2-3/4 **cups all-purpose flour**
 1/3 **cup ground cinnamon**

In a large bowl, cream butter and sugar until light and fluffy. Add eggs, one at a time, beating well after each addition. Combine flour and cinnamon; gradually add to creamed mixture and mix well. Cover and refrigerate for 1 hour or until easy to handle.

On a lightly floured surface, roll out to 1/4-in. thickness. Cut with a 2-1/2-in. star-shaped cookie cutter dipped in flour. Place 1 in. apart on the ungreased baking sheets.

Bake at 350° for 15-18 minutes or until edges are firm and bottom of cookies are lightly browned. Remove to wire racks to cool. **Yield: 5 dozen.**

cinnamon stars

prep: 15 minutes + chilling | **bake:** 15 min./batch

These cookies fill your home with an irresistible aroma as they bake. My grandmother made them every Christmas when I was a child. I have fond memories of helping her in the kitchen.

Jean Jones
Peachtree City, Georgia

1 cup cold butter

4 cups all-purpose flour

2 cups vanilla ice cream, softened

1 can (12 ounces) cherry cake and pastry filling

Sugar

In a large bowl, cut butter into flour until mixture resembles coarse crumbs. Stir in ice cream. Divide into four portions. Cover and refrigerate for 2 hours.

On a lightly floured surface, roll each portion to 1/8-in. thickness. With a fluted pastry cutter, cut into 2-in. squares. Place about 1/2 teaspoon filling in the center of each square. Overlap two opposite corners of dough over the filling and seal. Sprinkle lightly with sugar.

Place on ungreased baking sheets. Bake at 350° for 10-12 minutes or until bottoms are light brown. Cool on wire racks. **Yield:** about 5 dozen.

Editor's Note: This recipe was tested with Solo brand cake and pastry filling. Look for it in the baking aisle at your local grocery store.

italian horn cookies

prep: 30 minutes + chilling | **bake:** 10 min./batch + cooling

My family has been making these delicate fruit-filled cookies for generations. Light and flaky, they have the look of petite and elegant pastries.

Gloria Siddiqui
Houston, Texas

|||Ultimate**TIP**

Ice cream is often softened before being used in recipes or when it is too hard to scoop for eating. To soften in the refrigerator, transfer the ice cream from the freezer to the refrigerator 20-30 minutes before using. Or let it stand at room temperature for 10-15 minutes. Hard ice cream can also be softened in the microwave at 30% power for about 30 seconds.

chocolate mousse balls

prep: 20 minutes + chilling

I love working with my grandkids in the kitchen. I've found that the key is using recipes like this one that really let them get involved and have yummy results.

Michael Nye
Upper Sandusky, Ohio

6 milk chocolate candy bars (1.55 ounces *each*)

1 container (12 ounces) frozen whipped topping, thawed

1 cup crushed vanilla wafers (about 30 wafers)

In a saucepan over low heat, melt candy bars. Cool for 10 minutes. Fold into the topping. Cover and chill for 3 hours.

Shape into 1-in. balls and roll in the wafer crumbs. Refrigerate or freeze. **Yield:** about 3 dozen.

salted nut squares

prep: 15 minutes + chilling

A favorite of young and old, this recipe came from my sister-in-law. It's simple to prepare and delicious. There's no need to keep it warm or cold, so it's perfect for the potluck that has you traveling longer distances.

Kathy Tremel
Earling, Iowa

3 cups salted peanuts without skins, *divided*
2-1/2 tablespoons butter
2 cups peanut butter chips
1 can (14 ounces) sweetened condensed milk
2 cups miniature marshmallows

Place half of the peanuts in an ungreased 11-in. x 7-in. baking pan; set aside. In a large saucepan, melt butter and peanut butter chips over low heat; stir until smooth. Remove from the heat. Add milk and marshmallows; stir until melted.

Pour over peanuts. Sprinkle the remaining peanuts. Cover and refrigerate until chilled. Cut into bars. **Yield:** 30 servings.

chewy macaroons

prep: 15 minutes | **bake:** 25 minutes

I think that a perfectly prepared macaroon is lightly crisp on the outside and tender on the inside. These easy-to-make treats fit the bill.

Herbert Borland
Des Moines, Washington

2 egg whites
1/2 teaspoon vanilla extract
Pinch salt
6 tablespoons sugar
1 cup flaked coconut

In a small bowl, beat egg whites, vanilla and salt on medium speed until soft peaks form. Gradually add sugar, one tablespoon at time, beating until stiff peaks form. Fold in the coconut.

Drop by tablespoonfuls 2 in. apart onto well-greased baking sheets. Bake at 300° for 25 minutes or until lightly browned. Immediately remove to wire racks to cool. **Yield:** about 2 dozen.

terrific toffee

prep: 10 minutes | **cook:** 25 minutes + standing

This buttery toffee is one of those must-make treats my family requests for the holidays. You can also try variations to make English or hazelnut toffee.

Carol Gillespie
Chambersburg, Pennsylvania

1-1/2 teaspoons plus 1 cup butter, *divided*
  1 cup semisweet chocolate chips
  1 cup milk chocolate chips
  1 cup sugar
  3 tablespoons water
  2 cups coarsely chopped almonds, toasted, *divided*

Butter a large baking sheet with 1-1/2 teaspoons butter; set aside. In a small bowl, combine the semisweet and milk chocolate chips; set aside.

In a heavy saucepan, combine the sugar, water and remaining butter. Cook and stir over medium heat until a candy thermometer reaches 290° (soft-crack stage). Remove from the heat; stir in 1 cup almonds. Immediately pour onto prepared baking sheet.

Sprinkle with chocolate chips; spread the chocolate with a knife when melted. Sprinkle with remaining almonds. Let stand until set, about 1 hour. Break into 2-in. pieces. Store in an airtight container. **Yield: about 2 pounds.**

English Toffee: Omit the semisweet chocolate chips and almonds. Prepare toffee as directed; omit stirring in the almonds. Spread in pan and cool. Melt 1 cup milk chocolate chips in a microwave at 30% power or in a saucepan over low heat; stir until smooth. Spread over toffee and sprinkle with 1 cup chopped pecans. Let stand until set, about 1 hour.

Hazelnut Toffee: Omit milk chocolate chips and almonds. Prepare the toffee as directed; stir in 1/3 cup chopped hazelnuts. Spread in pan and allow to cool. Melt 2 cups semisweet chocolate chips in a microwave at 50% power or in a saucepan over low heat; stir until smooth. Spread over toffee; sprinkle with 1/2 cup finely chopped hazelnuts. Let stand until set, about 1 hour.

Editor's Note: We recommend that you test your candy thermometer before each use by bringing water to a boil; the thermometer should read 212°. Adjust your recipe temperature up or down based on your test.

gooey chip bars

prep: 15 minutes | **bake:** 20 minutes + cooling

always know that I can satisfy a sweet tooth in a jiffy with my chewy chocolaty bars. You'll never believe how easy they are to assemble.

Beatriz Boggs
Delray Beach, Florida

- 2 **cups graham cracker crumbs**
- 1 **can (14 ounces) sweetened condensed milk**
- 1 **cup (6 ounces) semisweet chocolate chips, *divided***
- 1/2 **cup chopped walnuts *or* pecans, optional**

In a large bowl, combine cracker crumbs and milk. Stir in 1/2 cup chocolate chips and nuts if desired (batter will be very thick).

Pat onto the bottom of a well-greased 8-in. square baking pan. Sprinkle with remaining chocolate chips. Bake at 350° for 20-25 minutes or until golden brown. Cool on a wire rack; cut into bars. **Yield:** 1-1/2 dozen.

- 1 **package (11-1/2 ounces) milk chocolate chips**
- 2 **tablespoons shortening**
- 1 **pound white confectionery coating, cut into 1/2-inch pieces**
- 1/2 **cup heavy whipping cream**

In a double boiler or microwave, melt chips and shortening. Stir until smooth; cook for 5 minutes. With a narrow pastry brush, "paint" the chocolate mixture on the inside of 1-in. foil candy cups. Place on a tray and refrigerate until firm, about 45 minutes.

Remove about 12 cups at a time from the refrigerator; remove and discard foil cups. Return chocolate cups to the refrigerator. For filling, melt the confectionery coating and cream; stir until smooth.

Transfer to a bowl; cover and refrigerate for 30 minutes or until mixture begins to thicken. Beat filling for 1-2 minutes or until light and fluffy. Use a pastry star tube or spoon to fill the chocolate cups. Store in the refrigerator. **Yield:** 5 dozen.

truffle cups

prep: 30 minutes + chilling

When I serve this elegant confection, it never fails to draw compliments. Delightfully tempting, the cups are a fun, fluffy variation on traditional truffles. They are truly delectable!

Katie Dowler
Birch Tree, Missouri

1 package (8 ounces) cream cheese, softened

2 tablespoons butter

2 pounds white almond bark, broken into small pieces

1 to 1-1/2 cups chopped pecans, walnuts *or* hickory nuts

In a bowl, beat the cream cheese until fluffy; set aside. In the top of a double boiler, melt the butter. Add almond bark; heat and stir until melted and smooth. Pour over the cream cheese; beat until smooth and glossy, about 7-10 minutes. Stir in nuts. Pour into a greased 9-in. square pan. Store in the refrigerator. **Yield:** 64 pieces (about 1 inch).

dairy state fudge

prep: 20 minutes + chilling

I grew up on a dairy farm in Wisconsin, so it's only natural that I have a lot of recipes that use dairy ingredients. I make this confection nearly every Christmas. You'll find it's hard to eat just one piece.

Jan Vande Slunt
Waupun, Wisconsin

||| Ultimate**TIP**

When a recipe calls for chopped nuts, here's a good rule of thumb. If the word "chopped" comes before the ingredient listed in a recipe, chop the ingredient before measuring. If the word "chopped" comes after the ingredient, then chop after measuring. For "1 cup chopped nuts," you should chop the nuts first, then measure out 1 cup of the chopped nuts.

honey cereal bars

prep: 20 minutes + chilling

Honey sweetens and holds together my five-ingredient bars. I think they are great for an after-school snack when the kids are hungry but I don't want to spoil appetites for dinner.

Ellie Conlon, ThistleDew Farm
Proctor, West Virginia

3/4 cup honey

3/4 cup peanut butter

1 teaspoon vanilla extract

3 cups Special K cereal

1 cup (6 ounces) semisweet chocolate chips, melted

In a large saucepan over medium heat, bring the honey and peanut butter to a boil. Remove from the heat; stir in vanilla extract and cereal.

Press into an ungreased 9-in. square pan. Spread chocolate over bars. Chill until firm. **Yield:** 20 bars.

crunchy chocolate cups

prep: 25 minutes + chilling

These sweet, crunchy morsels are super-easy to make and are always popular on my treat tray for the holidays.

Elizabeth Prestie
Preeceville, Saskatchewan

- 1 **package (12 ounces) semisweet chocolate chips**
- 1 **package (11 ounces) butterscotch chips**
- 1 **package (10 ounces) peanut butter chips**
- 1 **cup coarsely crushed cornflakes**
- 1/2 **cup chopped peanuts, optional**

In a large heavy saucepan, melt the chocolate chips, butterscotch chips and peanut butter chips over low heat. Remove from the heat; stir in the cornflakes. Add the peanuts if desired. Let stand for 10-15 minutes or until slightly cooled.

Drop by teaspoonful into miniature foil cups placed on a 15-in. x 10-in. x 1-in. baking sheet. Refrigerate until firm. **Yield:** about 5 dozen.

---

microwave oatmeal bars

prep: 10 minutes + chilling | **cook:** 10 minutes

A perfect bite on a fall afternoon, these rustic bars go great with hot coffee and cold milk alike. Using the microwave really speeds up the process.

Annette Self
Junction City, Ohio

- 2 **cups quick-cooking oats**
- 1/2 **cup packed brown sugar**
- 1/2 **cup butter, melted**
- 1/4 **cup corn syrup**
- 1 **cup (6 ounces) semisweet chocolate chips**

In a bowl, combine oats and brown sugar. Stir in butter and corn syrup. Press into a greased 9-in. square microwave-safe dish.

Rotate a half turn; microwave 1-1/2 minutes longer. Sprinkle with the chocolate chips. Microwave at 30% power for 4-1/2 minutes or until the chips are glossy; spread chocolate evenly over top. Refrigerate 15-20 minutes before cutting. **Yield:** 8-10 servings.

Editor's Note: This recipe was tested in a 1,100-watt microwave.

chocolate pudding sandwiches

prep: 15 minutes + freezing

These cookies are a favorite after-school snack for my kids...and even my diabetic husband enjoys one now and then.

Jan Thomas
Richmond, Virginia

1-1/2   **cups cold fat-free milk**
   1   **package (1.4 ounces) sugar-free instant chocolate pudding mix**

   1   **carton (8 ounces) frozen reduced-fat whipped topping, thawed**
   1   **cup miniature marshmallows**
   2   **packages (9 ounces *each*) chocolate wafers**

In a bowl, whisk milk and pudding mix for 2 minutes or until slightly thickened. Fold in whipped topping and marshmallows.

For each sandwich, spread about 2 tablespoons of pudding mixture on a chocolate wafer; top with another wafer. Stack sandwiches in an airtight container. Freeze until firm, about 3 hours. Remove from the freezer 5 minutes before serving. **Yield: 43 sandwiches.**

s'mores crumb bars

prep: 10 minutes | **bake:** 10 minutes + cooling

You don't have to be camping to enjoy the great taste of s'mores. Better yet, since you can whip up a batch of these tempting bars in your kitchen, you don't have to put up with mosquitoes!

Darlene Brenden
Salem, Oregon

3 cups graham cracker crumbs

3/4 cup butter, melted

1/3 cup sugar

3 cups miniature marshmallows

2 cups (12 ounces) semisweet cho chips

In a small bowl, combine the crumbs, butter and sugar; press half into a greased 13-in. x 9-in. baking pan. Sprinkle with marshmallows and chocolate chips. Top with remaining crumb mixture; press firmly.

Bake at 375° for 10 minutes. Remove to a wire rack; immediately press top firmly with spatula. Cool completely. Cut into bars. **Yield:** 3 dozen.

||| Ultimate**TIP**

Here are a few tips so that your cookies turn out great! Measure ingredients accurately and avoid overmixing the dough (if handled too much, the cookies can turn tough). Use heavy-gauge, dull aluminum baking sheets with one or two low sides. For greased baking sheets, use shortening or nonstick cooking spray. And for even baking, make cookies the same size and thickness.

5 cups all-purpose flour
1 cup sugar
1/2 teaspoon salt
2 cups cold butter

In a large bowl, combine the flour, sugar and salt. Cut in the cold butter until the mixture resembles fine crumbs. Pat into an ungreased 15-in. x 10-in. x 1-in. baking pan. Prick all over with a fork.

Bake at 325° for 35 minutes or until the center is set. Cool for 10-15 minutes. Cut into small squares. Continue to cool cookies to room temperature. **Yield: 5 dozen.**

holiday
shortbread cookies

prep: 10 minutes | **bake:** 35 minutes + cooling

This special treat came to me from Scotland through a relative. I compared this recipe with one a friend makes,

ltimate**TIP**

drop cookies, fill a table-
ith dough and use a spoon or
bber spatula to push the
ff the spoon onto a cool bak-
et. A 1 tablespoon-sized ice
coop is great for making uni-
ized drop cookies. Just scoop
gh, even off the top with the
a metal spatula and release
aking sheet.

mbine the cake mix, egg and
ng until well combined. Place
rs' sugar in a shallow dish.
gh by tablespoonfuls into the
coat. Place 2 in. apart on
sheets. Bake at 350° for 10-12
l lightly browned around the edges. Remove to wire racks to cool. **Yield: about 5 dozen.**

butterscotch taffy

prep: 10 minutes | **cook:** 15 minutes + cooling

It's a good thing that this recipe isn't a lot of fuss...the soft tempting taffy goes so fast, I sometimes don't even get to wrap the pieces!

Teri Lindquist
Wildwood, Illinois

1/2 **cup butter**
48 **large marshmallows**
1 **tablespoon water**
1/2 **teaspoon salt**
2 **cups (12 ounces) butterscotch chips**

In a heavy saucepan, combine the butter, marshmallows, water and salt; cook and stir over low heat until smooth. Add chips; stir until melted. Pour into a buttered 8-in. square baking pan; cool. Cut into 1-in. squares. Wrap individually in waxed paper; twist ends. **Yield: about 5 dozen.**

nuts-about-you cookie sticks

prep/cook: 10 minutes

Here is a fancy meal finale that couldn't be quicker to whip up. Start with purchased Pirouette cookies, dip them in a rich, creamy chocolate and peanut-butter coating, dust with nuts or sprinkles and serve with your favorite after-dinner beverage.

Taste of Home Test Kitchen
Greendale, Wisconsin

1/4 **cup semisweet chocolate chips**
3/4 **teaspoon shortening**
1-1/2 **teaspoons creamy peanut butter**
4 **French vanilla Pirouette cookies**
1/2 **cup chopped nuts**

In a microwave-safe bowl, melt the chocolate chips, shortening and peanut butter; stir until smooth. Dip one end of each cookie into chocolate mixture; sprinkle with nuts. Place on waxed paper; let stand until set. **Yield: 2 servings.**

christmas candies

prep: 20 minutes + chilling

During my childhood, my family lived in Brazil, where we relished these special treats. Roll the caramel-like bites in nuts or sprinkles.

Laura Beth Dean
Christiansburg, Virginia

3 **tablespoons baking cocoa**

1 **can (14 ounces) sweetened condensed milk**

2 **tablespoons butter**
Finely chopped pistachios

In a small heavy saucepan, bring the cocoa, milk and butter to a boil, stirring constantly. Reduce heat to low; cook and stir until thickened.

Transfer to a small bowl. Cover and refrigerate until chilled. Roll into 1-in. balls; roll in pistachios. Store in the refrigerator. **Yield:** about 2-1/2 dozen.

toffee crunch grahams

prep: 15 minutes | **bake:** 10 minutes + cooling

Only four ingredients make up these toffee bars loaded with crunchy almonds. My sister gave me the recipe years ago, and it's still a hit today.

Carol Ann Horne
Perth, Ontario

  12 **whole graham crackers**
-1/2 **cups butter, cubed**
   1 **cup packed brown sugar**
   2 **cups sliced almonds**

Line a 15-in. x 10-in. x 1-in. baking pan with heavy-duty foil. Place graham crackers in pan. In a saucepan, combine butter and brown sugar; bring to a boil, stirring constantly. Carefully pour over graham crackers. Sprinkle with almonds.

Bake at 400° for 6-8 minutes or until bubbly. Cool in pan for 4 minutes. Cut each cracker into four sections; transfer to wire racks to cool completely. **Yield:** 4 dozen.

---

sweetheart cookies

prep: 25 minutes | **bake:** 15 minutes

These rounds filled with fruit preserves were blue-ribbon winners at the county fair 2 years running. A family favorite, they never last very long.

Pamela Esposito
Smithville, New Jersey

 3/4 **cup butter, softened**
 1/2 **cup sugar**
   1 **egg yolk**
-1/2 **cups all-purpose flour**
   2 **tablespoons raspberry *or*
        strawberry preserves**

In a bowl, cream butter and sugar. Add egg yolk; mix well. Stir in the flour by hand. On a lightly floured surface, gently knead dough for 2-3 minutes or until thoroughly combined.

Roll into 1-in. balls. Place 2 in. apart on greased baking sheets. Using the end of a wooden spoon handle, make an indention in the center of each. Fill each with 1/4 teaspoon preserves.

Bake at 350° for 13-15 minutes or until edges are lightly browned. Remove to wire racks. Cool. **Yield:** about 2 dozen.

no-bake cereal bars

prep/cook: 20 minutes

With crisp rice cereal and peanut butter, these treats taste almost like candy. Perfect for a big crowd, they make great potluck contributions, bake-sale items or a quick pick-me-up.

Pauline Christiansen
Columbus, Kansas

2 **cups sugar**

2 **cups corn syrup**

1 **jar (40 ounces) chunky peanut butter**

6 **cups Cheerios**

6 **cups crisp rice cereal**

In a large saucepan, cook and stir sugar and corn syrup until the sugar is dissolved. Remove from the heat. Add peanut butter; mix well. Stir in cereals. Spread quickly into two lightly greased 15-in. x 10-in. x 1-in. pans. Cut into bars while warm. **Yield:** about 10 dozen.

quick toffee bars

prep: 15 minutes | **bake:** 10 minutes + cooling

These buttery, beautiful, quick bars are my all-time favorite snack...and a fast way to fill the cookie jar when company's coming!

Jeanette Wubbena
Standish, Michigan

12 whole graham crackers, broken into quarters
1 cup butter
1/2 cup sugar
1 cup chopped nuts
1 cup (6 ounces) semisweet chocolate chips

Line a 15-in. x 10-in. x 1-in. jelly-roll pan with waxed paper and grease the paper. Arrange the graham crackers in pan and set aside.

In a saucepan, melt butter and sugar over medium heat; let boil gently for 3 minutes. Spread evenly over graham crackers. Sprinkle nuts on top.

Bake at 325° for 10 minutes. Cool. Meanwhile, melt chocolate chips; spread over bars and allow to cool again. After chocolate is set, pan can be turned over so waxed paper can be peeled off. Bars can be frozen. **Yield:** 4 dozen.

black walnut butter cookies

prep: 20 minutes | **bake:** 20 minutes

This part of the Show-Me State has an abundance of black walnuts, so I make these cookies pretty often. I created the recipe after a lot of experimentation...and my family thinks they're a hit!

Patsy Bell Hobson
Liberty, Missouri

3/4 cup butter, softened
1 cup all-purpose flour
1/2 cup cornstarch
1/2 cup plus 1 tablespoon confectioners' sugar, *divided*
1/2 cup chopped black walnuts *or* walnuts

In a bowl, cream the butter. Combine the flour, cornstarch and 1/4 cup sugar; add to butter and mix well. Stir in walnuts. Roll into 3/4-in. balls and place 1 in. apart on greased baking sheets.

Bake at 300° for 20-25 minutes or until set. Cool on wire racks. Dust with additional confectioners' sugar. **Yield:** 6 dozen.

cakes & pies

pg. 216

fresh strawberry pie 212
tropical fruit cream pie 213
frosty chocolate pie 213
strawberry chiffon pie 214
candy bar pie .214
frosty peach pie supreme 215
apple german chocolate cake 215
chocolate swirl delight 216
mile-high lime pie 217
cherry cheesecake tarts 217
fruit-filled angel food torte 218
lemon cheese pie 218
creamy watermelon pie 219
berry-banana cheese pie 219
tangy lemonade pie 220
no-bake chocolate torte 220
peach cream pie 221
cherry cream cheese tarts 221
cookie ice cream pie 222
rhubarb cherry pie 222
chocolate peppermint pie 223
rainbow sherbet cake roll 223
fourth of july ice cream cake 224
double chocolate pie 225
rapid raspberry torte 225
chocolate cherry cupcakes 226
chocolate peanut dream pie 226
pear gingerbread cake 227
italian torte 227
cherry angel cake roll 228
apple graham dessert 228
raspberry lime pie 229
cookie ice cream cake 229

pg. 215

pg. 229

fresh strawberry pie

prep: 10 minutes | **cook:** 5 minutes + cooling

If you ask me, this festive fruit pie is almost too pretty to eat! No one seems to be able to resist the juicy whole strawberries and delightfully sweet glaze. Once the strawberry filling comes to a boil, I stir in a few drops of red food coloring for extra flair!

Judy Watson
Newmarket, Ontario

- 1 **cup plus 3 pints fresh strawberries,** *divided*
- 1 **pastry shell (9 inches), baked**
- 2/3 **cup sugar**
- 1/2 **cup water**
- 2 **tablespoons cornstarch**
- 2 **tablespoons cold water**
- 1/2 **cup reduced-fat whipped topping**

With a fork, mash 1 cup strawberries; set aside. Arrange the remaining berries in pastry shell.

In a saucepan, combine sugar and water; cook and stir until sugar is dissolved. Add mashed strawberries and bring to a boil. Combine cornstarch and cold water until smooth. Gradually stir into strawberry mixture. Bring to a boil; cook and stir for 2 minutes or until thickened.

Cool mixture for 15-20 minutes, stirring occasionally. Spoon over berries in pastry. Refrigerate for at least 2 hours. Garnish with whipped topping. **Yield:** 8 servings.

tropical fruit cream pie

prep/cook: 10 minutes

I use crunchy toasted coconut to add a special touch to this sweet and fruity pie. Try it yourself, and you'll see that it can be stirred up in a jiffy with handy pantry staples.

Carolyn Dixon
Wilmar, Arkansas

- 2 cups cold milk
- 1 package (3.4 ounces) instant coconut cream pudding mix
- 1 can (15-1/4 ounces) mixed tropical fruit, drained
- 1/2 cup flaked coconut, toasted
- 1 graham cracker crust (9 inches)

In a bowl, beat the milk and pudding mix for 2 minutes or until smooth. Let stand until slightly thickened, about 2 minutes. Add fruit and coconut; mix well. Pour into crust. Refrigerate until serving. **Yield:** 6-8 servings.

|||UltimateTIP

Toasting adds a deliciously nutty flavor to the popular dessert ingredient, coconut. To toast, spread in a 15-in. x 10-in. x 1-in. baking pan. Bake at 350° for 5-10 minutes or until lightly browned, stirring occasionally. Or, spread in a dry nonstick skillet and heat over low heat until lightly browned, stirring occasionally. Be sure to watch the coconut carefully so it doesn't burn.

- 15 cream-filled chocolate sandwich cookies, crushed
- 1/4 cup butter, melted
- 1 cup cold milk
- 1 package (3.9 ounces) instant chocolate pudding mix
- 2 cups vanilla ice cream, softened

In a large bowl, combine the cookie crumbs and melted butter until crumbly. Press into a greased 9-in. pie plate.

In a large bowl, beat milk and pudding mix on low speed for 2 minutes. Fold in ice cream. Spoon into prepared crust. Cover and freeze for 4 hours or until firm.

Remove the pie from the freezer 15 minutes before serving. **Yield:** 6-8 servings.

frosty chocolate pie

prep: 15 minutes + freezing

This chilled treat takes me back to my childhood because it tastes like a Fudgsicle. With sandwich cookies, chocolate pudding and vanilla ice cream, it's one dessert guaranteed to satisfy the kid in everyone. I like to garnish it with whipped topping and grated chocolate.

Maria Regakis
Somerville, Massachusetts

1 package (.3 ounces)
sugar-free strawberry gelatin

3/4 cup boiling water

1-1/4 cups cold water

1 cup frozen reduced-fat
whipped topping, thawed

2-1/4 cups sliced fresh strawberries,
divided

1 reduced-fat graham cracker
crust (8 inches)

In a large bowl, dissolve gelatin in boiling water. Stir in cold water. Refrigerate until slightly thickened. Fold in the whipped topping and 2 cups of strawberries. Pour into the crust. Refrigerate for 3 hours or until set. Garnish with the remaining strawberries. **Yield:** 8 servings.

strawberry chiffon pie

prep: 15 minutes + chilling

This recipe was given to me by a friend many years ago while we were attending a weight-loss class. I always feel guilt-free when I eat this light, fluffy strawberry pie...and my family loves it.

Gale Spross
Wills Point, Texas

candy bar pie

prep/cook: 20 minutes

Chocolate-almond candy bars in a pie! What's not to like? I love how this rich, impressive pie comes together in less than half an hour. It's the perfect way to complete any meal.

Rosalind Hamilton
Iowa, Louisiana

6 **chocolate bars with almonds
(1.45 ounces *each*)**

1 **container (8 ounces) frozen whipped
topping, thawed**

1 **tablespoon vanilla extract**

1 **prepared graham cracker crust
(8 *or* 9 inches)**

Shaved chocolate, optional

⫴UltimateTIP

When entertaining, it's fun to focus on the presentation of food. Here's a tip for a smooth, clean cut on a chiffon or other refrigerator-type pie. Warm the blade of a sharp knife in a tall glass of hot water, dry the knife blade and make a cut. It's important to clean and rewarm the knife before you make each cut. Voila! You'll have a picture-perfect slice of pie every time.

In a microwave oven, melt the chocolate bars; stir until smooth. Quickly fold into the whipped topping. Stir in the vanilla extract. Spoon into pie crust. Garnish with shaved chocolate, if desired. Chill until ready to serve. **Yield:** 6-8 servings.

frosty peach pie supreme

prep: 10 minutes + freezing

This impressive dessert is just peachy! With only four ingredients, it's a snap to make and always receives thumbs-up approval.

June Formanek
Belle Plaine, Iowa

- **1 cup sliced fresh *or* frozen peaches, *divided***
- **2 cups (16 ounces) fat-free reduced-sugar peach yogurt**
- **1 carton (8 ounces) frozen reduced-fat whipped topping, thawed**
- **1 reduced-fat graham cracker crust (8 inches)**

Finely chop half of the peaches; place in a bowl. Stir in the yogurt. Fold in whipped topping. Spoon into the crust. Cover and freeze for 4 hours or until firm. Refrigerate for 45 minutes before slicing. Top with remaining peaches. **Yield:** 8 servings.

- **1 can (21 ounces) apple pie filling**
- **1 package (18-1/4 ounces) German chocolate cake mix**
- **3 eggs**
- **3/4 cup coarsely chopped walnuts**
- **1/2 cup miniature semisweet chocolate chips**

Place pie filling in a blender; cover and process until the apples are in 1/4-in. chunks. Pour into a bowl; add dry cake mix and eggs. Beat on medium speed for 5 minutes. Pour into a greased 13-in. x 9-in. baking pan. Sprinkle with the nuts and the chocolate chips.

Bake at 350° for 40-45 minutes or until a toothpick inserted near the center comes out clean. Cool completely on a wire rack before cutting. **Yield:** 12-15 servings.

apple german chocolate cake

prep: 15 minutes | **bake:** 40 minutes

This delectable dessert is perfect to bake when unexpected guests stop by. A boxed cake mix and canned pie filling make the moist snack cake a cinch to put together, while mini chocolate chips and walnuts create the quick-and-easy topping.

Shirley Weaver
Zeeland, Michigan

chocolate swirl delight

prep: 20 minutes + chilling

I made a few alterations to a great recipe and ended up with an impressive dessert. Everyone loves its light texture and chocolaty flavor.

Lynne Bargar
Saegertown, Pennsylvania

  1 **package (13 ounces) Swiss cake rolls**
2-3/4 **cups cold milk**
  2 **packages (3.9 ounces *each*) instant chocolate fudge pudding mix**
  2 **cups whipped topping**

Cut each cake roll into eight slices; set aside any chocolate coating that separates from rolls for garnish. Line a 9-in. springform pan with cake slices, completely covering the bottom and sides.

In a small bowl, whisk milk and pudding mixes for 2 minutes. Let stand for 2 minutes or until soft-set. Pour over cake. Spread with whipped topping; sprinkle with any reserved chocolate coating. Cover and refrigerate for at least 2 hours before serving. **Yield:** 12 servings.

mile-high lime pie

prep: 10 minutes + chilling

Convenience items speed along the preparation of this light and fluffy make-ahead pie. The lime filling is very sweet, creamy and piles high in the crust. Add a few drops of green food color to the milk mixture if you'd like.

Candi Smith
Blue Springs, Missouri

1   can (14 ounces) fat-free sweetened condensed milk
1   cup (8 ounces) reduced-fat sour cream
1/3   cup plus 2 tablespoons lime juice
1   carton (8 ounces) frozen reduced-fat whipped topping, thawed
1   reduced-fat graham cracker crust (8 inches)

In a large bowl, combine the milk, sour cream and lime juice. Fold in whipped topping. Pour into the crust. Refrigerate for at least 12 hours. **Yield: 8 servings.**

1   package (10 ounces) frozen puff pastry shells
2   packages (3 ounces *each*) cream cheese, softened
1/4   cup plus 1 tablespoon confectioners' sugar, *divided*
1/2   teaspoon almond extract
1   can (21 ounces) cherry pie filling

Bake pastry shells according to package directions. In a small bowl, beat cream cheese, 1/4 cup sugar and extract. With a fork, carefully remove the circular top of each baked shell and set aside. Remove any soft layers of pastry inside shells and discard.

Spoon the cream cheese filling into shells; place on a baking sheet. Bake at 400° for 5 minutes. Cool for 1 hour. Refrigerate until serving.

Just before serving, spoon pie filling into shells. Top with reserved pastry circles. Dust with remaining sugar. Refrigerate leftovers. **Yield: 6 servings.**

cherry cheesecake tarts

prep: 15 minutes | **bake:** 20 minutes + cooling

Frozen puff pastry shells, cream cheese and cherry pie filling make these attractive tarts simple to prepare. The recipe can easily be doubled if you're entertaining a larger group.

Mary Lindell
Sanford, Michigan

1 carton (12 ounces) frozen reduced-fat whipped topping, thawed, *divided*

1 can (15 ounces) reduced-sugar fruit cocktail, drained

1 prepared angel food cake (10 inches)

1 can (11 ounces) mandarin oranges, drained

1 large navel orange, sliced, optional

Fresh mint, optional

Fold 1-1/2 cups whipped topping into fruit cocktail just until blended. Split cake horizontally into three layers; place one layer on a serving plate. Spread with half of the fruit mixture. Repeat layers. Top with remaining cake layer.

Frost top and sides with remaining whipped topping. Arrange mandarin oranges on top. Refrigerate until serving. Serve with orange slices and mint if desired. **Yield: 12 servings.**

fruit-filled angel food torte

prep/cook: 15 minutes

Tired of eating plain angel food cake or fruit for dessert, I decided to combine the two with a little whipped topping. The result is this scrumptious and refreshing torte. It tastes as good as it looks!

Hettie Johnson
Jacksonville, Florida

lemon cheese pie

prep/cook: 30 minutes

Because this luscious pie can be made ahead and frozen, it's not unusual for me to have one ready to serve in the freezer. I simply remove it from the freezer a few minutes before slicing.

Laura Odell
Eden, North Carolina

1 package (8 ounces) cream cheese, softened

2 cups cold milk, *divided*

1 package (3.4 ounces) instant lemon pudding mix

1/2 teaspoon grated lemon peel

1 graham cracker crust (9 inches)

||| UltimateTIP

There are a few things to look for when buying lemons. Look for ones that are firm, feel heavy for their size and have a bright yellow color. Avoid any with bruises or wrinkles. Store at room temperature for about 3 days. For longer storage, place in your refrigerator's crisper drawer up to 2 to 3 weeks. Lemon juice or grated peel can be frozen for up to 1 year.

In a bowl, beat the cream cheese until smooth. Gradually add 1/2 cup milk. Sprinkle the pudding mix over all. Gradually add the remaining milk and lemon peel; beat until thickened, about 5 minutes. Pour into the crust. Freeze until ready to serve. **Yield: 6-8 servings.**

creamy watermelon pie

prep: 15 minutes + chilling

This simple pie is so refreshing that it never lasts long on warm summer days. Watermelon and a few convenience items make it a delightful dessert that doesn't take much effort. It's perfect for on-the-go cooks.

Velma Beck
Carlinville, Illinois

1 package (3 ounces) watermelon gelatin

1/4 cup boiling water

1 carton (12 ounces) frozen whipped topping, thawed

2 cups cubed seeded watermelon

1 graham cracker crust (9 inches)

In a large bowl, dissolve gelatin in boiling water. Cool to room temperature. Whisk in whipped topping; fold in watermelon. Spoon into crust. Refrigerate for 2 hours or until set. **Yield:** 6-8 servings.

berry-banana cheese pie

prep: 10 minutes + chilling

I made up this recipe from ingredients I had on hand, and we really like it. Strawberry-banana gelatin gives fruity flavor and pretty color to the smooth cheesecake-like pie.

Sharon McClatchery
Muskogee, Oklahoma

1 package (3 ounces) strawberry-banana gelatin

1/4 cup sugar

1 cup boiling water

1 package (8 ounces) cream cheese, cubed

1 carton (8 ounces) whipped topping, thawed

1 extra-serving-size graham cracker crust (9 ounces)

In a large bowl, dissolve the gelatin and sugar in boiling water. Beat in the cubed cream cheese until smooth. Fold in the whipped topping. Pour into crust. Refrigerate for 2 hours or until set. **Yield:** 8 servings.

1 package (.3 ounces)
   sugar-free lemon gelatin

1 package (8 ounces) reduced-
   fat cream cheese, cubed

1-3/4 teaspoons sugar-free
   lemonade drink mix

1 reduced-fat graham cracker
   crust (8 inches)

6 tablespoons reduced-fat
   whipped topping

Prepare gelatin according to package directions. Chill until almost set. Transfer to a blender or food processor. Add cream cheese and lemonade mix; cover and process until smooth. Pour into crust. Refrigerate overnight. Serve with whipped topping. **Yield:** 6 servings.

tangy lemonade pie

prep: 15 minutes + chilling

I really enjoy lemon pie, but I have to watch my sugar intake. I experimented with sugar-free gelatin and lemonade mix to come up with this light pie that's absolutely delicious.

Carol Anderson
West Chicago, Illinois

no-bake chocolate torte

prep/cook: 20 minutes

Here's a delightful dessert that looks and tastes like you fussed all day. With its attractive appearance and wonderful taste, no one will suspect that you saved time by spreading an easy-to-prepare frosting on a store-bought pound cake. For extra flavor and flair, top the treat with toasted almonds.

Taste of Home Test Kitchen
Greendale, Wisconsin

||| Ultimate**TIP**

There are two types of unsweetened cocoa powder: natural and Dutch-processed. Natural cocoa powder tastes bitter and imparts an intense chocolate flavor. If you like a strong chocolate flavor, use it. Dutch processed cocoa powder is alkalized, which neutralizes the cocoa's acidity; it has a milder flavor and is easier to dissolve in liquids.

1 frozen pound cake (10-3/4 ounces),
   thawed

2 cups heavy whipping cream

6 tablespoons confectioners' sugar

6 tablespoons baking cocoa

1/2 teaspoon almond extract

Slice pound cake lengthwise into three layers and set aside. In a large bowl, beat the cream until soft peaks form. Gradually add sugar and cocoa; beat until stiff peaks form. Stir in extract.

Place one layer of cake on a serving platter; top with 1 cup of the frosting. Repeat layers. Frost top and sides with remaining frosting. Chill at least 15 minutes. Refrigerate any leftovers. **Yield:** 4-6 servings.

peach cream pie

prep: 10 minutes | **bake:** 40 minutes

My family loves this dessert and asks for it often. It's a breeze to make and delicious served warm or cold.

Karen Odom
Melbourne, Florida

6 medium ripe peaches, peeled and sliced
1 unbaked deep-dish pastry shell (9 inches)
1/2 cup sugar
3 tablespoons all-purpose flour
1/4 teaspoon salt
3/4 cup heavy whipping cream

Arrange peaches in the pastry shell. In a small bowl, combine sugar, flour and salt; stir in cream until smooth. Pour over peaches.

Bake at 400° for 40-45 minutes or until filling is almost set. Serve warm or cold. Refrigerate leftovers. **Yield:** 6-8 servings.

|||UltimateTIP

To peel peaches, place them in a large pot of boiling water for 10-20 seconds or until the skin splits. Remove with a slotted spoon. Immediately place in an ice water bath to cool the peaches and stop the cooking process. Use a paring knife to peel the skin, which should easily come off. If stubborn areas of skin won't peel off, just return fruit to the boiling water for a few more seconds.

---

cherry cream cheese tarts

prep/cook: 10 minutes

It's hard to believe that just five ingredients and a few minutes of preparation can result in these delicate and scrumptious tarts! They're the perfect dessert for two.

Cindi Mitchell
Waring, Texas

1 package (3 ounces) cream cheese, softened
1/4 cup confectioners' sugar
1/8 to 1/4 teaspoon almond *or* vanilla extract
2 individual graham cracker shells
1/4 cup cherry pie filling

In a small bowl, beat the cream cheese, sugar and extract until smooth. Spoon into shells. Top with pie filling. Refrigerate until serving. **Yield:** 2 servings.

10 cream-filled chocolate
  sandwich cookies, finely
  crushed

3 tablespoons butter, melted

14 whole cream-filled chocolate
  sandwich cookies

FILLING:

1/2 gallon raspberry ripple ice
  cream, softened, *divided*

1/2 cup prepared fudge topping,
  divided

Combine crushed cookies and butter; mix well. Press onto bottom only of a 9-in. pie plate. Stand whole cookies up around edges, pressing lightly into crust. Freeze 1 hour.

For filling, spread half of ice cream over crushed cookies. Drizzle with 1/4 cup of fudge topping. Freeze 1 hour. Spread remaining ice cream on top. Drizzle with remaining fudge topping. Freeze several hours or overnight.

Let pie stand at room temperature about 15 minutes before cutting. **Yield:** 8 servings.

cookie ice cream pie

prep: 25 minutes + freezing

This cool and creamy pie is fun to make with two already prepared ingredients—ice cream and cookies. Because you use your freezer, not your oven, preparing the crunchy, creamy treat on warm days won't heat up the kitchen.

Debbie Walsh
Madison, Wisconsin

rhubarb cherry pie

prep: 10 minutes + standing | **bake:** 40 minutes

Here's a special treat that combines two mouth-watering tastes—rhubarb and cherries. Not only is it a great way to use up rhubarb, but it's a heartwarming dessert you'll turn to time and again.

Eunice Hurt
Murfreesboro, Tennessee

|||UltimateTIP

If using frozen rhubarb in the Rhubarb Cherry Pie, measure it while still frozen, then thaw. Drain in a colander, but do not press the liquid out. If using fresh, look for stalks that are crisp and brightly colored. Wrap in plastic and refrigerate up to 3 days. Wash the stalks and remove the poisonous leaves before using. One pound yields about 3 cups chopped.

3 cups sliced fresh *or* frozen rhubarb
  (1/2-inch pieces)

1 can (16 ounces) pitted tart red
  cherries, drained

1-1/4 cups sugar

1/4 cup quick-cooking tapioca

Pastry for double-crust pie (9 inches)

In a bowl, combine first four ingredients; let stand for 15 minutes. Line a 9-in. pie plate with pastry; add filling. Top with a lattice crust; flute the edges.

Bake at 400° for 40-50 minutes or until crust is golden and filling is bubbling. **Yield:** 8 servings.

chocolate peppermint pie

prep: 15 minutes + freezing

This delightful dessert will satisfy a chocolate lover's craving. The frosty sensation is great during the holidays.

Kristine Dorazio
Chepachet, Rhode Island

- 1 quart chocolate-chocolate chip ice cream, softened
- 1 chocolate cookie crust (9 inches)
- 3 packages (1.84 ounces *each*) chocolate-covered peppermint candies
- 1 cup whipping cream, *divided*

Spoon ice cream into crust. Freeze until firm, about 2 hours. Meanwhile, in a small saucepan, heat candies with 3-4 tablespoons of cream; stir until smooth. Cool. Whip the remaining cream; spoon over ice cream. Drizzle with some of the chocolate-peppermint sauce; serve pie with the remaining sauce. **Yield:** 6-8 servings.

---

rainbow sherbet cake roll

prep: 20 minutes + freezing | **bake:** 20 minutes + cooling

A cake roll doesn't have to be complicated, especially when you start out with an angel food cake mix. For added convenience, this sherbet-filled dessert can be kept in the freezer for weeks.

Karen Edland
McHenry, North Dakota

- 1 package (16 ounces) angel food cake mix
- 1 to 2 tablespoons confectioners' sugar
- 1/2 gallon berry rainbow sherbet

Coat two 15-in. x 10-in. x 1-in. baking pans with cooking spray; line pans with waxed paper and spray the paper. Prepare cake mix according to package directions; spread batter into prepared pans. Bake at 375° for 18-22 minutes or until the top springs back when lightly touched and entire top appears dry.

Cool in pans for 5 minutes. Turn each cake onto a kitchen towel dusted with confectioners' sugar. Gently peel off waxed paper. Roll up cakes in the towels jelly-roll style, starting with a short side. Cool completely on a wire rack.

Unroll cakes; spread each with 4 cups sherbet to within 1/2 in. of edges. Roll up again. Place with seam side down on plastic wrap. Wrap securely; freeze until firm, about 6 hours. Remove from freezer 15 minutes before serving. Cut into 1-in. slices. Freeze leftovers. **Yield:** 20 servings.

fourth of july ice cream cake

prep: 20 minutes + freezing

This eye-catching dessert keeps well in the freezer for days, making it the perfect treat to make before a get-together. Plus, it's nice to be able to serve cake and ice cream in one slice.

Anne Scholovich
Waukesha, Wisconsin

- 1 **prepared angel food cake (10 inches)**
- 2 **quarts strawberry ice cream, softened**
- 1 **quart vanilla ice cream, softened**
- 2-1/2 **cups whipping cream**
- 2 **tablespoons confectioners' sugar**

Cut cake horizontally into four equal layers. Place bottom layer on a serving plate; spread with half of the strawberry ice cream. Immediately place in freezer. Spread second cake layer with vanilla ice cream; place over strawberry layer in freezer. Spread third cake layer with remaining strawberry ice cream; place over vanilla layer in freezer. Top with remaining cake layer.

In a bowl, beat cream until soft peaks form. Add sugar; beat until stiff peaks form. Frost top and sides of cake. Freeze until serving. **Yield:** 12-14 servings.

double chocolate pie

prep: 15 minutes + chilling

If you're watching your weight and you thought your days of luscious chocolate pies were over, think again! This light pudding pie is a rich and creamy treat.

Carol LaNaye Burnette
Sylvan Springs, Alabama

1-1/2 cups cold fat-free milk, *divided*

1 package (1.4 ounces) sugar-free instant chocolate fudge pudding mix

1 carton (8 ounces) frozen fat-free whipped topping, thawed, *divided*

1 reduced-fat graham cracker crust (8 inches)

1 package (1 ounce) sugar-free instant white chocolate *or* vanilla pudding mix

In a bowl, whisk 3/4 cup milk and chocolate pudding mix for 2 minutes or until thickened. Fold in 1-3/4 cups whipped topping. Spread into crust.

In another bowl, whisk the remaining milk and the white chocolate pudding mix for 2 minutes or until slightly thickened. Fold in the remaining whipped topping. Spread over the chocolate layer. Refrigerate for 4 hours or until set. **Yield: 8 servings.**

3/4 cup heavy whipping cream

1 tablespoon confectioners' sugar

2 snack-size cups (3-1/2 ounces *each*) lemon pudding

1 loaf (10-3/4 ounces) frozen pound cake, thawed

1/3 cup raspberry jam, *divided*

rapid raspberry torte

prep/cook: 15 minutes

This tasty, layered dessert is simple to assemble, because it calls for a frozen pound cake, raspberry jam and little cups of prepared lemon pudding.

Ruth Peterson
Jenison, Michigan

In a small bowl, beat cream until soft peaks form. Add confectioners' sugar; beat until stiff peaks form. Place pudding in a bowl; fold in whipped cream.

Cut cake horizontally into three layers. Place bottom layer on a serving plate; top with half the jam. Repeat layers. Top with third cake layer. Cut into slices; dollop with the pudding mixture. **Yield: 7-10 servings.**

Editor's Note: This recipe was tested with Hunt's Snack Pack lemon pudding.

chocolate cherry cupcakes

prep: 15 minutes | **bake:** 20 minutes

A convenient cake mix helps me whip up these special treats. Inside each of my cupcakes is a fruity surprise that everyone seems to enjoy.

Bertille Cooper
California, Maryland

1 package (18-1/4 ounces) chocolate cake mix
1-1/3 cups water
1/2 cup canola oil
3 eggs
1 can (21 ounces) cherry pie filling
1 can (16 ounces) vanilla frosting

In a large bowl, combine the cake mix, water, oil and eggs; beat on low speed for 30 seconds. Beat on medium for 2 minutes.

Spoon batter by 1/4 cupfuls into paper-lined muffin cups. Spoon a rounded teaspoon of pie filling onto the center of each cupcake. Set remaining pie filling aside.

Bake at 350° for 20-25 minutes or until a toothpick inserted on an angle toward the center comes out clean. Remove from pans to wire racks to cool completely.

Frost the cupcakes; top each with one cherry from the pie filling. Serve the additional pie filling with the cupcakes or refrigerate for another use. **Yield:** 2 dozen.

chocolate peanut dream pie

prep: 10 minutes + chilling

I love the flavor of peanut butter cups, so I dreamed up this creamy, rich pie to serve to company. It's wonderfully simple to make and always gets rave reviews.

Rosanne Marshall
Depew, New York

1 package (3.4 ounces) cook-and-serve chocolate pudding mix
1/2 cup creamy peanut butter
1 cup whipped topping
1 graham cracker crust (9 inches)
Peanuts and additional whipped topping, optional

Prepare pudding according to package directions. Remove from the heat; whisk in peanut butter. Place pan in a bowl of ice water for 5 minutes, stirring occasionally. Fold in whipped topping. Pour into the crust. Cover and refrigerate for 1 hour or until set. Garnish with peanuts and whipped topping if desired. **Yield:** 6-8 servings.

pear gingerbread cake

prep: 10 minutes | **bake:** 30 minutes + cooling

You'll need just four items to stir up this tasty gingerbread cake topped with canned pears. You can also use fresh ripe pears when they're in season.

Cindy Reams
Philipsburg, Pennsylvania

1/4 **cup butter, melted**

2 **cans (15-1/4 ounces *each*) sliced pears, drained and patted dry**

1/3 **cup sugar**

1 **package (14-1/2 ounces) gingerbread cake mix**

Spread the butter in a 9-in. square baking dish. Arrange pear slices in rows over the butter. Sprinkle with sugar. Prepare cake mix batter according to package directions. Carefully pour over the pears.

Bake at 350° for 30-35 minutes or until a toothpick inserted near the center comes out clean. Cool on a wire rack for 10 minutes before inverting onto a serving plate. **Yield:** 9 servings.

italian torte

prep/cook: 15 minutes

This is one of my favorite dessert recipes because it's quickly prepared, yet it's very different, delicious and good for any occasion. It is sure to impress your guests as it does mine.

Theresa Stewart
New Oxford, Pennsylvania

1 **cup ricotta cheese**

3 **tablespoons sugar**

1/4 **cup miniature chocolate chips**

1 **loaf (10-3/4 ounces) frozen pound cake, thawed**

In a bowl, combine the ricotta cheese and sugar; mix well. Stir in chocolate chips. Split cake into three horizontal layers. Place bottom layer on a serving plate; top with half of the cheese mixture. Repeat layers. Top with the remaining cake layer. Cover and refrigerate until serving. **Yield:** 6 servings.

cherry angel cake roll

prep: 25 minutes + chilling | **bake:** 10 minutes + cooling

I keep up a fast pace at college but still like to entertain. These pretty party cakes require a handful of ingredients, yet always seem to impress guests.

Lisa Ruehlow
Madison, Wisconsin

- 1 **package (16 ounces) angel food cake mix**
- 4 **tablespoons confectioners' sugar,** *divided*
- 1 **carton (8 ounces) frozen reduced-fat whipped topping, thawed,** *divided*
- 1 **can (20 ounces) reduced-sugar cherry pie filling**
- 1/4 **teaspoon almond extract**

Line two 15-in. x 10-in. x 1-in. baking pans with ungreased parchment paper. Prepare cake batter according to package directions. Spread evenly in prepared pans. Bake at 375° for 12-15 minutes or until cake springs back when lightly touched. Cool for 5 minutes.

Invert the jelly roll onto two kitchen towels dusted with 3 tablespoons confectioners' sugar. Gently peel off parchment paper. Roll up cakes in the towels jelly-roll style, starting with a short side. Cool completely on a wire rack.

Unroll cakes; spread each with 1 cup whipped topping to within 1/2 in. of edges. Combine the pie filling and almond extract; spread over whipped topping on each cake. Roll up again. Place each seam side down on a serving platter. Cover and refrigerate for 1 hour.

Dust the tops of the cakes with remaining confectioners' sugar. Slice, then garnish with the remaining whipped topping. **Yield:** 2 cakes (8 slices each).

raspberry lime pie

prep/cook: 20 minutes

Who can resist a creamy berry pie? Even when time is tight, you'll be able to serve a homemade dessert with this recipe at your fingertips. Add a little red food coloring to the whipped topping if you'd like.

Jane Zempel
Midland, Michigan

- 1 **can (14 ounces) sweetened condensed milk**
- 1/2 **cup lime juice**
- 1 **container (8 ounces) frozen whipped topping, thawed**
- 1 **cup fresh raspberries**
- 1 **graham cracker pie crust (9 inches)**

In a large bowl, stir together milk and lime juice. Mixture will begin to thicken. Beat in whipped topping. Gently fold in raspberries. Spoon into pie crust. Chill. **Yield:** 8 servings.

apple graham dessert

prep: 10 minutes + chilling

My favorite after-school snack was applesauce with graham crackers. I started cooking and baking when I was a very young child, and as far as I can remember, this cake was one of my first creations.

Rita Ferro
Alameda, California

- 6 whole cinnamon graham crackers
- 1 cup applesauce
- 1 cup whipped topping

Chopped walnuts, optional

Place one graham cracker on a serving plate. Spread with 2 heaping tablespoons of applesauce. Repeat layers, ending with applesauce. Spread the whipped topping over top and sides. Sprinkle the dessert with nuts if desired. Refrigerate for 2 hours before slicing. **Yield: 2 servings.**

cookie ice cream cake

prep: 35 minutes + freezing

I discovered this recipe online and changed it a little to suit my family's tastes. It always gets lots of compliments because people love the hot fudge topping and unique cookie crust. My husband says it's the best ice cream cake he's ever had.

Heather McKillip
Auroroa, Illinois

- 44 miniature chocolate chip cookies
- 1/4 cup butter, melted
- 1 cup hot fudge topping, *divided*
- 1 quart vanilla ice cream, softened
- 1 quart chocolate ice cream, softened

Crush 25 cookies; set remaining cookies aside. In a bowl, combine cookie crumbs and butter. Press onto the bottom of a greased 10-in. springform pan. Freeze for 15 minutes.

In a microwave-safe bowl, heat 3/4 cup hot fudge topping on high for 15-20 seconds or until pourable; spread over crust. Arrange reserved cookies around the edge of pan. Freeze for 15 minutes. Spread vanilla ice cream over fudge topping; freeze for 30 minutes. Spread with chocolate ice cream. Cover and freeze until firm. May be frozen for up to 2 months.

Remove from the freezer 10 minutes before serving. Remove sides of pan. Warm the remaining hot fudge topping; drizzle over the top. **Yield: 10-12 servings.**

delightful desserts

pg. 234

ice cream supreme 232
lemon berry trifle 233
cranberry sherbet 233
orange whip 234
refreshing lemon cream 234
strawberry lemon parfaits 235
mint chocolate chip pie 235
citrus sherbet torte 236
minister's delight 237
pound cake cobbler 237
very berry parfaits 238
apple pan betty 238
make-ahead s'mores 239
tropical banana compote 239
individual strawberry trifles 240
toffee coffee ice cream 241
coffee mousse 241
quicker caramel flan 242
cappuccino pudding 242
melon mousse 243
microwave cherry crisp 243
heavenly chocolate mousse 244
apple crisp for two 245
coffee ice cream torte 245
cream puff pyramids 246
blueberry raspberry crunch 246
peanut butter cookie parfait 247
cherry mallow dessert 247

pg. 237

pg. 244

ice cream supreme

prep: 15 minutes + freezing

Summers here in Maine are too short to spend a lot of time in the kitchen, so we're always looking for simple, quick recipes to make. This fast dessert fits our family of ice cream lovers fine.

Kathleen Clapp
Blue Hill, Maine

1 cup (6 ounces) chocolate chips
1/3 cup creamy peanut butter
3 cups crispy rice cereal
1/2 gallon vanilla ice cream, softened

In a small saucepan over low heat, melt chocolate and peanut butter. Add cereal; stir until coated. Spread on waxed paper to cool. Set aside 3/4 cup for topping; combine remaining mixture with ice cream. Spread into a 10-in. springform pan; sprinkle with topping. Freeze for 4 hours or overnight. **Yield:** 10 servings.

lemon berry trifle

prep/cook: 15 minutes

Here's a simple-to-make sweet that's perfect for summer. We enjoy it so much, I make it all year. If fresh berries are not available, use the quick-frozen varieties or just use peaches or nectarines.

Nanci Keatley
Salem, Oregon

5 cups cubed angel food cake
1 carton (8 ounces) lemon yogurt
1 cup whipping topping, *divided*
3 cups mixed fresh berries
Lemon peel, optional

Place cake cubes in a 2-qt. serving bowl or individual dishes. Combine yogurt and 3/4 cup whipped topping; spoon over cake. Top with berries. Top with remaining whipped topping and lemon peel if desired. **Yield:** 4-6 servings.

‖UltimateTIP

Fresh berries should be stored covered in your refrigerator and washed just before using. Use them within 10 days of purchase. To wash berries, place a few at a time in a colander in the sink. Gently wash, then spread on paper towels to pat dry. To remove the stems from strawberries, use a strawberry huller or the tip of a serrated grapefruit spoon.

---

cranberry sherbet

prep: 25 minutes + freezing | **cook:** 10 minutes + cooling

Tired of making the same desserts time after time? Try this sweet and tart sherbet. It's festive, light and a refreshing change of pace.

Heather Clement
Indian River, Ontario

1 package (12 ounces) fresh *or* frozen cranberries
2-3/4 cups water, *divided*
2 cups sugar
1 envelope unflavored gelatin
1/2 cup orange juice

In a saucepan, combine the cranberries and 2-1/2 cups of water. Bring to a boil; cook gently until all the cranberries have popped, about 10 minutes. Remove from heat; cool slightly. Press mixture through a sieve or food mill, reserving juice and discarding skins and seeds.

In another saucepan, combine the cranberry juice and sugar; cook over medium heat until the sugar dissolves. Remove from the heat and set aside.

Combine gelatin and remaining 1/4 cup water; stir until softened. Add cranberry mixture and orange juice to gelatin; mix well. Pour into a 2-qt. container; freeze 4-5 hours or until mixture is slushy. Remove from freezer; beat with electric mixer until sherbet is a bright pink color. Freeze until firm. **Yield:** about 6 cups.

1 can (11 ounces) mandarin oranges, drained and patted dry
1 cup (8 ounces) vanilla yogurt
2 tablespoons orange juice concentrate
2 cups whipped topping

In a large bowl, combine the oranges, yogurt and orange juice concentrate. Fold in the whipped topping. Spoon into serving dishes. Cover and freeze until firm. Remove from the freezer 10 minutes before serving. **Yield:** 4 servings.

orange whip

prep: 10 minutes + freezing

It takes just a few minutes to blend together this silky and smooth whip. Yogurt adds a nice tang to this light, refreshing orange-flavored dessert that's so pretty. It's a real treat to have on warm summer days.

Sue Thomas
Casa Grande, Arizona

|||UltimateTIP

To add a special finishing touch to a variety of desserts, make sugared cranberries and orange peels. First, in a bowl, combine several orange peel strips, 1/3 cup fresh cranberries and 1/2 cup sugar. Stir gently to combine. Cover and refrigerate for 1 hour. Arrange the orange peel strips and cranberries on top of the dessert just before serving.

refreshing lemon cream

prep: 10 minutes + freezing

Fresh lemon juice provides the tart flavor in this cool and rich ice cream recipe. The refreshing make-ahead treat can be prepared without an ice cream maker and looks splendid and summery when served in individual cups made from lemon halves.

Taste of Home Test Kitchen
Greendale, Wisconsin

2 cups heavy whipping cream
1 cup sugar
1/3 cup lemon juice
1 tablespoon grated lemon peel
Lemon boats, optional

In a bowl, stir the cream and sugar until sugar is dissolved. Stir in the lemon juice and peel (mixture will thicken slightly). Cover and freeze until firm, about 4 hours. Remove from the freezer 15 minutes before serving. Serve in lemon boats or individual dishes. **Yield:** 6 servings.

strawberry lemon parfaits

prep/cook: 10 minutes

No one will believe this fruit-and-citrus treat came from only three ingredients. Surprise your gang with the layered delight tonight.

Joy Beck
Cincinnati, Ohio

1 **pint fresh strawberries**

3 **tablespoons sugar**

3 **cartons (8 ounces *each*) lemon yogurt**

In a food processor, combine strawberries and sugar. Process for 20-30 seconds or until berries are coarsely chopped. Divide half of the mixture into four parfait glasses or bowls; top with yogurt. Garnish with additional berries if desired. **Yield: 4 servings.**

mint chocolate chip pie

prep: 10 minutes + freezing

You'll need only a few ingredients to fix this yummy dessert that features a cool combination of mint and chocolate. When time is short, it's so handy to pull this no-fuss pie out of the freezer.

Dolores Scofield
West Shokan, New York

6 **to 8 cups mint chocolate chip ice cream, softened**

1 **chocolate crumb crust (9 inches)**

2 **squares (1 ounce *each*) semisweet chocolate**

Spoon ice cream into crust. In a microwave-safe bowl, melt chocolate; stir until smooth. Drizzle over ice cream. Freeze for 6-8 hours or overnight. Remove from the freezer 15 minutes before serving. Pie may be frozen for up to 2 months. **Yield: 6-8 servings.**

citrus sherbet torte

prep: 15 minutes + freezing
bake: 40 minutes + cooling

When my mother-in-law first served this colorful torte, I thought it was the prettiest dessert I ever saw. Not only does it keep well in the freezer, but different flavors of sherbet can be used to reflect the colors of the season.

Betty Tabb
Mifflintown, Pennsylvania

- 1 **package (16 ounces) angel food cake mix**
- 2 **pints orange sherbet**
- 2 **pints lime sherbet**
- 1 **carton (12 ounces) frozen whipped topping, thawed**

Assorted cake decorator sprinkles, optional

Prepare and bake the cake according to package directions, using an ungreased 10-in. tube pan. Cool.

Immediately invert pan; cool completely, about 1 hour. Run a knife around side and center tube of pan; split horizontally into three layers.

Place bottom layer on a serving plate; spread with orange sherbet. Top with the second layer; spread with lime sherbet. Top with remaining cake layer. Frost top and side with whipped topping. Decorate with colored sprinkles if desired. Freeze until serving.
Yield: 12-14 servings.

minister's delight

prep: 5 minutes | **cook:** 2 hours

You'll need a can of cherry pie filling, a yellow cake mix and just two other ingredients to simmer up this warm dessert. A friend gave me the recipe several years ago, saying that a minister's wife fixed it every Sunday, so she named it accordingly.

Mary Ann Potter
Blue Springs, Missouri

1 can (21 ounces) cherry *or* apple pie filling

1 package (18-1/4 ounces) yellow cake mix

1/2 cup butter, melted

1/3 cup chopped walnuts, optional

Place pie filling in a 1-1/2-qt. slow cooker. Combine cake mix and butter (mixture will be crumbly); sprinkle over filling. Sprinkle with walnuts if desired. Cover and cook on low for 2-3 hours. Serve in bowls. **Yield:** 10-12 servings.

pound cake cobbler

prep/cook: 15 minutes

Frozen pound cake and canned pie filling take the work out of making dessert in this appealing delight. It's perfect for just about any occasion you can name, making it ideal for today's busy cooks.

Heidi Wilcox
Lapeer, Michigan

1 frozen pound cake (10-3/4 ounces), thawed

1 can (21 ounces) cherry *or* blueberry pie filling

1/3 cup water

1/2 teaspoon almond extract

Whipped topping

2 tablespoons sliced almonds, toasted

Cut cake into 1-in. cubes. Place in a microwave-safe 1-1/2-qt. dish or 9-in. pie plate. In a small bowl, combine the pie filling, water and extract; spoon over cake.

Cover and microwave on high for 2-4 minutes or until heated through. Spoon onto dessert plates; garnish with whipped topping and almonds. **Yield:** 4 servings.

Editor's Note: This recipe was tested in a 1,100-watt microwave.

1 package (.3 ounce) sugar-free strawberry gelatin

1 cup boiling water

1 cup cold water

2 cups fresh *or* frozen blueberries, *divided*

2 cups sliced fresh *or* frozen unsweetened strawberries, *divided*

1-3/4 cups cold fat-free milk

1 package (1 ounce) sugar-free instant vanilla pudding mix

In a large bowl, dissolve gelatin in boiling water. Stir in cold water. Pour into eight parfait glasses; refrigerate until firm, about 1 hour.

Top with half of the blueberries and half of the strawberries. In a large bowl, whisk milk and pudding mix for 2 minutes. Let stand for 2 minutes or until soft-set. Pour over berries. Top with remaining berries. Cover and refrigerate 1 hour longer. **Yield:** 8 servings.

very berry parfaits

prep: 15 minutes + chilling

When I asked drop-in company to stay for dinner, I happened to have all the ingredients on hand to create this elegant layered berry treat. Everyone raved about this yummy and refreshing low-sugar dessert.

Andree Garrett
Plymouth, Michigan

apple pan betty

prep/cook: 15 minutes

I found this recipe right after I was married. Forty-seven years later, it's still a favorite during fall and winter, when apples are at their best.

Shirley Leister
West Chester, Pennsylvania

1 medium apple, peeled and cubed

3 tablespoons butter

1 cup bread cubes

3 tablespoons sugar

1/4 teaspoon ground cinnamon

In a small skillet, saute the apple in butter for 2-3 minutes or until tender. Add the bread cubes. Sprinkle with sugar and cinnamon; toss to coat. Saute until bread is warmed. **Yield:** 2 servings.

|||UltimateTIP

Looking for ways to use up apples? Try one of these two-person desserts.

* For baked apples, core apples and stuff with brown sugar, cinnamon and butter. Place in a pan with a little water; bake until apples are tender.

* Blend a package of cream cheese with brown sugar and vanilla to taste. Serve as a dip with crisp apple slices.

make-ahead s'mores

prep/cook: 20 minutes

These are perfect little snacks to keep on hand for when unexpected company drops by.

Anne Sherman
Orangeburg, South Carolina

- 8 ounces semisweet chocolate
- 1 can (14 ounces) sweetened condensed milk
- 1 teaspoon vanilla extract
- 16 whole graham crackers, halved
- 2 cups miniature marshmallows

In a heavy saucepan, melt chocolate over low heat. Add milk; cook and stir until smooth. Stir in vanilla. Making one s'more at a time, spread 1 tablespoon chocolate mixture over each of two graham cracker halves. Place eight or nine marshmallows on one cracker; gently press the other cracker on top. Repeat. Wrap in plastic wrap; store at room temperature. **Yield:** 16 s'mores.

- 3 medium firm bananas
- 1/4 cup orange juice
- 2 tablespoons butter
- 3 tablespoons brown sugar
- 2 tablespoons flaked coconut, toasted

Cut the bananas in half lengthwise, then cut widthwise into quarters. Arrange in a greased 11-in. x 7-in. baking dish.

In a saucepan, combine orange juice, butter and brown sugar; cook and stir until sugar is dissolved and butter is melted. Pour over the bananas.

Bake, uncovered, at 350° for 10-12 minutes. Spoon into individual serving dishes; sprinkle with coconut. **Yield:** 4 servings.

tropical banana compote

prep/cook: 20 minutes

Don't limit your use of bananas to the cereal bowl. Instead, send your taste buds on a "trip" to the tropics with this special and speedy dessert. Bananas are available during every season, so this is bound to become a favorite all year round.

Taste of Home Test Kitchen
Greendale, Wisconsin

individual strawberry trifles

prep/cook: 20 minutes

These delicious little trifles are loaded with berries and pound cake cubes then drizzled with a decadent homemade chocolate sauce. I like to sprinkle each one with a little confectioners' sugar.

Karen Scaglione
Nanuet, New York

1/2 **cup semisweet chocolate chips**
1/2 **cup heavy whipping cream**
  2 **tablespoons orange juice**
  2 **cups sliced fresh strawberries**
  4 **slices pound cake, cubed**

In a small saucepan, melt chocolate chips with cream over low heat; stir until blended. Remove from the heat; stir in orange juice. Cool to room temperature.

In four dessert glasses or bowls, layer the strawberries, cake cubes and chocolate mixture. **Yield:** 4 servings.

toffee coffee ice cream

prep/cook: 10 minutes

Need an afternoon pick-me-up? Try this perky ice cream with almonds, toffee and miniature marshmallows. It'll make the rest of the day a little sweeter.

Taste of Home Test Kitchen
Greendale, Wisconsin

- 1 **pint coffee ice cream, softened**
- 1/4 **cup miniature marshmallows**
- 1/4 **cup milk chocolate-covered almonds, halved**
- 1 **English toffee candy bar, chopped**

In a bowl, combine ice cream, marshmallows, almonds and chopped candy bar until blended. Serve immediately. **Yield:** 5 servings.

- 1 **envelope unflavored gelatin**
- 1/4 **cup cold water**
- 2 **teaspoons instant coffee granules**
- 1/4 **cup boiling water**

Sugar substitute equivalent to 2 teaspoons sugar

- 2 **ice cubes**
- 2 **cups plus 4 tablespoons reduced-fat whipped topping,** *divided*

Additional coffee granules, crushed

In a small bowl, sprinkle the gelatin over cold water; let stand for 2 minutes. In a small saucepan, dissolve the coffee granules in boiling water. Add gelatin mixture; cook and stir just until the gelatin is dissolved (do not boil).

Remove from the heat; stir in the sugar substitute. Add ice cubes; stir until ice is melted and mixture begins to thicken. Transfer to a large bowl; add 2/3 cup whipped topping. Beat until blended. Fold in 1-1/3 cups whipped topping.

Spoon into four individual serving dishes; top each with 1 tablespoon whipped topping. Refrigerate for at least 2 hours. Just before serving, dust with crushed coffee granules. **Yield:** 4 servings.

Editor's Note: This recipe was tested with Splenda no-calorie sweetener.

coffee mousse

prep: 15 minutes + chilling

The recipe for this very low-sugar dessert comes from my daughter. Its texture is light as a cloud, and its flavor is perfect for coffee lovers.

Vernette Dechaine
Pittsfield, Maine

5 eggs
1/2 cup sugar
1 teaspoon vanilla extract
1/8 teaspoon salt
2-1/2 cups milk
2 tablespoons caramel ice cream topping

In a small bowl, whisk the eggs, sugar, vanilla and salt. Gradually stir in milk. Spoon 1 teaspoon caramel topping into each of six ungreased 6-oz. custard cups.

Place cups in a 13-in. x 9-in. baking dish. Pour egg mixture into each cup (cups will be full). Fill baking dish with 1 in. of hot water.

Bake, uncovered, at 350° for 30-35 minutes or until centers are almost set (mixture will jiggle). Remove custard cups from water to a wire rack; cool for 30 minutes.

Refrigerate for 3 hours or until thoroughly chilled. Invert and unmold onto rimmed dessert dishes. **Yield:** 6 servings.

quicker caramel flan

prep: 15 minutes | **bake:** 30 minutes + chilling

Like to order flan at restaurants? Now you can enjoy the popular dish in your home…without much effort!

Taste of Home Test Kitchen
Greendale, Wisconsin

|||Ultimate**TIP**

Two keys to perfect custard are timing and proper oven temperature. Underbaking results in a runny custard, while overbaking can cause a watery custard. To check for proper doneness, insert a clean knife near the center before the recommended baking time. When the knife comes out clean, the custard is done. The center may jiggle, but will firm up as it cools.

---

cappuccino pudding

prep/cook: 20 minutes

With its fun combination of chocolate, coffee and cinnamon, this smooth dessert is one of my most requested dishes. Garnish it with whipped topping and chocolate wafer crumbs for additional appeal.

Cindy Bertrand
Floydada, Texas

4 teaspoons instant coffee granules
1 tablespoon boiling water
1-1/2 cups cold fat-free milk
1 package (1.4 ounces) sugar-free instant chocolate (fudge) pudding mix
1/2 teaspoon ground cinnamon
1 cup reduced-fat whipped topping

Dissolve coffee in water; set aside. In a bowl, combine milk, pudding mix and cinnamon. Beat on low speed for 2 minutes. Stir in coffee. Fold in whipped topping. Spoon into serving dishes. **Yield:** 4 servings.

melon mousse

prep: 15 minutes + chilling

This unique summer dessert is low in fat and a creative way to use cantaloupe. I think it's best when made with very ripe melon, which gives the sweetest flavor.

Sandra McKenzie
Braham, Minnesota

2 **envelopes unflavored gelatin**

3 **tablespoons lemon juice**

4 **cups cubed ripe cantaloupe**

1 **tablespoon sugar**

1 **carton (8 ounces) fat-free lemon yogurt**

In a small saucepan, sprinkle gelatin over lemon juice; let stand for 1 minute. Heat over low heat, stirring until gelatin is completely dissolved.

In a blender, combine gelatin mixture, cantaloupe and sugar; cover and process until smooth.

Transfer to a bowl; stir in the lemon yogurt. Spoon into individual parfait glasses; chill until firm. **Yield: 6 servings.**

microwave cherry crisp

prep/cook: 20 minutes

My tasty treat uses a time-saving method to produce old-fashioned flavor. It tastes just like an oven-baked crisp with half the fuss and mess. Serve it warm alongside a scoop of ice cream.

Debra Morello
Edwards, California

1 **can (21 ounces) cherry pie filling**

3/4 **cup packed brown sugar**

2/3 **cup quick-cooking oats**

1/3 **cup all-purpose flour**

1/4 **cup butter, cubed**

Spoon filling into a greased 9-in. pie plate. In a small bowl, combine the brown sugar, oats and flour; cut in the butter until crumbly. Sprinkle over filling. Microwave on high for 7-9 minutes. **Yield: 4-6 servings.**

Editor's Note: This recipe was tested in a 1,100-watt microwave.

heavenly
chocolate mousse

prep: 30 minutes + cooling

"Heaven on a spoon" is how one friend describes this chocolaty dessert. My husband, Allen, rates it best of all the special treats I've made. The filling can also be used for a pie.

Christy Freeman
Central Point, Oregon

8 **squares (1 ounce *each*) semisweet chocolate, coarsely chopped**

1/2 **cup water, *divided***

2 **tablespoons butter**

3 **egg yolks**

2 **tablespoons sugar**

1-1/4 **cups heavy whipping cream, whipped**

In a microwave-safe bowl, microwave the chocolate, 1/4 cup water and butter until the chocolate and butter are melted; stir until smooth. Cool for 10 minutes.

In a small heavy saucepan, whisk egg yolks, sugar and remaining water. Cook and stir over medium heat until mixture reaches 160° or is thick enough to coat the back of a metal spoon. Remove from the heat; whisk in chocolate mixture.

Set saucepan in ice and stir until cooled, about 5-10 minutes. Fold in whipped cream. Spoon into dessert dishes. Refrigerate for 4 hours or overnight. **Yield:** 6-8 servings.

apple crisp for two

prep: 10 minutes | **bake:** 25 minutes

I like to make this dessert in autumn, when the apple crop is fresh and delicious. I often bake it while we are having dinner so it can be served warm. It's perfect for the two of us. We like ours topped with rich whipped cream and a sprinkle of cinnamon.

Emma Crowder
Anaheim, California

2 medium tart apples, peeled and sliced
3 tablespoons water
3 tablespoons graham cracker crumbs
3 tablespoons sugar
1/4 teaspoon ground cinnamon
2 tablespoons cold butter

Place apples in a greased 1-qt. baking dish; pour water over apples. In a bowl, combine the graham cracker crumbs, sugar and cinnamon. Cut in butter until crumbly. Sprinkle over apples.

Bake, uncovered, at 350° for 25-30 minutes or until apples are tender. **Yield:** 2 servings.

---

2 packages (3 ounces *each*) ladyfingers
1 cup chocolate-covered English toffee bits *or* 4 Heath candy bars (1.4 ounces *each*), crushed, *divided*
1/2 gallon coffee ice cream, softened
1 carton (8 ounces) frozen whipped topping, thawed

Place ladyfingers around the edge of a 9-in. springform pan. Line the bottom of the pan with remaining ladyfingers. Stir 1/2 cup toffee bits into the ice cream; spoon into prepared pan. Cover with plastic wrap; freeze overnight or until firm. May be frozen for up to 2 months.

Just before serving, remove sides of pan. Garnish with the whipped topping and remaining toffee bits. **Yield:** 16 servings.

coffee ice cream torte

prep: 20 minutes + freezing

This make-ahead dessert goes over big with company, and calls for only four ingredients. If you can't find coffee-flavored ice cream, dissolve instant coffee granules in warm water and stir into plain vanilla ice cream.

Janet Hutts
Gainesville, Georgia

Delightful Desserts

2 cans (21 ounces *each*) cherry pie filling

24 to 32 frozen cream-filled miniature cream puffs, thawed

1 cup (6 ounces) semisweet chocolate chips, melted

3 tablespoons confectioners' sugar

Whipped cream in a can

In a small saucepan, warm the cherry pie filling over medium-low heat just until heated through. Place three or four cream puffs on each dessert plate.

Place the melted chocolate in a small resealable plastic bag; cut a small hole in a corner of the bag. Spoon about 1/4 cup of warm pie filling over cream puffs; drizzle with chocolate. Dust with confectioners' sugar; garnish with whipped cream. **Yield:** 8 servings.

cream puff pyramids

prep/cook: 15 minutes

I love that that these quick-to-assemble desserts call for only a handful of ingredients, including store-bought miniature cream puffs and whipped cream. Nothing could be simpler or more elegant for a special occasion.

Saundra Busby
West Columbia, South Carolina

⫼UltimateTIP

Before melting chocolate chips, be sure that all of your equipment and utensils are completely dry. Any moisture may cause the chocolate to stiffen or "seize." Chocolate that has seized can sometimes be saved by immediately adding 1 tablespoon vegetable oil for each 6 ounces of chocolate. Slowly heat the mixture and stir until smooth.

blueberry raspberry crunch

prep/cook: 30 minutes

Canned pie filling and a cake mix take the work out of preparing this heartwarming delight.

Harriett Catlin
Nanticoke, Maryland

1 can (21 ounces) blueberry pie filling

1 can (21 ounces) raspberry pie filling

1 package (18-1/4 ounces) white cake mix

1/2 cup chopped walnuts

1/2 cup butter, melted

Combine pie fillings in a greased 13-in. x 9-in. baking dish. In a bowl, combine the cake mix, walnuts and butter until crumbly; sprinkle over filling.

Bake at 375° for 25-30 minutes or until the filling is bubbly and topping is golden brown. Serve warm. **Yield:** 12 servings.

peanut butter cookie parfait

prep/cook: 15 minutes

You'll need just a few moments to assemble this cool, creamy and crunchy dessert. The single-serving sundae is a perfect way to treat yourself...or someone special.

Jamie Wright
Kalamazoo, Michigan

- 3 peanut butter cookies, coarsely chopped
- 2/3 cup vanilla ice cream
- 3 tablespoons hot fudge ice cream topping, warmed

Set aside one large cookie piece. Sprinkle half of the chopped cookies in a parfait glass; top with half of the ice cream and hot fudge topping. Repeat. Garnish with the reserved cookie piece. **Yield: 1 serving.**

cherry mallow dessert

prep: 25 + freezing

For a swift treat, I spread a homemade graham cracker crust with pie filling, then top it with a fun marshmallow and whipped cream layer. You can also prepare it with blueberry pie filling.

Carol Heppner
Caronport, Saskatchewan

- 1-1/2 cups graham cracker crumbs
- 1/3 cup butter, melted
- 1 can (21 ounces) cherry pie filling
- 3 cups miniature marshmallows
- 1 cup heavy whipping cream, whipped

Set aside 1 tablespoon graham cracker crumbs for topping. Place the remaining crumbs in a bowl; stir in butter until combined. Press into a greased 9-in. square baking pan. Bake at 350° for 10-12 minutes or until lightly browned. Cool completely.

Spread pie filling over crust. Fold marshmallows into the whipped cream; spread over filling. Sprinkle with the reserved crumbs. Refrigerate for at least 6 hours. **Yield: 9 servings.**

general recipe index

APPETIZERS

Dips & Spreads
Baked Asparagus Dip, 6
Brie in Puff Pastry, 7
Coconut Fruit Dip, 15
Dairy Delicious Dip, 33
Dreamy Fruit Dip, 20
Easy Black Bean Salsa, 18
Guacamole Dip, 20
Refreshing Fruit Dip, 30
Smoked Salmon Dip, 9
Taffy Apple Dip, 13

Hot Appetizers
Asparagus in Puff Pastry, 19
Basil-Buttered French Bread, 168
Black Bean Quesadillas, 11
Buffet Meatballs, 28
Buttery French Bread, 162
Cheddar Bacon Toasts, 172
Cheddar-Salsa Biscuit Strips, 171
Cheese Bread, 176
Cheese Toast, 167
Cheesy Zucchini Bites, 16
Crispy Garlic Breadsticks, 177
Crunchy Cheese Toasts, 173
Garlic Bread, 157
Italian Sausage Mushrooms, 37
Like 'Em Hot Wings, 26
Mozzarella Pepperoni Bread, 156
Mushroom Bread Wedges, 159
Mushroom Puffs, 24
Pizza Sticks, 166
Poppy Seed French Bread, 164
Ranch Garlic Bread, 156
Ricotta Tart, 27
Sausage-Stuffed Jalapenos, 31
Shrimp with Basil-Mango Sauce, 23
Speedy Pizza Rings, 34
Sweet & Saucy Meatballs, 26
Turkey Nachos, 15

Snacks
Apple Cartwheels, 10
California Fried Walnuts, 17
Cheese Crisps, 165
Colorful Fruit Kabobs, 25
Confetti Snack Mix, 9
Crunchy Cheese Nibblers, 16
Crunchy Trail Mix, 35
Dragon Dippers, 29
Parmesan Popcorn, 11
Sweet Graham Snacks, 206
Tortilla Snack Strips, 13

APPLES
Apple Cartwheels, 10
Apple Cinnamon Bismarcks, 168
Apple Crisp for Two, 245
Apple German Chocolate Cake, 215
Apple Graham Dessert, 228
Apple Grape Drink, 7
Apple Pan Betty, 238
Apple Pinwheels, 167
Brie in Puff Pastry, 7
Broccoli Apple Salad, 55
Cran-Apple Sauce, 146
Taffy Apple Dip, 13

APRICOTS
Apricot Cashew Clusters, 189
Apricot-Glaze Chicken, 105

ASPARAGUS
Asparagus in Puff Pastry, 19
Asparagus with Blue Cheese
    Sauce, 134
Baked Asparagus Dip, 6

AVOCADOS
Avocado Bacon Sandwiches, 63
Guacamole Dip, 20

BACON
Avocado Bacon Sandwiches, 63
Ballpark Baked Beans, 137
Baby Corn Romaine Salad, 49
Beans with Celery Bacon Sauce, 135
BLT Pasta Salad, 55
Cheddar Bacon Toasts, 172
Stuffed Bacon Burgers, 79
Sweet-Sour Lettuce Salad, 44
Tortellini Carbonara, 84

BANANAS
Banana Cocoa Smoothies, 37
Berry-Banana Cheese Pie, 219
Cherry Yogurt Smoothies, 14
Chocolate Banana Smoothies, 14
Grandmother's Orange Salad, 54
Smooth Vanilla Shakes, 19
Tropical Banana Compote, 239

BARS
Caramel Corn Chocolate Bars, 183
Cherry Squares, 190
Chewy Walnut Bars, 186
Chocolate Chip Cheese Bars, 181
Chocolate-Covered Peanut Butter Bars, 186
Chocolate Marshmallow Squares, 206
Crispy Kiss Squares, 190
German Chocolate Bars, 205
Gooey Chip Bars, 197
Honey Cereal Bars, 198
Microwave Oatmeal Bars, 199
No-Bake Cereal Bars, 208
Quick Toffee Bars, 209
Salted Nut Squares, 195
S'mores Crumb Bars, 201
Sweet Graham Snacks, 206
Toffee Crunch Grahams, 207
White Chocolate Cereal Bars, 191

BEANS & LENTILS
Baked Bean Corn Bread, 158
Black Bean Quesadillas, 11
Easy Black Bean Salsa, 18
Two-Bean Salad, 41
Vegetarian Pasta, 120

BEEF *(also see Ground Beef)*
Barbecued Beef Sandwiches, 79
Beef 'n' Cheese Tortillas, 71
Beef Onion Soup, 68
Beef Veggie Casserole, 91
Fiesta Rib Eye Steaks, 92
Flavorful Beef Brisket, 94
Italian Beef Sandwiches, 76
Party Chicken, 102
Roast Beef and Gravy, 85
Slow-Cooked Swiss Steak, 94

BEVERAGES & SMOOTHIES
Apple Grape Drink, 7
Banana Cocoa Smoothies, 37
Berry Yogurt Shakes, 17
Butterscotch Coffee, 8
Cherry Yogurt Smoothies, 14
Chocolate Banana Smoothies, 14
Creamy Strawberry Breeze, 8
Easy Mint Hot Chocolate, 23
Frappe Mocha, 12
Frosted Chocolate Malted Shakes, 21
Fruity Red Smoothies, 25
Pear Cooler, 34
Raspberry Lemon Smoothie, 29
Raspberry Mint Cooler, 22
Smooth Vanilla Shakes, 19
Sparkling Rhubarb Spritzer, 32
Special Lemonade, 33
Springtime Lime Slushy, 28
Strawberry Cooler, 10

Ultimate**Five**Ingredient Recipes

Strawberry Lemonade Slush, 36
Sunny Slush, 31
Sunset Cooler, 27
Winter Warmer, 21

BISCUITS & POPOVERS
Apple Cinnamon Bismarcks, 168
Beefy Biscuit Cups, 169
Beer 'n' Brat Biscuits, 161
Biscuit Bites, 165
Cheddar-Salsa Biscuit Strips, 171
Garlic Crescent Rolls, 174
Kid's Favorite Biscuits, 163
Paprika Cheese Biscuits, 168
Popovers, 173

BLUEBERRIES
Blueberry Raspberry Crunch, 246
Chilled Blueberry Soup, 66
Sour Cream Blueberry Muffins, 160
Very Berry Parfaits, 238

BROCCOLI
Baby Corn Romaine Salad, 49
Broccoli Apple Salad, 55
Broccoli Casserole, 131
Broccoli with Mock Hollandaise, 143
Broccoli with Orange Sauce, 148

BURGERS (see Sandwiches)

CABBAGE & SAUERKRAUT
Country Cabbage Soup, 58
Reuben Burgers, 65
Simple Cabbage Slaw, 45

CAKES & CUPCAKES
Apple German Chocolate Cake, 215
Cappuccino Chip Cupcakes, 32
Cherry Angel Cake Roll, 228
Chocolate Cherry Cupcakes, 226
Chocolate Swirl Delight, 216
Cookie Ice Cream Cake, 229
Fourth of July Ice Cream Cake, 224
Pear Gingerbread Cake, 227
Pound Cake Cobbler, 237
Rainbow Sherbet Cake Roll, 223

CANDIES
Apricot Cashew Clusters, 189
Butterscotch Peanut Candy, 182
Butterscotch Taffy, 203
Cherry Almond Bark, 185
Chocolate Mousse Balls, 194
Chocolate Truffles, 182
Christmas Candies, 204
Crisp Peanut Candies, 181
Crunchy Chocolate Cups, 199
Dairy State Fudge, 198
Layered Mint Candies, 188
Marshmallow Fudge, 192
Old-Time Butter Crunch Candy, 189
Peanut Butter Chocolate Cups, 187
Peanut Butter Fudge, 185
Terrific Toffee, 196
Truffle Cups, 197

CARROTS
Baked Carrots, 131
Buttery Peas and Carrots, 151
Skillet Ranch Vegetables, 139
Spiced Carrot Strips, 145

CASSEROLES
Main Dishes
Beef & Rice Enchiladas, 89
Beef Veggie Casserole, 91
Enchilada Casserole, 84
Hamburger Casserole, 87
Italian Bow Tie Bake, 115
Lazy Lasagna, 118
Save a Penny Casserole, 82
Spinach Ravioli Bake, 95
Spinach Rice Ham Bake, 90
Tomato Macaroni Casserole, 123
Wild Rice Mushroom Chicken, 99
Side Dishes
Broccoli Casserole, 131
Cheesy Hash Brown Bake, 139
Double Cheddar Hash Browns, 130
Perfect Scalloped Oysters, 135
Potatoes Supreme, 138

CHEESE
(also see Cream Cheese)
Asparagus with Blue Cheese Sauce, 134
Baked Swiss Chicken, 107
Barbecue Jack Chicken, 101
Beef 'n' Cheese Tortillas, 71
Black Bean Quesadillas, 11
Blue Cheese Salad Dressing, 41
Brie in Puff Pastry, 7
Budget Macaroni and Cheese, 125
Cheddar Bacon Toasts, 172
Cheddar Cheese Sauce, 130
Cheddar Chili Braid, 166
Cheddar-Salsa Biscuit Strips, 171
Cheese Bread, 176
Cheese Crisps, 165
Cheese Danish Dessert, 175
Cheese Potato Puff, 133
Cheese Toast, 167
Cheesy Hash Brown Bake, 139
Cheesy Zucchini Bites, 16
Creamy Parmesan Sauce, 136
Crunchy Cheese Nibblers, 16
Crunchy Cheese Toasts, 173
Double Cheddar Hash Browns, 130
Green Chili Grilled Cheese, 62
Grilled Chicken Cordon Bleu, 110
Ham 'n' Cheddar Corn Bread, 59
Italian Grilled Cheese, 61
Jalapeno Swiss Burgers, 68
Mini Blue Cheese Rolls, 172
Mozzarella Ham Stromboli, 86
Mozzarella Pepperoni Bread, 156
Paprika Cheese Biscuits, 168
Parmesan Cheese Straws, 177
Parmesan Noodles, 151
Parmesan Popcorn, 11

Prosciutto Provolone Panini, 72
Ricotta Tart, 27
Speedy Pizza Rings, 34
Spinach Rice Ham Bake, 90
Tailgate Sausages, 93

CHERRIES
Cherry Almond Bark, 185
Cherry Angel Cake Roll, 228
Cherry Cheesecake Tarts, 217
Cherry Cream Cheese Tarts, 221
Cherry Danish, 155
Cherry Mallow Dessert, 247
Cherry Squares, 190
Cherry Yogurt Smoothies, 14
Chocolate Cherry Cupcakes, 226
Fruity Green Salad, 49
Microwave Cherry Crisp, 243
Minister's Delight, 237
Pound Cake Cobbler, 237
Rhubarb Cherry Pie, 222

CHICKEN
Apricot-Glaze Chicken, 105
Baked Lemon Chicken, 100
Baked Swiss Chicken, 107
Barbecue Jack Chicken, 101
Chicken in a Haystack, 102
Chicken in Baskets, 106
Chicken Rice Soup, 60
Chicken Salsa Pizza, 101
Cranberry Chicken, 111
Easy Chicken and Noodles, 104
Garlic Chicken Penne, 103
Grilled Chicken Cordon Bleu, 110
Grilled Chicken with Peach Sauce, 103
Honey Baked Chicken, 99
Honey Mustard Chicken, 105
Lemon Chicken Soup, 78
Like 'Em Hot Wings, 26
Party Chicken, 102
Pecan-Crusted Chicken, 111
Pesto Chicken Pasta, 109
Salsa Chicken Soup, 73
Savory Chicken Dinner, 98
Simple Salsa Chicken, 110
Southern Fried Chicken, 109
Stuffing-Coated Chicken, 108
Wild Rice Mushroom Chicken, 99

CHOCOLATE
Apple German Chocolate Cake, 215
Banana Cocoa Smoothies, 37
Cappuccino Chip Cupcakes, 32
Caramel Corn Chocolate Bars, 183
Cherry Almond Bark, 185
Chocolate Banana Smoothies, 14
Chocolate Cherry Cupcakes, 226
Chocolate Chip Cheese Bars, 181
Chocolate-Covered Peanut Butter Bars, 186
Chocolate Marshmallow Squares, 206
Chocolate Mousse Balls, 194
Chocolate Peanut Dream Pie, 226
Chocolate Peppermint Pie, 223

CHOCOLATE *(continued)*
Chocolate Pudding Sandwiches, 200
Chocolate Swirl Delight, 216
Chocolate Truffles, 182
Christmas Candies, 204
Confetti Snack Mix, 9
Crispy Kiss Squares, 190
Crunchy Chocolate Cups, 199
Crunchy Trail Mix, 35
Dairy State Fudge, 198
Double Chocolate Pie, 225
Easy Mint Hot Chocolate, 23
Frosted Chocolate Malted Shakes, 21
Frosty Chocolate Pie, 213
German Chocolate Bars, 205
Gooey Chip Bars, 197
Heavenly Chocolate Mousse, 244
Layered Mint Candies, 188
Make-Ahead S'mores, 239
Marshmallow Fudge, 192
Mint Chocolate Chip Pie, 235
No-Bake Chocolate Torte, 220
Peanut Butter Berry Delights, 35
Peanut Butter Chocolate Cups, 187
Peanut Butter Kiss Cookies, 180
S'mores Crumb Bars, 201
Terrific Toffee, 196
Truffle Cups, 197
White Chocolate Cereal Bars, 191
Winter Warmer, 21

COCONUT
Cherry Squares, 190
Chewy Macaroons, 195
Coconut Fruit Dip, 15
Tropical Fruit Cream Pie, 213

CONDIMENTS
Asparagus with Blue Cheese Sauce, 134
Baked Cranberry Relish, 138
Beans with Celery Bacon Sauce, 135
Broccoli with Mock Hollandaise, 143
Broccoli with Orange Sauce, 148
Cheddar Cheese Sauce, 130
Cran-Apple Sauce, 146
Creamy Parmesan Sauce, 136
Dill Mustard, 140
Garlic Lemon Butter, 129
Herbed Corn on the Cob, 141
Hollandaise Sauce, 129
Kettle Gravy, 132
Pear Cranberry Sauce, 136
Spiced Honey Butter, 144
Sweet-and-Sour Mustard, 150

COOKIES
Angel Wings, 184
Black Walnut Butter Cookies, 209
Buttery Yeast Spritz, 183
Chewy Macaroons, 195
Chocolate Pudding Sandwiches, 200
Cinnamon Stars, 193
Cookie Ice Cream Cake, 229
Cookie Ice Cream Pie, 222

Flourless Peanut Butter Cookies, 201
Holiday Shortbread Cookies, 202
Holiday Wreath Cookies, 187
Italian Horn Cookies, 194
Lemon Snowflakes, 205
Nuts-About-You Cookie Sticks, 203
Peanut Butter Cookie Parfait, 247
Peanut Butter Kiss Cookies, 180
Strawberry Cookies, 202
Sugar Cookie Slices, 191
Sweetheart Cookies, 207

CORN
Baby Corn Romaine Salad, 49
Herbed Corn on the Cob, 141
Spicy Fish Soup, 73
Zucchini Corn Medley, 143

CORN BREAD
Baked Bean Corn Bread, 158
Chive Corn Bread, 159
Ham 'n' Cheddar Corn Bread, 59

CRANBERRIES
Baked Cranberry Relish, 138
Berry Barbecued Pork Roast, 90
Cran-Apple Sauce, 146
Cranberry Chicken, 111
Cranberry Sherbet, 233
Pear Cranberry Sauce, 136

CREAM CHEESE
Asparagus in Puff Pastry, 19
Berry-Banana Cheese Pie, 219
Cherry Cream Cheese Tarts, 221
Chocolate Chip Cheese Bars, 181
Dairy Delicious Dip, 33
Dreamy Fruit Dip, 20
Hoppin' Good Salad, 53
Italian Sausage Mushrooms, 37
Lemon Cheese Pie, 218
Mushroom Puffs, 24
Sausage-Stuffed Jalapenos, 31
Taffy Apple Dip, 13
Thanksgiving Turkey Sandwich, 77

CUCUMBERS
Italian Cucumber Salad, 42
Tangy Cucumber Gelatin, 50

CUPCAKES
(see Cakes & Cupcakes)

DESSERTS
(also see Cakes & Cupcakes; Ice Cream & Sherbet; Pies & Tarts)
Apple Crisp for Two, 245
Apple Graham Dessert, 228
Apple Pan Betty, 238
Blueberry Raspberry Crunch, 246
Cappuccino Pudding, 242
Cheese Danish Dessert, 175
Cherry Mallow Dessert, 247
Citrus Sherbet Torte, 236
Coffee Ice Cream Torte, 245
Coffee Mousse, 241

Cream Puff Pyramids, 246
Fruit-Filled Angel Food Torte, 218
Heavenly Chocolate Mousse, 244
Ice Cream Supreme, 232
Individual Strawberry Trifles, 240
Italian Torte, 227
Lemon Berry Trifle, 233
Make-Ahead S'mores, 239
Melon Mousse, 243
Microwave Cherry Crisp, 243
Minister's Delight, 237
No-Bake Chocolate Torte, 220
Orange Whip, 234
Peanut Butter Cookie Parfait, 247
Pound Cake Cobbler, 237
Quicker Caramel Flan, 242
Rapid Raspberry Torte, 225
Strawberry Lemon Parfaits, 235
Tropical Banana Compote, 239
Very Berry Parfaits, 238

SWEET BREADS
Apple Cinnamon Bismarcks, 168
Apple Pinwheels, 167
Cheese Danish Dessert, 175
Cherry Danish, 155
Monkey Bread, 163
Simple Pecan Rolls, 171

EGGS
Egg Drop Soup, 65
Hollandaise Sauce, 129
Old-Fashioned Egg Salad, 47

FISH & SEAFOOD
Baked Cod, 125
BBQ Chip-Crusted Orange Roughy, 124
Blackened Fish Salad, 122
Caribbean Rice 'n' Shrimp, 119
Crumb-Topped Haddock, 114
Firecracker Shrimp, 115
Greek Grilled Catfish, 116
Honey Grilled Shrimp, 123
Honey Walleye, 124
Italian Orange Roughy, 116
Italian Tuna Pasta Salad, 53
Minty Peach Halibut, 119
New England Clam Chowder, 69
Perfect Scalloped Oysters, 135
Pesto Halibut, 117
Shrimp with Basil-Mango Sauce, 23
Smoked Salmon Dip, 9
Spicy Fish Soup, 73
Tarragon Flounder, 117
Tomato Salmon Bake, 121
Trout Baked in Cream, 120

FRUIT *(also see specific kinds)*
Apple Grape Drink, 7
Coconut Fruit Dip, 15
Colorful Fruit Kabobs, 25
Dreamy Fruit Dip, 20
Fresh Fruit Bowl, 51
Fruit-Filled Angel Food Torte, 218
Fruit Salad Dressing, 45

Fruity Green Salad, 49
Lemon Berry Trifle, 233
Refreshing Fruit Dip, 30
Shrimp with Basil-Mango Sauce, 23
Tropical Fruit Cream Pie, 213

GARLIC
Crispy Garlic Breadsticks, 177
Garlic Bread, 157
Garlic Brussels Sprouts, 137
Garlic Chicken Penne, 103
Garlic Crescent Rolls, 174
Garlic Lemon Butter, 129

GREEN BEANS
Beans with Celery Bacon Sauce, 135
Greek Green Beans, 140
Red, White and Green Salad, 44
Two-Bean Salad, 41

GRILLED
Barbecue Jack Chicken, 101
Barbecued Baby Back Ribs, 93
Fiesta Rib Eye Steaks, 92
Firecracker Shrimp, 115
Greek Grilled Catfish, 116
Grilled Chicken Cordon Bleu, 110
Grilled Chicken with Peach Sauce, 103
Honey Grilled Shrimp, 123
Italian Grilled Cheese, 61
Maple Ham Steak, 88
Reuben Burgers, 65
Stuffed Bacon Burgers, 79
Tailgate Sausages, 93
Zippy Pork Chops, 87

GROUND BEEF
Beef & Rice Enchiladas, 89
Beefy Biscuit Cups, 169
Country Cabbage Soup, 58
Enchilada Casserole, 84
Hamburger Casserole, 87
Hamburger Skillet Supper, 83
Jalapeno Swiss Burgers, 68
Quick Pizza Soup, 77
Save a Penny Casserole, 82
Spicy Potato Soup, 62
Stuffed Bacon Burgers, 79
Sweet & Saucy Meatballs, 26
Tomato Hamburger Soup, 67
Vegetable Beef Pie, 83

HAM
Grilled Chicken Cordon Bleu, 110
Ham 'n' Cheddar Corn Bread, 59
Maple Ham Steak, 88
Marmalade Baked Ham, 95
Mozzarella Ham Stromboli, 86
Prosciutto Provolone Panini, 72
Spinach Rice Ham Bake, 90
Sugar-Glazed Ham, 91

HONEY
Honey Baked Chicken, 99
Honey Cereal Bars, 198

Honey Grilled Shrimp, 123
Honey Mustard Chicken, 105
Honey Oatmeal Bread, 155
Honey Walleye, 124
Spiced Honey Butter, 144

ICE CREAM & SHERBET
Citrus Sherbet Torte, 236
Coffee Ice Cream Torte, 245
Cookie Ice Cream Cake, 229
Cookie Ice Cream Pie, 222
Cranberry Sherbet, 233
Fourth of July Ice Cream Cake, 224
Ice Cream Supreme, 232
Mint Chocolate Chip Pie, 235
Rainbow Sherbet Cake Roll, 223
Refreshing Lemon Cream, 234
Sunny Slush, 31
Toffee Coffee Ice Cream, 241

LEMONS & LIMES
Baked Lemon Chicken, 100
Cool Lime Salad, 43
Garlic Lemon Butter, 129
Lemon Berry Trifle, 233
Lemon Cheese Pie, 218
Lemon Chicken Soup, 78
Lemon Poppy Seed Bread, 154
Lemon Snowflakes, 205
Mile-High Lime Pie, 217
Raspberry Lemon Smoothie, 29
Raspberry Lime Pie, 229
Raspberry Mint Cooler, 22
Refreshing Lemon Cream, 234
Special Lemonade, 33
Springtime Lime Slushy, 28
Strawberry Lemon Parfaits, 235
Strawberry Lemonade Slush, 36
Tangy Lemonade Pie, 220

MARSHMALLOWS
Cherry Mallow Dessert, 247
Chocolate Marshmallow Squares, 206
Hoppin' Good Salad, 53
Make-Ahead S'mores, 239
Marshmallow Fudge, 192
S'mores Crumb Bars, 201

MEAT LOAF & MEATBALLS
Buffet Meatballs, 28
Meat Loaf Sandwiches, 66
Mushroom Meatball Soup, 71
Sweet & Saucy Meatballs, 26

MEATLESS ENTRESS
Budget Macaroni and Cheese, 125
Italian Bow Tie Bake, 115
Lazy Lasagna, 118
Savory Soup Spuds, 141
Tomato Pizza Bread, 164
Tomato Spinach Spirals, 121
Vegetarian Pasta, 120

MELON
Colorful Fruit Kabobs, 25
Creamy Watermelon Pie, 219

Fresh Fruit Bowl, 51
Melon Mousse, 243
Sparkling Melon, 52

MICROWAVE ENTREES
Chicken in a Haystack, 102
Chicken in Baskets, 106
Pepperoni Rigatoni, 85

MINT
Chocolate Peppermint Pie, 223
Easy Mint Hot Chocolate, 23
Layered Mint Candies, 188
Mint Chocolate Chip Pie, 235
Minty Peach Halibut, 119
Raspberry Mint Cooler, 22

MUFFINS
(see Quick Breads & Muffins)

MUSHROOMS
Creamy Mushroom Bow Ties, 128
Italian Sausage Mushrooms, 37
Mushroom Bread Wedges, 159
Mushroom Meatball Soup, 71
Mushroom Puffs, 24
Snappy Peas 'n' Mushrooms, 149
Wild Rice Mushroom Chicken, 99

NUTS & PEANUT BUTTER
Apricot Cashew Clusters, 189
Black Walnut Butter Cookies, 209
Brussels Sprouts with Pecans, 150
Butterscotch Peanut Candy, 182
California Fried Walnuts, 17
Cherry Almond Bark, 185
Chewy Walnut Bars, 186
Chocolate-Covered Peanut Butter Bars, 186
Chocolate Peanut Dream Pie, 226
Christmas Candies, 204
Confetti Snack Mix, 9
Crisp Peanut Candies, 181
Crunchy Trail Mix, 35
Dairy State Fudge, 198
Flourless Peanut Butter Cookies, 201
Grilled PBJ Sandwiches, 63
No-Bake Cereal Bars, 208
Nuts-About-You Cookie Sticks, 203
Old-Time Butter Crunch Candy, 189
Peanut Butter Berry Delights, 35
Peanut Butter Chocolate Cups, 187
Peanut Butter Cookie Parfait, 247
Peanut Butter Fudge, 185
Peanut Butter Kiss Cookies, 180
Pecan-Crusted Chicken, 111
Quick Toffee Bars, 209
Salted Nut Squares, 195
Simple Pecan Rolls, 171
Swift Strawberry Salad, 48
Terrific Toffee, 196
Toffee Crunch Grahams, 207

OATS
Honey Oatmeal Bread, 155
Maple Oatmeal Bread, 157
Microwave Oatmeal Bars, 199

ORANGES

Broccoli with Orange Sauce, 148
Fresh Fruit Bowl, 51
Grandmother's Orange Salad, 54
Hoppin' Good Salad, 53
Mandarin Fluff, 47
Marmalade Baked Ham, 95
Orange Whip, 234
Sunset Cooler, 27

OVEN ENTREES *(also see Casseroles; Slow Cooker; Skillet & Stovetop Entrees)*

Apricot-Glaze Chicken, 105
Baked Cod, 125
Baked Lemon Chicken, 100
Baked Swiss Chicken, 107
BBQ Chip-Crusted Orange Roughy, 124
Berry Barbecued Pork Roast, 90
Blackened Fish Salad, 122
Chicken Salsa Pizza, 101
Cranberry Chicken, 111
Crumb-Topped Haddock, 114
Flavorful Beef Brisket, 94
Greek Grilled Catfish, 116
Honey Baked Chicken, 99
Italian Orange Roughy, 116
Italian Pork Hoagies, 67
Marmalade Baked Ham, 95
Minty Peach Halibut, 119
Mozzarella Ham Stromboli, 86
Party Chicken, 102
Pecan-Crusted Chicken, 111
Pesto Halibut, 117
Savory Chicken Dinner, 98
Simple Salsa Chicken, 110
Stuffed Spinach Loaf, 69
Stuffing-Coated Chicken, 108
Sugar-Glazed Ham, 91
Sweet & Saucy Meatballs, 26
Tarragon Flounder, 117
Tomato Salmon Bake, 121
Trout Baked in Cream 120
Vegetable Beef Pie, 83
Wild Rice Mushroom Chicken, 99

PASTA

ABC Vegetable Soup, 61
BLT Pasta Salad, 55
Budget Macaroni and Cheese, 125
Creamy Mushroom Bow Ties, 128
Easy Chicken and Noodles, 104
Garlic Chicken Penne, 103
Hamburger Skillet Supper, 83
Homemade Noodles, 144
Italian Bow Tie Bake, 115
Italian Tuna Pasta Salad, 53
Lazy Lasagna, 118
Parmesan Noodles, 151
Pepperoni Rigatoni, 85
Pesto Chicken Pasta, 109
Ranch Turkey Pasta Dinner, 108
Spaghetti with Homemade Turkey
  Sausage, 104

Spinach Ravioli Bake, 95
Tomato Macaroni Casserole, 123
Tomato Spinach Spirals, 121
Tortellini Carbonara, 84
Tortellini Toss, 43
Vegetarian Pasta, 120

PEACHES

Frosty Peach Pie Supreme, 215
Grilled Chicken with Peach Sauce, 103
Minty Peach Halibut, 119
Peach Cream Pie, 221
Refreshing Fruit Dip, 30

PEARS

Fruity Green Salad, 49
Pear Cooler, 34
Pear Cranberry Sauce, 136
Pear Gingerbread Cake, 227

PEAS

Buttery Peas and Carrots, 151
Garlic Chicken Penne, 103
Snappy Peas 'n' Mushrooms, 149

PEPPERS

Jalapeno Swiss Burgers, 68
Sausage Pepper Sandwiches, 64
Sausage-Stuffed Jalapenos, 31

PIES & TARTS

Berry-Banana Cheese Pie, 219
Candy Bar Pie, 214
Cherry Cheesecake Tarts, 217
Cherry Cream Cheese Tarts, 221
Chocolate Peanut Dream Pie, 226
Chocolate Peppermint Pie, 223
Cookie Ice Cream Pie, 222
Creamy Watermelon Pie, 219
Double Chocolate Pie, 225
Fresh Strawberry Pie, 212
Frosty Chocolate Pie, 213
Frosty Peach Pie Supreme, 215
Lemon Cheese Pie, 218
Mile-High Lime Pie, 217
Mint Chocolate Chip Pie, 235
Peach Cream Pie, 221
Raspberry Lime Pie, 229
Rhubarb Cherry Pie, 222
Strawberry Chiffon Pie, 214
Tangy Lemonade Pie, 220
Tropical Fruit Cream Pie, 213

PINEAPPLE

Cool Lime Salad, 43
Fresh Fruit Bowl, 51
Grandmother's Orange Salad, 54
Sparkling Rhubarb Spritzer, 32
Spiced Pineapple, 147
Sunny Slush, 31

PORK *(also see Bacon; Ham; Sausage & Pepperoni)*

Barbecued Baby Back Ribs, 93
Berry Barbecued Pork Roast, 90
Chili Barbecue Chops, 88

Italian Pork Hoagies, 67
Pigs in a Blanket, 60
Reuben Burgers, 65
Sweet and Savory Ribs, 92
Zippy Pork Chops, 87

POTATOES & SWEET POTATOES

Beef Veggie Casserole, 91
Cheese Potato Puff, 133
Cheesy Hash Brown Bake, 139
Double Cheddar Hash Browns, 130
Hamburger Casserole, 87
Herbed Potato Wedges, 132
Potatoes Supreme, 138
Red, White and Green Salad, 44
Sausage Hash, 89
Savory Chicken Dinner, 98
Savory Soup Spuds, 141
Seasoned Fries, 149
Spicy Potato Soup, 62
Spinach Sausage Soup, 70
Sunday Dinner Mashed Potatoes, 142
Sweet Potato Salad, 40

QUICK BREADS & MUFFINS *(also see Biscuits & Popovers; Corn Bread)*

Fluffy Biscuit Muffins, 161
Lemon Poppy Seed Bread, 154
Parmesan Cheese Straws, 177
Sour Cream Blueberry Muffins, 160

RASPBERRIES

Berry Yogurt Shakes, 17
Blueberry Raspberry Crunch, 246
Fruity Red Smoothies, 25
Rapid Raspberry Torte, 225
Raspberry Ice Tea, 22
Raspberry Lemon Smoothie, 29
Raspberry Lime Pie, 229
Raspberry Mint Cooler, 22
Raspberry Tossed Salad, 42

RHUBARB

Rhubarb Cherry Pie, 222
Sparkling Rhubarb Spritzer, 32

RICE

Beef & Rice Enchiladas, 89
Caribbean Rice 'n' Shrimp, 119
Chicken Rice Soup, 60
Spinach Rice Ham Bake, 90
Vegetable Rice Medley, 146
Wild Rice Mushroom Chicken, 99

SALADS & SALAD DRESSINGS
Bean & Vegetable Salads

Broccoli Apple Salad, 55
Catalina Tomato Salad, 51
Italian Cucumber Salad, 42
Red, White and Green Salad, 44
Sweet Potato Salad, 40
Two-Bean Salad, 41

Dressings
Blue Cheese Salad Dressing, 41
Fruit Salad Dressing, 45
Milly's Salad Dressing, 46
Simple Salad Dressing, 50
Thousand Island Dressing, 54
Fruit & Gelatin Salads
Cool Lime Salad, 43
Fresh Fruit Bowl, 51
Grandmother's Orange Salad, 54
Hoppin' Good Salad, 53
Mandarin Fluff, 47
Seven-Layer Gelatin Salad, 46
Sparkling Melon, 52
Swift Strawberry Salad, 48
Tangy Cucumber Gelatin, 50
Green Salads & Egg Salad
Baby Corn Romaine Salad, 49
Blackened Fish Salad, 122
Fruity Green Salad, 49
Old-Fashioned Egg Salad, 47
Raspberry Tossed Salad, 42
Simple Cabbage Slaw, 45
Speedy Spinach Salad, 48
Sweet-Sour Lettuce Salad, 44
Pasta Salads
BLT Pasta Salad, 55
Italian Tuna Pasta Salad, 53
Tortellini Toss, 43

SANDWICHES
Burgers
Jalapeno Swiss Burgers, 68
Reuben Burgers, 65
Stuffed Bacon Burgers, 79
Cold Sandwiches
Avocado Bacon Sandwiches, 63
Beef 'n' Cheese Tortillas, 71
Taco Turkey Wraps, 78
Thanksgiving Turkey Sandwich, 77
Hot Sandwiches
Barbecued Beef Sandwiches, 79
Green Chili Grilled Cheese, 62
Grilled PBJ Sandwiches, 63
Italian Beef Sandwiches, 76
Italian Grilled Cheese, 61
Italian Pork Hoagies, 67
Meat Loaf Sandwiches, 66
Mozzarella Ham Stromboli, 86
Mozzarella Pepperoni Bread, 156
Pigs in a Blanket, 60
Prosciutto Provolone Panini, 72
Sausage Pepper Sandwiches, 64
Stuffed Spinach Loaf, 69

SAUSAGE & PEPPERONI
Beer 'n' Brat Biscuits, 161
Italian Sausage Mushrooms, 37
Mozzarella Pepperoni Bread, 156
Pepperoni Rigatoni, 85
Sausage Hash, 89
Sausage Pepper Sandwiches, 64
Sausage-Stuffed Jalapenos, 31
Speedy Pizza Rings, 34

Spinach Sausage Soup, 70
Stuffed Spinach Loaf, 69
Tailgate Sausages, 93

SIDE DISHES
(also see Casseroles)
Baked Carrots, 131
Ballpark Baked Beans, 137
Basil Cherry Tomatoes, 147
Beans with Celery Bacon Sauce, 135
Broccoli with Mock Hollandaise, 143
Broccoli with Orange Sauce, 148
Brussels Sprouts with Pecans, 150
Buttery Peas and Carrots, 151
Cheese Potato Puff, 133
Creamy Mushroom Bow Ties, 128
Garlic Brussels Sprouts, 137
Greek Green Beans, 140
Herbed Potato Wedges, 132
Homemade Noodles, 144
Italian Mixed Vegetables, 133
Italian Vegetable Saute, 145
Parmesan Noodles, 151
Seasoned Fries, 149
Skillet Ranch Vegetables, 139
Snappy Peas 'n' Mushrooms, 149
Spiced Carrot Strips, 145
Spiced Pineapple, 147
Sunday Dinner Mashed Potatoes, 142
Vegetable Rice Medley, 146
Zucchini Corn Medley, 143

SLOW COOKER
(also see Oven Entrees)
Buffet Meatballs, 28
Enchilada Casserole, 84
Italian Beef Sandwiches, 76
Minister's Delight, 237
Roast Beef and Gravy, 85
Sausage Pepper Sandwiches, 64
Slow-Cooked Swiss Steak, 94
Sweet and Savory Ribs, 92
Tomato Hamburger Soup, 67

SKILLET & STOVETOP ENTREES
Barbecued Baby Back Ribs, 93
Breaded Turkey Slices, 107
Budget Macaroni and Cheese, 125
Caribbean Rice 'n' Shrimp, 119
Chili Barbecue Chops, 88
Dilled Turkey Breast, 100
Easy Chicken and Noodles, 104
Garlic Chicken Penne, 103
Hamburger Skillet Supper, 83
Honey Mustard Chicken, 105
Honey Walleye, 124
Pesto Chicken Pasta, 109
Ranch Turkey Pasta Dinner, 108
Sausage Hash, 89
Southern Fried Chicken, 109
Spaghetti with Homemade Turkey
   Sausage, 104
Tomato Spinach Spirals, 121

Tortellini Carbonara, 84
Vegetarian Pasta, 120
Wild Rice Mushroom Chicken, 99

SOUPS
ABC Vegetable Soup, 61
Beef Onion Soup, 68
Chicken Rice Soup, 60
Chilled Blueberry Soup, 66
Country Cabbage Soup, 58
Creamy Tomato Soup, 72
Curried Zucchini Soup, 59
Egg Drop Soup, 65
Lemon Chicken Soup, 78
Mushroom Meatball Soup, 71
New England Clam Chowder, 69
Quick Pizza Soup, 77
Salsa Chicken Soup, 73
Savory Soup Spuds, 141
Spicy Fish Soup, 73
Spicy Potato Soup, 62
Spinach Sausage Soup, 70
Tomato Hamburger Soup, 67

SPINACH
Speedy Spinach Salad, 48
Spinach Ravioli Bake, 95
Spinach Rice Ham Bake, 90
Spinach Sausage Soup, 70
Stuffed Spinach Loaf, 69
Tomato Spinach Spirals, 121

SQUASH & ZUCCHINI
Cheesy Zucchini Bites, 16
Curried Zucchini Soup, 59
Italian Tuna Pasta Salad, 53
Skillet Ranch Vegetables, 139
Speedy Pizza Rings, 34
Zucchini Corn Medley, 143

STRAWBERRIES
Colorful Fruit Kabobs, 25
Creamy Strawberry Breeze, 8
Fresh Fruit Bowl, 51
Fresh Strawberry Pie, 212
Fruity Red Smoothies, 25
Individual Strawberry Trifles, 240
Lemon Berry Trifle, 233
Peanut Butter Berry Delights, 35
Refreshing Fruit Dip, 30
Strawberry Chiffon Pie, 214
Strawberry Cookies, 202
Strawberry Cooler, 10
Strawberry Lemon Parfaits, 235
Strawberry Lemonade Slush, 36
Swift Strawberry Salad, 48
Very Berry Parfaits, 238

TOMATOES
Basil Cherry Tomatoes, 147
BLT Pasta Salad, 55
Catalina Tomato Salad, 51
Creamy Tomato Soup, 72
Easy Black Bean Salsa, 18

TOMATOES *(continued)*
Italian Cucumber Salad, 42
Red, White and Green Salad, 44
Tomato Hamburger Soup, 67
Tomato Macaroni Casserole, 123
Tomato Pizza Bread, 164
Tomato Salmon Bake, 121
Tomato Spinach Spirals, 121
Tortellini Toss, 43

TORTILLAS
Beef 'n' Cheese Tortillas, 71
Beef & Rice Enchiladas, 89
Black Bean Quesadillas, 11
Dragon Dippers, 29
Enchilada Casserole, 84
Fiesta Rib Eye Steaks, 92
Quick Elephant Ears, 193
Taco Turkey Wraps, 78
Tortilla Snack Strips, 13

TURKEY
Breaded Turkey Slices, 107
Dilled Turkey Breast, 100
Ranch Turkey Pasta Dinner, 108
Spaghetti with Homemade Turkey
    Sausage, 104
Taco Turkey Wraps, 78
Thanksgiving Turkey Sandwich, 77
Turkey Nachos, 15

VEGETABLES
(also see specific kinds)
ABC Vegetable Soup, 61
Beef Veggie Casserole, 91
Garlic Brussels Sprouts, 137
Hamburger Skillet Supper, 83
Italian Mixed Vegetables, 133
Italian Vegetable Saute, 145
Ranch Turkey Pasta Dinner, 108
Save A Penny Casserole, 82

Skillet Ranch Vegetables, 139
Tomato Hamburger Soup, 67
Vegetable Beef Pie, 83
Vegetable Rice Medley, 146
Vegetarian Pasta, 120

YEAST BREADS & ROLLS
(also see Sweet Breads)
Bread Bowls, 175
Cheddar Chili Braid, 166
Country White Bread, 158
Crusty French Bread, 176
French Onion Bread, 170
Honey Oatmeal Bread, 155
Maple Oatmeal Bread, 157
Mini Blue Cheese Rolls, 172
Overnight Rolls, 162

ZUCCHINI
(see Squash & Zucchini)

alphabetical recipe index

A
ABC Vegetable Soup, 61
Angel Wings, 184
Apple Cartwheels, 10
Apple Cinnamon Bismarcks, 168
Apple Crisp for Two, 245
Apple German Chocolate Cake, 215
Apple Graham Dessert, 228
Apple Grape Drink, 7
Apple Pan Betty, 238
Apple Pinwheels, 167
Apricot Cashew Clusters, 189
Apricot-Glaze Chicken, 105
Asparagus in Puff Pastry, 19
Asparagus with Blue Cheese Sauce, 134
Avocado Bacon Sandwiches, 63

B
Baby Corn Romaine Salad, 49
Baked Asparagus Dip, 6
Baked Bean Corn Bread, 158
Baked Carrots, 131
Baked Cod, 125
Baked Cranberry Relish, 138
Baked Lemon Chicken, 100
Baked Swiss Chicken, 107
Ballpark Baked Beans, 137
Banana Cocoa Smoothies, 37
Barbecue Jack Chicken, 101
Barbecued Baby Back Ribs, 93
Barbecued Beef Sandwiches, 79
Basil-Buttered French Bread, 168
Basil Cherry Tomatoes, 147
BBQ Chip-Crusted Orange Roughy, 124
Beans with Celery Bacon Sauce, 135
Beef 'n' Cheese Tortillas, 71

Beef & Rice Enchiladas, 89
Beef Onion Soup, 68
Beef Veggie Casserole, 91
Beefy Biscuit Cups, 169
Beer 'n' Brat Biscuits, 161
Berry-Banana Cheese Pie, 219
Berry Barbecued Pork Roast, 90
Berry Yogurt Shakes, 17
Biscuit Bites, 165
Black Bean Quesadillas, 11
Black Walnut Butter Cookies, 209
Blackened Fish Salad, 122
BLT Pasta Salad, 55
Blue Cheese Salad Dressing, 41
Blueberry Raspberry Crunch, 246
Bread Bowls, 175
Breaded Turkey Slices, 107
Brie in Puff Pastry, 7
Broccoli Apple Salad, 55
Broccoli Casserole, 131
Broccoli with Mock Hollandaise, 143
Broccoli with Orange Sauce, 148
Brussels Sprouts with Pecans, 150
Budget Macaroni and Cheese, 125
Buffet Meatballs, 28
Butterscotch Coffee, 8
Butterscotch Peanut Candy, 182
Butterscotch Taffy, 203
Buttery French Bread, 162
Buttery Peas and Carrots, 151
Buttery Yeast Spritz, 183

C
California Fried Walnuts, 17
Candy Bar Pie, 214
Cappuccino Chip Cupcakes, 32

Cappuccino Pudding, 242
Caramel Corn Chocolate Bars, 183
Caribbean Rice 'n' Shrimp, 119
Catalina Tomato Salad, 51
Cheddar Bacon Toasts, 172
Cheddar Cheese Sauce, 130
Cheddar Chili Braid, 166
Cheddar-Salsa Biscuit Strips, 171
Cheese Bread, 176
Cheese Crisps, 165
Cheese Danish Dessert, 175
Cheese Potato Puff, 133
Cheese Toast, 167
Cheesy Hash Brown Bake, 139
Cheesy Zucchini Bites, 16
Cherry Almond Bark, 185
Cherry Angel Cake Roll, 228
Cherry Cheesecake Tarts, 217
Cherry Cream Cheese Tarts, 221
Cherry Danish, 155
Cherry Mallow Dessert, 247
Cherry Squares, 190
Cherry Yogurt Smoothies, 14
Chewy Macaroons, 195
Chewy Walnut Bars, 186
Chicken in a Haystack, 102
Chicken in Baskets, 106
Chicken Rice Soup, 60
Chicken Salsa Pizza, 101
Chili Barbecue Chops, 88
Chilled Blueberry Soup, 66
Chive Corn Bread, 159
Chocolate Banana Smoothies, 14
Chocolate Cherry Cupcakes, 226
Chocolate Chip Cheese Bars, 181
Chocolate-Covered Peanut Butter Bars, 186

Chocolate Marshmallow Squares, 206
Chocolate Mousse Balls, 194
Chocolate Peanut Dream Pie, 226
Chocolate Peppermint Pie, 223
Chocolate Pudding Sandwiches, 200
Chocolate Swirl Delight, 216
Chocolate Truffles, 182
Christmas Candies, 204
Cinnamon Stars, 193
Citrus Sherbet Torte, 236
Coconut Fruit Dip, 15
Coffee Ice Cream Torte, 245
Coffee Mousse, 241
Colorful Fruit Kabobs, 25
Confetti Snack Mix, 9
Cookie Ice Cream Cake, 229
Cookie Ice Cream Pie, 222
Cool Lime Salad, 43
Country Cabbage Soup, 58
Country White Bread, 158
Cran-Apple Sauce, 146
Cranberry Chicken, 111
Cranberry Sherbet, 233
Cream Puff Pyramids, 246
Creamy Mushroom Bow Ties, 128
Creamy Parmesan Sauce, 136
Creamy Strawberry Breeze, 8
Creamy Tomato Soup, 72
Creamy Watermelon Pie, 219
Crisp Peanut Candies, 181
Crispy Garlic Breadsticks, 177
Crispy Kiss Squares, 190
Crumb-Topped Haddock, 114
Crunchy Cheese Nibblers, 16
Crunchy Cheese Toasts, 173
Crunchy Chocolate Cups, 199
Crunchy Trail Mix, 35
Crusty French Bread, 176
Curried Zucchini Soup, 59

D

Dairy Delicious Dip, 33
Dairy State Fudge, 198
Dill Mustard, 140
Dilled Turkey Breast, 100
Double Cheddar Hash Browns, 130
Double Chocolate Pie, 225
Dragon Dippers, 29
Dreamy Fruit Dip, 20

E

Easy Black Bean Salsa, 18
Easy Chicken and Noodles, 104
Easy Mint Hot Chocolate, 23
Egg Drop Soup, 65
Enchilada Casserole, 84

F

Fiesta Rib Eye Steaks, 92
Firecracker Shrimp, 115
Flavorful Beef Brisket, 94
Flourless Peanut Butter Cookies, 201
Fluffy Biscuit Muffins, 161
Fourth of July Ice Cream Cake, 224

Frappe Mocha, 12
French Onion Bread, 170
Fresh Fruit Bowl, 51
Fresh Strawberry Pie, 212
Frosted Chocolate Malted Shakes, 21
Frosty Chocolate Pie, 213
Frosty Peach Pie Supreme, 215
Fruit-Filled Angel Food Torte, 218
Fruit Salad Dressing, 45
Fruity Green Salad, 49
Fruity Red Smoothies, 25

G

Garlic Bread, 157
Garlic Brussels Sprouts, 137
Garlic Chicken Penne, 103
Garlic Crescent Rolls, 174
Garlic Lemon Butter, 129
German Chocolate Bars, 205
Gooey Chip Bars, 197
Grandmother's Orange Salad, 54
Greek Green Beans, 140
Greek Grilled Catfish, 116
Green Chili Grilled Cheese, 62
Grilled Chicken Cordon Bleu, 110
Grilled Chicken with Peach Sauce, 103
Grilled PBJ Sandwiches, 63
Guacamole Dip, 20

H

Ham 'n' Cheddar Corn Bread, 59
Hamburger Casserole, 87
Hamburger Skillet Supper, 83
Heavenly Chocolate Mousse, 244
Herbed Corn on the Cob, 141
Herbed Potato Wedges, 132
Holiday Shortbread Cookies, 202
Holiday Wreath Cookies, 187
Hollandaise Sauce, 129
Homemade Noodles, 144
Honey Baked Chicken, 99
Honey Cereal Bars, 198
Honey Grilled Shrimp, 123
Honey Mustard Chicken, 105
Honey Oatmeal Bread, 155
Honey Walleye, 124
Hoppin' Good Salad, 53

I

Ice Cream Supreme, 232
Individual Strawberry Trifles, 240
Italian Beef Sandwiches, 76
Italian Bow Tie Bake, 115
Italian Cucumber Salad, 42
Italian Grilled Cheese, 61
Italian Horn Cookies, 194
Italian Mixed Vegetables, 133
Italian Orange Roughy, 116
Italian Pork Hoagies, 67
Italian Sausage Mushrooms, 37
Italian Torte, 227
Italian Tuna Pasta Salad, 53
Italian Vegetable Saute, 145

J

Jalapeno Swiss Burgers, 68

K

Kettle Gravy, 132
Kid's Favorite Biscuits, 163

L

Layered Mint Candies, 188
Lazy Lasagna, 118
Lemon Berry Trifle, 233
Lemon Cheese Pie, 218
Lemon Chicken Soup, 78
Lemon Poppy Seed Bread, 154
Lemon Snowflakes, 205
Like 'Em Hot Wings, 26

M

Make-Ahead S'mores, 239
Mandarin Fluff, 47
Maple Ham Steak, 88
Maple Oatmeal Bread, 157
Marmalade Baked Ham, 95
Marshmallow Fudge, 192
Meat Loaf Sandwiches, 66
Melon Mousse, 243
Microwave Cherry Crisp, 243
Microwave Oatmeal Bars, 199
Mile-High Lime Pie, 217
Milly's Salad Dressing, 46
Mini Blue Cheese Rolls, 172
Minister's Delight, 237
Mint Chocolate Chip Pie, 235
Minty Peach Halibut, 119
Monkey Bread, 163
Mozzarella Ham Stromboli, 86
Mozzarella Pepperoni Bread, 156
Mushroom Bread Wedges, 159
Mushroom Meatball Soup, 71
Mushroom Puffs, 24

N

New England Clam Chowder, 69
No-Bake Cereal Bars, 208
No-Bake Chocolate Torte, 220
Nuts-About-You Cookie Sticks, 203

O

Old-Fashioned Egg Salad, 47
Old-Time Butter Crunch Candy, 189
Orange Whip, 234
Overnight Rolls, 162

P

Paprika Cheese Biscuits, 168
Parmesan Cheese Straws, 177
Parmesan Noodles, 151
Parmesan Popcorn, 11
Party Chicken, 102
Peach Cream Pie, 221
Peanut Butter Berry Delights, 35
Peanut Butter Chocolate Cups, 187
Peanut Butter Cookie Parfait, 247
Peanut Butter Fudge, 185
Peanut Butter Kiss Cookies, 180

Pear Cooler, 34
Pear Cranberry Sauce, 136
Pear Gingerbread Cake, 227
Pecan-Crusted Chicken, 111
Pepperoni Rigatoni, 85
Perfect Scalloped Oysters, 135
Pesto Chicken Pasta, 109
Pesto Halibut, 117
Pigs in a Blanket, 60
Pizza Sticks, 166
Popovers, 173
Poppy Seed French Bread, 164
Potatoes Supreme, 138
Pound Cake Cobbler, 237
Prosciutto Provolone Panini, 72

Q
Quick Elephant Ears, 193
Quick Pizza Soup, 77
Quick Toffee Bars, 209
Quicker Caramel Flan, 242

R
Rainbow Sherbet Cake Roll, 223
Ranch Garlic Bread, 156
Ranch Turkey Pasta Dinner, 108
Rapid Raspberry Torte, 225
Raspberry Ice Tea, 22
Raspberry Lemon Smoothie, 29
Raspberry Lime Pie, 229
Raspberry Mint Cooler, 22
Raspberry Tossed Salad, 42
Red, White and Green Salad, 44
Refreshing Fruit Dip, 30
Refreshing Lemon Cream, 234
Reuben Burgers, 65
Rhubarb Cherry Pie, 222
Ricotta Tart, 27
Roast Beef and Gravy, 85

S
Salsa Chicken Soup, 73
Salted Nut Squares, 195
Sausage Hash, 89
Sausage Pepper Sandwiches, 64
Sausage-Stuffed Jalapenos, 31
Save A Penny Casserole, 82
Savory Chicken Dinner, 98

Savory Soup Spuds, 141
Seasoned Fries, 149
Seven-Layer Gelatin Salad, 46
Shrimp with Basil-Mango Sauce, 23
Simple Cabbage Slaw, 45
Simple Pecan Rolls, 171
Simple Salad Dressing, 50
Simple Salsa Chicken, 110
Skillet Ranch Vegetables, 139
Slow-Cooked Swiss Steak, 94
Smoked Salmon Dip, 9
Smooth Vanilla Shakes, 19
S'mores Crumb Bars, 201
Snappy Peas 'n' Mushrooms, 149
Sour Cream Blueberry Muffins, 160
Southern Fried Chicken, 109
Spaghetti with Homemade Turkey
   Sausage, 104
Sparkling Melon, 52
Sparkling Rhubarb Spritzer, 32
Special Lemonade, 33
Speedy Pizza Rings, 34
Speedy Spinach Salad, 48
Spiced Carrot Strips, 145
Spiced Honey Butter, 144
Spiced Pineapple, 147
Spicy Fish Soup, 73
Spicy Potato Soup, 62
Spinach Ravioli Bake, 95
Spinach Rice Ham Bake, 90
Spinach Sausage Soup, 70
Springtime Lime Slushy, 28
Strawberry Chiffon Pie, 214
Strawberry Cookies, 202
Strawberry Cooler, 10
Strawberry Lemon Parfaits, 235
Strawberry Lemonade Slush, 36
Stuffed Bacon Burgers, 79
Stuffed Spinach Loaf, 69
Stuffing-Coated Chicken, 108
Sugar Cookie Slices, 191
Sugar-Glazed Ham, 91
Sunday Dinner Mashed Potatoes, 142
Sunny Slush, 31
Sunset Cooler, 27
Sweet & Saucy Meatballs, 26
Sweet and Savory Ribs, 92

Sweet-and-Sour Mustard, 150
Sweet Graham Snacks, 206
Sweet Potato Salad, 40
Sweet-Sour Lettuce Salad, 44
Sweetheart Cookies, 207
Swift Strawberry Salad, 48

T
Taco Turkey Wraps, 78
Taffy Apple Dip, 13
Tailgate Sausages, 93
Tangy Cucumber Gelatin, 50
Tangy Lemonade Pie, 220
Tarragon Flounder, 117
Terrific Toffee, 196
Thanksgiving Turkey Sandwich, 77
Thousand Island Dressing, 54
Toffee Coffee Ice Cream, 241
Toffee Crunch Grahams, 207
Tomato Hamburger Soup, 67
Tomato Macaroni Casserole, 123
Tomato Pizza Bread, 164
Tomato Salmon Bake, 121
Tomato Spinach Spirals, 121
Tortellini Carbonara, 84
Tortellini Toss, 43
Tortilla Snack Strips, 13
Tropical Banana Compote, 239
Tropical Fruit Cream Pie, 213
Trout Baked in Cream 120
Truffle Cups, 197
Turkey Nachos, 15
Two-Bean Salad, 41

V
Vegetable Beef Pie, 83
Vegetable Rice Medley, 146
Vegetarian Pasta, 120
Very Berry Parfaits, 238
White Chocolate Cereal Bars, 191

W
Wild Rice Mushroom Chicken, 99
Winter Warmer, 21

Z
Zippy Pork Chops, 87
Zucchini Corn Medley, 143